LIVING RHETORIC AND COMPOSITION
Stories of the Discipline

LIVING RHETORIC AND COMPOSITION

Stories of the Discipline

Edited by

Duane H. Roen
Arizona State University

Stuart C. Brown
New Mexico State University

Theresa Enos
University of Arizona

 LAWRENCE ERLBAUM ASSOCIATES, PUBLISHERS
1999   Mahwah, New Jersey   London

Lawrence Erlbaum Associates, Inc., Publishers
10 Industrial Avenue
Mahwah, New Jersey 07430

Cover design by Kathryn Houghtaling Lacey

Library of Congress Cataloging-in-Publication Data

Living rhetoric and composition : stories of the discipline / edited
by Duane H. Roen, Stuart C. Brown, Theresa Enos.
   p.   cm.
  Includes bibliographical references and index.
  ISBN 0-8058-2372-7 (alk. paper). — ISBN 0-8058-2373-5 (pbk. :
alk. paper).
   1. English language—Rhetoric—Study and teaching—United States.
2. English language—Composition and exercises. 3. English
teachers—United States—Biography. I. Roen, Duane H. II. Brown,
Stuart C. (Stuart Cameron), 1955–   . III. Enos, Theresa.
PE1405.U6L58 1999
808′.042′07—dc21   98-43355
                                   CIP

Books published by Lawrence Erlbaum Associates are printed on acid-free paper,
and their bindings are chosen for strength and durability.

Printed in the United States of America
10 9 8 7 6 5 4 3 2 1

We dedicate this book to those who forged our way and left us a legacy, to those who now are living that legacy and shaping it further, and to those who will live and shape it in the future.

Contents

Foreword

Andrea A. Lunsford
Ohio State University

Where were you when you "fell in love" with the theory and/or practice of rhetoric and composition? What were you doing at the very moment when you claimed the teaching of writing/reading as your way of life? What stories can you tell about coming into and helping to shape this field of study? These are some of the questions explored by the nineteen chapters collected in this volume, chapters that tell a truth but, like Emily Dickinson, "tell it slant"—from unique individual perspectives enriched by an opportunity to call a momentary halt to the busyness of everyday professional life, take a steady look backward, and report on the landscape. Do you wonder what Wendy Bishop was doing with a lime green Fiat or just what led Duane Roen to become such an advocate and practitioner of collaboration? Do you want to know why Harry Caplan's hat is so important to Rich Enos or what it is between Bob Barker and Bill Covino? Do you have a hard time imagining Win Horner, complete with typewriter, in a playpen? Or what Vic Vitanza is (not) talking about? The chapters here tell all and, in addition, provide reminiscences about how these scholar-teachers came to composition and rhetoric as well as retrospective snapshots of a field in the making.

Certainly the familiar narratives of "rhet/comp" are here, too: the journey from other fields (philosophy, classics, religion, and most of all literature) to a new field of study; the institutional struggles and punishments that Chuck Bazerman says "seem to go with the territory"; the role that the GI Bill, 1960s activism, and programs like open admissions played in helping scholars (re)imagine themselves as rhetoricians and compositionists; the shock of recognition that teaching, really teaching, seems to have brought to many, along with a growing realization that the teaching of writing and literacies offers rich and compelling rewards; the struggles for disciplinary recognition and legitimacy and the (very) troubled marriage of literature and composition; the battles for tenure and promotion . . . always the battles for tenure and promotion. For those who joined the field during the 1960s and 1970s, even the early 1980s, these narratives will be familiar territory: Indeed, I can recognize my own journey whispering between the lines of many chapters in this volume. For those who have come to rhetoric and composition in the last decade, however, these narratives may be less familiar: For most of the writers in *Living Rhetoric and Composition: Stories of the Discipline*, formal graduate programs in rhetoric and composition were either unimaginable or very new; for others, the kind of professionalism that graduate students now probably experience as the status quo (frequent appearances at conferences, multiple publications during graduate school, extensive preparation for the job market, etc.) was largely unknown. Perhaps most important, the self-reflexiveness of teaching assistant mentoring programs and the intense (and I think most beneficial) examination of just how closely rhetoric and composition have been tied to the reproduction of the status quo, to exclusionary practices, and to "standards" of all kinds are moves that were imaginable to only a very few during the early years of this discipline.

So it is instructive to read this volume not only with delight at what it includes but also with attention to what it does not include. For many understandable reasons, the authors represented here do not worry a great deal about the hegemonic impulses discernible in our discipline's history. And although many reflect on important teachers in their lives (and this aspect I found particularly interesting, even uplifting), they reflect less often on particularly important students, usually preferring to speak of students in general or even of teaching (which implies an attention to students, of course). There are other omissions that every contributor is no doubt aware of as well. A quick glance at the table of contents reveals 19 contributors—14 White men and 5 White women. Where are colleagues of color in the story of rhetoric and composition? Where are all the women who have devoted their careers to teaching, especially the teaching of writing? Where are students, and especially the students of color? In the conclusion to her chapter, Kathleen Welch faces these questions squarely, insisting that "The composition/rhetoric democratic vista must contain the vision of gender equality, race equality, and ethnic equality. The *kairic* moment is now."

Indeed it is. And although we have miles to go before we rest, as Welch notes, we also have a vibrant group of scholar-teachers who have recently entered or are entering our field, including tenure-track and graduate student colleagues. Many others are living their ways into rhetoric and composition—in very different ways than I or many of the contributors to this volume did, ways that will make a difference in the way composition and rhetoric get historicized, theorized, and storied. Theirs are stories that need to be told and, more important, need to be heard if the field of rhetoric and composition is to realize the democratic and inclusionary goals articulated by many in this volume.

So perhaps readers can look forward to sequels, maybe even prequels, to *Living Rhetoric and Composition.* If the contemporary fascination with memoir is any indication (see everything from *Oprah* to the *New York Review of Books* or the *AARP Bulletin,* which recently announced that " 'Memoir fever' proves infectious, sweep[ing] the country"), there will be readers aplenty for such additional volumes, and I first among them.

Preface:
Scholar/Teacher/Storyteller

This is a collection of stories, stories of scholars who have found a lifelong commitment to the teaching of writing. The idea for the book first occurred to Duane while he was on a campus visit to Syracuse University in the spring of 1993. While there, he had a chat with Sam Gorovitz, a professor of philosophy and then dean of arts and sciences. Sitting on a table in Sam's office was a copy of David Karnos and Robert Shoemaker's newly published collection *Falling in Love With Wisdom: American Philosophers Talk About Their Calling.* In it, 62 contemporary philosophers, including Sam, explained how they fell in love with philosophy. Our view is that every field needs a book like *Falling in Love With Wisdom.*

This volume includes the professional histories of 19 rhetoricians and compositionists who explain how they came to fall in love with the written word and with teaching. Their stories are filled with personal anecdotes—some funny, some touching, some mundane. All of the stories are fascinating, however, because they demonstrate how scholars' personal and professional lives intertwine. These stories also help to situate the scholars, their work, and, importantly, the development of the profession.

These chapters reflect the progression of rhetoric and composition studies from the ad hoc scrambling of post-World War II teachers into a vibrant and growing discipline with more than 70 doctoral programs producing specialized scholars, researchers, and teachers of writing. The chapter authors represent the variety of the camps that now compose the diverse discipline of rhetoric and composition. Whether historian, researcher, theorist, or practitioner, each of these contributors is, however, a teacher.

We have collected narratives from senior members of the profession so that their stories can be preserved for future generations of scholars and teachers in the field. They provide a sense of the changes, the historical development of the profession as it has been transformed over the last 50 years. It is especially important to capture these voices and their record at this time as many of the senior leaders of the profession are now retiring. This collection is not only a record of their contributions and some of the benchmark moments in the field but also an opportunity for them to provide us with their reflections and retrospections.

The dramatic increase in the number of doctoral programs in the 1970s and 1980s is notable in these narratives. That is, there is a difference in the role that graduate training had in the lives of more junior and more senior members of the profession. To reflect this, we have included contributions from several newer members of the profession because their stories illustrate how today's young scholars gain entry into the profession. These contributors represent the many younger scholars who will be expected to carry the profession into the 21st century.

As in any collection, we recognize that there are limitations. In our case, it is the limited representation of how the profession is now being configured along gender, ethnic, and class lines. The writers here are predominantly White and male and tenured (or retired from tenured positions), reflective of a not-too-distant past when most college professors were members of those groups. In chronicling the history and development of rhetoric and composition, we must recognize that the profession mirrored the academy in these earlier times.

However, as recent surveys show, women are making significant gains in tenure-track positions. Graduate courses and tenure-track positions are attracting more and more ethnic diversity. Our discipline is growing and changing and diversifying at a startling pace. And we did try to include more women and people of color in this volume to portray this changing dynamic. Unfortunately, a number of contributors dropped out of the project, primarily women and people of color, which upset the more equitable portrayal for which we strove. As for class issues, we simply failed to recognize this inherent discrimination in the purpose of our project. Should someone 10 or 20 years in the future do a similar collection, gender, ethnic, and class representation will be much different, perhaps to the point where it is not even necessary to draw attention to these issues.

We have compiled this collection with multiple audiences in mind. First, experienced scholars and teachers in rhetoric and composition will be interested in reading about some of the more visible members of the field. Second, graduate students in rhetoric and composition should find the book appealing as they begin to follow in the footsteps of people such as those who appear in this collection, many whose work these students study. Because some of the major graduate programs in the country—those described in the spring 1994 issue of *Rhetoric Review*—have professional development courses, the book might serve students in those courses. Some programs have a series of noncredit professional development workshops for which the book may be suited. Generally, we hope that each contributor to this collection will in some way serve as mentor to those just entering the field. Students and instructors of writing will find the book useful in their composition methods courses because many of the contributors describe teachers, course work, and scholarship that influenced their own development as writers. Further, we hope that the book will help graduate students recognize that they are like the scholars and teachers included in the book. And that the scholars presented here are not resting on their laurels but are still struggling with professional issues and scholarly concerns. As Wendy Bishop observes, "You tell me I'm a prominent scholar and I pinch myself." That, we hope, will offer comfort.

We hope that the contributions—individually and collectively—will encourage young scholars to ponder the possibilities of their lives as teachers. Eric Waggoner, a young scholar who helped us with research and editing for this anthology, offers his response to reading the chapters. The chapters have given him a new perspective on how we compose our lives as teachers:

> As a graduate student, I don't often find myself thinking about teachers' lives, the lives they bring into the classroom, their personal histories, teaching histories, families, homes, other careers, and the like. I think I—we—most usually assume some congenital teaching trait among the best, an inborn talent which those instructors possess. They could never, we feel, have done anything else. Doubtless this has something to do with a fear of falling during our own slow progress. Working with these manuscripts has reminded me of what I should have known already: We all move towards this field, this study, this profession, in fits and starts. We worry, and we plan, and we try to anticipate both failure and success; but we can rarely guess at where we'll end up. We move forward, we let the work take us where we need to be because we trust it, because it connects us. I'm reminded that the work, the important and lasting part of that journey—the work matters to us, and for us. I've learned from these lives.

One must remember that these are narratives for the most part, and, as such, are transient. These stories take us to a certain point in the writer's life, but they stop, whereas the writer goes on. Still, they provide an orientation to the profession while revealing the scholar behind the scholarship. Some have chosen to take liberties with the constraints and conventions of academic writing. Others note important attitudes and their origins that shape a particular scholar's approach, such as Duane Roen's emphasis on collaboration. Or they choose to focus on their early years—Richard Enos, for example, describes how the formal study of rhetoric retroactively shaped his perceptions of his childhood experiences. Frank D'Angelo and William Covino point to childhood as entry points for their love of language and detail how that love eventually turned into careers.

Others have chosen to note defining moments in the development of the National Council of Teachers of English (NCTE) and the Conference on College Composition and Communication (CCCC). Richard Lloyd-Jones marks key events in the 1960s that have led to the profession as we now know it. Some point to broader implications that now define the profession, such as Charles Bazerman's observations about the tensions between literary studies and rhetoric and composition. John Trimbur reveals how his overt political interests have shaped his work as scholar-teacher. Theresa Enos describes her struggles as a woman entering the profession and the status of women as teachers of writing.

The chapters here reveal how rhetoric and composition are shaped by the confluences of various disciplines, such as literary study, creative writing, philosophy, and education. Of note are the disparate paths and backgrounds that people have taken to achieve their professional stature. These contributions, however, are most revelatory in describing the forging of a discipline as it reasserts its value within the academy and to the students it serves.

ACKNOWLEDGMENTS

I thank Hanna, Nick, and Maureen for their love and patience. I am fortunate to have them in my life. I also thank Sam Gorovitz, professor of philosophy at Syracuse University, for the kernel idea for this collection, and my mentors—Joyce King, Claire Stein, Nick Karolides, Gene Pichè, Mike Graves, Les Whipp, Bob Shafer, Leo Lambert—who have provided many years of guidance and friendship. They have made my writing and teaching possible.

—*Duane Roen*

To my students, past and present, from whom I learn so much, I express a special and continuing thanks.

—*Theresa Enos*

I thank Leslie for many years of intellectual support and companionship.

—*Stuart Brown*

We all thank Naomi Silverman of Lawrence Erlbaum Associates for encouraging us to undertake this project. She has just the right combination of enthusiasm and patience for an editor. We thank the scholar-teachers who reviewed an earlier manuscript of this collection. Their questions and comments were invaluable. We would also like to thank the dedicated staff of Lawrence Erlbaum Associates for their hard work and attention while reviewing this manuscript. Special thanks to Sondra Guideman, our production editor.

We thank our students, friends, and colleagues at Arizona State University, New Mexico State University, and the University of Arizona for all they have shared with us. We are especially grateful to our department chairs—Nancy Gutierrez, Reed Way Dasenbrock, and Larry Evers—for supporting our work as scholars and teachers.

We thank Eric Waggoner, Papatya Bucak, Deborah Ackerman, Susan Heck, and Rebecca Busker for assisting us with research and manuscript preparation. Their diligence, skill, and good humor are all admirable.

—Duane Roen
—Stuart Brown
—Theresa Enos

CHAPTER ONE

How I Became a Teacher of Composition

Edward P. J. Corbett
Ohio State University

At the 1996 Convention of the Conference on College Composition and Communication (CCCC) in Milwaukee, Wisconsin, I was so enthralled by the talk given by James Kinneavy, the 1995 winner of the Exemplar Award, that after the meeting I wrote and asked him if he would send me a copy of his address. I eventually received a copy of that talk, titled "A Backward Look at 55 Years of Teaching Writing." After reading that fascinating talk, I decided that for my Exemplar Award address, I would present a narrative account of how I became a teacher of composition. At the Watson Conference at the University of Louisville in October 1996, I was on a panel that included such distinguished members of our profession as James Kinneavy, Winifred Horner, and Frank D'Angelo, and all four of us gave an account of how and why we got involved in rhetoric and composition. In the December 1987 issue of *College Composition and Communication* (*CCC*), I published an article titled "Teaching Composition: Where We've Been and Where We're Going." In this chapter I repeat some of the things I discussed in that article and in my address at the Watson Conference, which was titled "My Relation to the Past of Rhetoric." I also add some other details about my fortunes as a teacher of composition.

Let me start out by confessing that, as an undergraduate, I never had a course in freshman English, but I was a fervent reader of essays, short stories, and novels. I also wrote several short stories and sent them off to such exalted magazines as the *Saturday Evening Post, Cosmopolitan,* and the *New Yorker.* All I have to show for that activity as a writer of fiction is a suitcase full of mimeographed rejection slips.

1

At the end of World War II, I spent the last 9 months of my service with the U.S. Marine Corps in North China, helping to repatriate the Japanese soldiers. When I learned that I would be sent back to the United States in June 1946 and would be honorably discharged from the service, I decided I would take advantage of the GI Bill by going back to college to earn a master's degree. I had married a Chicago girl during the war years, so I decided I would apply for graduate work at the University of Chicago. Because many of the American creative writers whom I most admired at that time—people like Ernest Hemingway, William Faulkner, and Sherwood Anderson—had done their apprenticeship as newspapermen, I decided that I would do graduate work in journalism. So I wrote to the University of Chicago and asked for information about their journalism program. Somebody in the admissions office wrote back to tell me that the University of Chicago did not have a journalism department but informed me that there were two first-rate journalism schools nearby, Northwestern University in Evanston, Illinois, and Marquette University in Milwaukee, Wisconsin. An alternative program, they told me, would be to get a master's degree in another subject and then pick up some essential journalism courses elsewhere. That suggestion intrigued me. But what subject did I want to pursue? Well, I always liked to read novels, short stories, plays, and poetry. Why not enroll in a graduate program in English?

The University of Chicago was an exciting place to be right after World War II. First of all, Robert Hutchins was the president of the university at that time, and Mortimer Adler was in the philosophy department there—both were especially notable at that time for their establishment of the Great Books program. The university was made even more exciting by the presence of hundreds of bright, eager veterans who resumed their educations after being discharged from the armed forces. Two of the graduate students who were there at the time were Wayne Booth, who later published his influential book *The Rhetoric of Fiction,* and James Miller, who later became the chairman of the English department at the University of Nebraska and the editor of *College English.*

I was an excited graduate student at that time, but I was far from being an exciting student. Because I had majored in philosophy in my undergraduate years, I had a lot of catching up to do in my graduate program in English. I took some courses in 18th-century literature, my favorite period of English literature. I also took a course in linguistics from James Hulbert, one of the editors, along with Sir William Craigie, of *The Dictionary of American English.* And I took a course in philosophy, where we read some texts of Aristotle and Plato. Like most students of English at the time, however, I was most interested in the study and criticism of English and American literature. At the time, one of the hottest systems of literary criticism was the so-called New Criticism, especially as that system emanated from the books and articles of Cleanth

Brooks and Robert Penn Warren. But the premier system of literary criticism that was popular with many of the English professors at the University of Chicago at that time was the system known as the "Chicago School of Criticism." In 1952, the University of Chicago Press published *Critics and Criticism: Ancient and Modern*, edited by Ronald S. Crane and featuring such other professors at Chicago as William Keast, Elder Olson, Richard McKeon, and Norman Maclean. All of the essays in this collection were solidly based on Aristotle's *Poetics*. Many of Aristotle's other works figured prominently in the Hutchins–Adler Great Books program, but curiously enough I never read Aristotle's *Rhetoric*. I later learned from a talk given by Gerald Nelms, a former graduate student of mine, that a number of professors at the University of Chicago tried to promote the institution of an undergraduate course in composition based on classical rhetoric but that the proposal was voted down by many of the senior professors at the university.

After I took my master's degree at Chicago in June 1948, I applied for a teaching job in one of the colleges and universities that at the time were desperate for faculty to staff their courses for the thousands of veterans who were enrolling in higher education under the GI Bill. I was offered a job as an instructor of English at Creighton University, a Jesuit university in Omaha, Nebraska, and I started teaching there in the autumn of 1948. In my first semester there, I was assigned to teach four sections of freshman English and one section of a survey course in English literature. I had never taken a course in writing in my undergraduate school nor had I taken one in how to teach composition. After teaching four sections of composition in a row, 3 days a week, I felt I was entering heaven when, at 3 in the afternoon, I got a chance to teach a sophomore survey course in English literature. In later years, when I reflected on how unprepared I was to teach a freshman writing course, I felt I owed all those students a profound apology for my ineptitude. In those classes I had them doing irrelevant things, such as diagramming sentences, a skill that I had acquired from the nun I had in my seventh- and eighth-grade classes in an elementary school in Milwaukee.

I have often spoken or written about how I serendipitously discovered rhetoric during that first semester of my teaching career. One day, in my sophomore literature course, I was scheduled to deal with the essays of Addison and Steele. As a result of my acquaintance with the New Criticism, I was able to analyze the life out of a poem or a play or a story, but I did not know how to analyze a piece of nonfictional prose. So in preparation for that class, I went to the criticism section of the Creighton library. In surveying the shelves, my eye fell on a calfskin-covered book titled *Lectures on Rhetoric and Belles Lettres*. This was a collection of the lectures that Hugh Blair had delivered to his classes at the University of Edinburgh during the second half of the 18th century. I did not know what *rhetoric* was, but I knew what *belles lettres* referred to. *Belles lettres* dealt with the kinds of texts I had been using with in the first half of the sophomore survey course that I was teaching, and the essays of Addison and Steele certainly qualified as *belles lettres*. So I took the book down from the shelf and opened it up. The book opened fortuitously to one of Hugh Blair's sentence-by-sentence analyses of one of Addison's *Spectator* essays. Voila! I stood there and read two of Blair's analyses of Addison's essays, and I was so impressed that I checked the book out of the library and brought it home and prepared my lecture for the next day on Addison's essays.

That was the beginning of my relation with rhetoric. Eventually, I went back to the beginning of the book and read all 47 of Blair's lectures. In the earlier chapters, Blair traced out the history of rhetoric, starting with the Greeks and Romans and then going on to the development of rhetoric studies in the Middle Ages and in the Renaissance. Ultimately, Blair presents the changes that the 18th-century rhetoricians like himself, George Campbell, and Adam Smith had made in the presentation of rhetoric to their students. The Scottish rhetoricians treated rhetoric first as the Greeks and Romans did, as it related to the courtroom and the public forum; then as the rhetoricians of the Middle Ages did, as it related to the pulpit and to letter writing; and finally as the rhetoricians of the Renaissance did, as it related to printed discourse. The major new contribution that the Scottish rhetoricians made to the development of rhetoric was their application of rhetoric to the analysis and creation of belletristic texts.

Blair got me interested enough in his review of the history of rhetoric that I went back to such rhetoricians as Aristotle, Isocrates, Cicero, and Quintilian and read their extant texts. I was so impressed and fascinated by their presentation of rhetoric that I began to apply some of their instruction not only to my literature courses but also to my writing courses. Eventually the chair of the English department assigned me to teach a course in the history of rhetoric to graduate students who were assigned to teach one or more sections of our freshman writing course. And as a result of my own reading and teaching, I improved immensely as a teacher of writing.

By the end of my second year at Creighton, I had abandoned my plan to become a journalist and decided I wanted to become a teacher. I realized, however, that if I wanted to pursue a career in teaching on the college and university level, I would have to get a doctorate. So I applied to Loyola University in Chicago and was accepted for the autumn of 1950 as a graduate student and as a teaching assistant (TA), assigned to teach two sections of freshman English. In my writing courses at Loyola, I began to use some of the techniques of classical rhetoric and some of the techniques of the rhetoric introduced by the Scottish rhetoricians. I discovered that I was now a much more effective teacher of composition than I had been at Creighton University.

By the time I finished the course work for my doctorate at Loyola and passed my qualifying examinations in June 1953, I had decided that I would write my dissertation on Blair. I found a professor who approved of that project and consented to be my director. By that time, I had two children and could no longer live on a TA's stipend, so I accepted an invitation to return to Creighton University as an assistant professor. Soon after returning there, I was appointed as the director of freshman English and began writing my dissertation. I finally took my doctoral degree in June 1956. The first chapter of my dissertation presented a survey of the rhetoric textbooks used in English schools in the 16th, 17th, and 18th centuries. That chapter became the basis for the "Survey of Rhetoric" from the time of the Greeks and Romans to the 20th century that I included in my book *Classical Rhetoric for the Modern Student*, first published by Oxford University Press in April 1965. That book is now going into its fourth edition, coauthored by a former graduate student of mine, Robert Connors.

That book was also responsible for my getting the job as director of freshman English at Ohio State University (OSU) in 1966. Albert Kuhn, chair of the English Department at OSU, used my book in the training course for the new crop of teaching assistants in the autumn of 1965. When I learned that the writing program at OSU had succeeded the program at the University of Minnesota as the largest freshman English program on a single campus, I was mightily intimidated; but the program was so well organized by Edwin Robbins, my predecessor, that I finally agreed to take the job. I just kept the ship afloat. Under the directorship of such people as Susan Miller, Frank O'Hare, and Andrea Lunsford, that freshman program in writing became one of the premier programs in the nation.

That is the story of the beginning of my relationship with rhetoric and of my career as a teacher of composition. I must now deal in a summary way with the remarkable development that has taken place since those early years in the training of teachers of writing and in the shaping of freshman English programs. One of the factors in that remarkable development is the growth in size and sophistication of the CCCC (4Cs). When I was the program chair of the 4Cs convention in Seattle, Washington, in the early 1970s, we were lucky if we could attract 300 people. The 4Cs now attracts somewhere between 3,000 and 4,000 people. And many of those in attendance and who participate in the program are graduate students.

As mentioned earlier, I will make use here of my article "Teaching Composition: Where We've Been and Where We're Going," which appeared in the December 1987 issue of *CCC*. The most economical way for me to use this nine-page article is to quote the headings of its eight major sections. I will briefly summarize the contents of each of these sections.

1. *The Enhanced Professionalism of the Composition Teacher:* We older teachers are well aware of how much better trained the younger teachers are today than we were.

2. *The Growth of Graduate Programs in Rhetoric and Composition:* In 1987 Gary Tate published a list of graduate programs in rhetoric and composition in the United States, and in 1994 Stuart C. Brown, Paul R. Meyer, and Theresa Enos updated the survey, showing the significant increases in programs. Both lists were published in *Rhetoric Review.*

3. *Books on the History, Theory, and Practice of Composition:* Those who read the ads in flyers and in journals about new books are well aware of the growing list.

4. *Special Conferences on Rhetoric and Composition:* Many of you have attended some of these special conferences.

5. *New Journals and New Research in Rhetoric and Composition:* In the April 1984 issue of *College English,* Robert Connors listed 15 new resources.

6. *Changes in What We Teach in the Composition Classroom:* (a) the teaching of business, professional, and technical writing, (b) the writing-across-the-curriculum movement, and (c) the TESOL programs.

7. *Changes in How We Teach Composition:* One of those significant changes was the shift of attention from the product of writing to the process of writing.

8. *A Negative Note About the Teaching of Composition:* In this section I expressed my growing doubts about whether I had done the students in my writing classes any good. Here I quote two of the final paragraphs of this article:

Lately, I have been giving myself the Marine Corps treatment. In Marine boot camp, the Drill Instructors had a marvelously effective way of communicating with their charges. On the parade ground, for instance, if anyone fouled up in the marching formation, the Drill Instructor would halt the platoon, would right-face us, and then while we all stood at quivering attention, he would stride down to the offending recruit, stick the tip of his nose right up against the tip of the recruit's nose, and for the next five minutes, he would subject the poor recruit to his wonderfully varied and emphatic ways of letting him know that he was an asshole.

Well, one morning recently while I was shaving—probably after a period of being conscience-stricken about my repeated failures as a teacher of writing—I stuck this big nose of mine against the tip of the nose reflected in the mirror and shouted at the top of my lungs, "CORBETT, YOU FRAUD!"

How does it make you feel when the man who was named for the 1996 Exemplar Award confesses, in a loud voice, that he is a fraud?

Columbus, Ohio
March 26, 1997

CHAPTER TWO

Getting to Know Rhetorica

Janice Lauer
Purdue University

I grew up in a family that loved words. My father, Vincent, at age 15, was president of the *Detroit News* Young Writers' Club, publishing short essays and cartoons in the early 1920s (see Appendix). Most early mornings as a child, I put in an hour or two reading stories before the rest of my family was awake; but writing did not come as naturally. When I was 10, my aunt Mercedes sculpted two statues, one of my sister, Carolann, with a dog and doll, and one of me holding a book. Was that a forecast?

During my elementary, high school, and college days, I don't remember ever meeting Rhetorica, but I spent a lot of time with Grammar. When I started teaching in 1954 as a member of a religious community, Rhetorica was a stranger to me—at times a distant suspicious figure, at times an over-dressed clown. In my undergraduate background, I had been enchanted with philosophy, committed to literature, a companion of Latin and French, and a disciple of social justice. During my first years of teaching elementary, junior high, and high school, however, I often felt a gap in my preparation as a teacher. My students in these years, whether in the inner-city school, small blue-collar town, or wealthy suburb, needed help in learning how to write. But my educational resources were silent. The textbooks showed to my students elegant pieces of prose, glistening in their stylistic sophistication, juxtaposed with ugly pages of exercises in grammar, spelling, and punctuation. I was frustrated. Why had my education left me so bankrupt in the face of one of my key responsibilities?

Having taught for 5 years, I was sent to get a master's in English at St. Louis University. During my first semester, I met the usual faculty crowd of New Critics, Shakespearean experts, modern poetry devotees. I became intrigued with modern and contemporary British and American poetry, eventually writing a master's essay on Wallace Stevens' poetry. In the second semester of my work, however, I met Rhetorica face to face in the most unlikely time and place—an 8 a.m. Saturday bibliography course taught by a Jesuit who had recently returned from studies in Europe—Walter Ong. Rhetorica wasn't formally introduced to our class but crept in the back way: One day I learned through the graduate student grapevine that our professor had written on the subject of rhetoric. When I sought out these publications, I caught my first glimpse of Rhetorica. During that semester, filled as it was with print fonts, recto and verso, research venues, and the like, I occasionally asked questions about the "extra" reading I had been doing and heard from Fr. Ong my first commentary on Rhetorica and her problems with Peter Ramus.

After finishing my degree, in 1960 I began teaching college English; one composition course in particular was touted as rigorous because it taught students how to think. The "subject matter" of the course was logic: categorical, hypothetical, and disjunctive syllogisms, and fallacies. I dutifully prepared and taught this course, drilling students on syllogisms, and awaited students' rigorously argued texts. I got a few, but most students were baffled about the relationship of logic to their writing. After giving this pedagogy a good chance, I turned to casebooks. I remember well a casebook on tragedy that my honors English class loved to discuss. They became excited about tragedies, and a few even wrote good pieces; but again the connection between tragedy and writing was tenuous. I then turned to another content for the composition class—linguistics, especially structural and transformational grammar. Following the latest pedagogical craze, I figured that knowing the structure of the language would surely help my students become better writers. Again disappointment.

In 1962, I entered the doctoral program at the University of Michigan as a commuting student while continuing to teach my classes. Through a mutual friend, I had an initial interview with Warner Rice, then in his last years as legendary head of the English department. When he asked what my area of interest was, I told him that I wanted to study rhetoric. He paused for some time and then said, "We don't teach rhetoric here anymore, but we used to be called a Department of Rhetoric." (Only much later, after I had finished my work, did I learn that he had been one of Fred Newton Scott's students!) He said, however, that there was an indirect way to study rhetoric if I followed a particular degree course, which would entail examinations in two areas of English (I chose modern British and American literature and English linguistics) and a few courses in education, with options for interdisciplinary studies. He offered to be my academic advisor. Although I never encountered Rhetorica in any of my courses in Ann Arbor, I made arrangements for private meetings, writing every paper on one of her aspects, gradually becoming more familiar with her. During these meetings, I became fascinated with rhetorical invention, beginning to understand Ong's point that Ramus' banishment of invention from rhetoric had been a major force in marginalizing rhetoric in the academy.

In my courses in Ann Arbor, none of my instructors seemed familiar with my new friend, although they tolerated the rhetorical emphases in my papers. One summer, when the Linguistics Society held its summer institute in Ann Arbor, I took three courses, including a psycholinguistics course taught by John Carroll from Harvard, one of the leading theorists in this subfield. I had high hopes that psycholinguistics would be a link to rhetorical invention. During the class, I asked questions about the relationship between knowledge and discourse and about invention but consistently received answers that limited linguistics to the sentence level, causing me to realize that linguistics would not provide a venue for exploring rhetoric, especially rhetorical invention.

In 1965, feeling rhetorically isolated, I attended a Conference on College Composition and Communication (CCCC), wandering from one session devoted to practical teaching tips to another. Unstimulated, I found myself listening to a panel of three people with exciting ideas: Pete Becker, Jim Moffett, and Richard Young. When I checked my program, I was surprised to see that two of them were at the University of Michigan. When I went up afterward to speak to them, I found that Becker and Young taught in the humanities department of the engineering school, at that time on another planet from the English department. The four of us went out for coffee and a long conversation about rhetoric and composition. In today's parlance, I had found the first members of my discourse community. I heard about Moffett's curriculum and about Young and Becker's rhetorical theory, called tagmemics.

Following that encounter, Richard Young and I had occasional conversations to continue our mutual interest in invention. I was just formulating my doctoral committee and requested that he serve as a member. The other members included James Downer, a broad-minded linguist who served as chair; Hugh English, then director of composition; and Ronald Tikofsky, the new head of psycholinguistics, who was studying aphasia in rats! In my dissertation, I narrated the fate of rhetorical invention from the classical period to the 20th century, linking the notion of rhetorical invention to the emerging study of heuristics and studying its features as a source for a new understanding of invention. I also surveyed contemporary rhetorical theories, such as Kenneth Burke's, and rhetoric as epistemic, seeking possible sources for a new inventional theory of writing. Finally, I analyzed the existence (or lack thereof) of invention in major composition textbooks and evaluated current theories and texts in terms of their inventional potential.

Rhetorica was now no longer a stranger to me. But our relationship needed a community in which to flourish; it came in the form of the newly started Rhetoric Society of America. When I attended the first organizational meeting at the CCCC (4Cs) in Minneapolis in 1968, I found rhetoric devotees from the fields of communication, philosophy, and English interested in forming a society to share issues and problems in discourse. At subsequent 4Cs meetings, this group met to discuss these rhetorical interests. A subgroup began to go out to dinner at the 4Cs; the regular members were Ed Corbett, Ross and Norma Winterowd, George and Mary Yoos, Richard Young, and me. Although I do not remember our specific conversations over wine and salmon, I do recall that from these events I gained a sense of community and a dedication to developing rhetorical studies within English departments. This group became a sustaining force, isolated as most of us were in English departments uninterested in Rhetorica and disdainful of Composition.

Our devotion to Rhetorica could not be kept under a bushel; it needed outlets, grounding, offspring. During the years since my 1967 dissertation, I have tried to introduce rhetoric in different situations: in my classes; through an inventional pedagogy that I shared with colleagues and graduate students at two schools, Marygrove College and the University of Detroit; at 13 summer rhetoric seminars that eventually enrolled 442 people from every state, as well as Canada and England, in a textbook and essays; and finally in a doctoral program in rhetoric and composition.

Over the years, Rhetorica has changed, responding to epistemological shifts and ideological developments. That was inevitable with her because she lives and breathes in context, situated and strategic, creating knowledge and effecting change palpably through discourse. Her changes have deepened our relationship, helping me to grow as a teacher and scholar. I am happy now seeing Rhetorica stroll the halls of academia, invigorating many fields and empowering students to inquire and work toward social justice. Little did my father realize that his love of words would "get me" and that I would join with others to help the academy and students to conclude that "'riting is not so bad."

West Lafayette, Indiana
January 13, 1997

APPENDIX

Items from the scrapbook of Vincent T. Lauer
(published in the *Detroit News*, 1920–1922)

1922 OFFICERS OF THE YOUNG WRITERS' CLUB

Vincent Lauer (center) was elected president of the Young Writers' Club; John Hicks (left), vice-president, and Betty O'Neil (right) secretary and treasurer. We are expecting great things from this trio of live Young Writers.

WINNERS OF THE 1921 CREDIT RACE

The prize of $25, awarded to the Young Writer for the highest number of credits earned during the past year, goes to Vincent Lauer, who had 340 credits; Marion Schleede second, 316; John Hicks third, 201, and Leland Jacobs fourth, 184.

Others who won high number of credits are as follows. Eva Calkins, 121; John Vogt, 102; Alwilda Nutt, 101.

Observations of the Schoolroom Clock.
by Vincent Lauer.

"Ho, Hum! There's that pretty schoolmistress, Miss Smith, winding me up again. Another five hour's work.
"Tick-tock! Here they come. 'Stuck-up' Alice Jones, Tommy Peters, Henry John Sullivan, Lucy Marshall, Mary Anderson, Lewis Johnson, Harry Wynn—all there. How they pester me!"Ho, Hum! If they only knew! If I could only drop to the floor and end it all, instead of remaining here, so far above all those pesky scholars!
"Tick-tock!
What! 'Rithmetic already! This is the class that worries me. Ouch! As soon as teacher turns her back to the class those impudent rascals plaster my face with spitballs. That's the tenth one that has struck me. Henry John has the surest aim of all. Oh, if I could get down and box his ears with my metal hands. Thank goodness, there's the bell for recess."
"Tick-tock! Tick-tock! Oh! Peace at last, even if it is short and sweet."
"Another class! Well, 'riting is not so bad. Now they pester each other and forget me for a while. Look at Tommy pulling Mary's braids. I'll wager he never gets a touch of the strap at home. Evidently his parents are familiar with that old saying, 'Spare the rod and spoil the child'—at least his actions show it. How glad I am that he can not reach me and try to pull my scanty gray locks! Horrors! A toad hopping up the aisle. I wonder if it can possibly jump this high. Ah, teacher is telling Harry to carry the ugly creature outside. Sure enough, there he goes."
"What can be causing all the excitement since Harry came in? Why even teacher is standing upon her chair shrieking! Oh, I see, it's a mouse Harry just brought in. Listen to their squeals. This means the end of school for today. My, how they can run. That door ought to be open a few feet wider to accommodate them all.
"Tick-tock! Tick-tock!"

What Happened When the School Clock Stopped.
by Vincent Lauer.

I am a school clock of uncertain age and ancestry. Of course, one of my social standing could only be located in a country school, and such is the place where I reside.
One day I had an idea that I would take a much-earned rest—in other words, I would stop ticking for a while. The day I determined upon was a warm September day about a week or so after school had reopened. Practically all the students, especially the boys, were feeling "blue"— there is no necessity for mentioning the cause of this feeling, as the reader himself may be familiar with it—and the teacher, too, was feeling quite "blue," for it was hard work to teach a class of grumpy, downcast students, whose minds were at least a half mile from the schoolhouse—the exact location being the "ole swimmin' hole," a much-frequented gathering place for the boys. I delayed the time for going on strike till after the students had eaten lunch. After classes had been resumed, suddenly, with a sharp whirring sound which only I can make, I stopped dead. Poor teacher now had no means of judging the length of the classes!
Fortunately (for the students, however), one of the boys had with him a large watch which he had, to all appearances, at least, set to the correct time in the morning, but I had observed his actions and noticed that he had set his timepiece about three-quarters of an hour ahead, so that, when the teacher asked for this watch to judge class time, the periods were speeded up quite a bit more than usual. Thus, when the teacher rang the dismissal bell at 4 o'clock it was really only a few minutes past 3, and the boys hurried to the "old swimming hole," rejoicing at the unexpected free time, and I knew I had earned the gratitude of all the class that day. The next morning, with the same unexpectedness I had previously exhibited, I resumed ticking again, to the extreme dismay of the entire class.

CHAPTER THREE

Looking at Writing; Writing What I See

Charles Bazerman
University of California, Santa Barbara

In Burma in the holy city of Pagan, a large Buddha sits in the Manuha temple, a building scarcely larger than the Buddha himself. The Buddha cannot stir without bumping into a wall, cannot even shake his head without being reminded of his containment. When you walk into the chamber you see only what is immediately in front of you—mostly Buddha's throne, or Buddha's knees. You cannot gain any view of the whole. There is no room to walk around. To see another aspect of the god, you have to exit and enter through another door. Only one person can comfortably occupy each entrance. Two people crowd each other and spoil the contemplation of the god.

Although there are larger Buddhas and smaller shrines elsewhere in that city of temples, one is left with a sense of the overwhelming immensity of this particular Buddha, a Buddha too large to perceive as a whole, and of the smallness of the space the Buddha is confined within. King Manuha built this temple in 1059 C.E. while imprisoned by King Anawrahta. It is said to have been built as an act of defiance and complaint under the guise of piety. Today it has become a political symbol, and small gifts to the temple are perceived as acts of defiance, which the repressive military regime overlooks to maintain its own veneer of piety.

All of us who have lived within the chambers of composition housed within the temples of literature daily witness the power of writing. We see the difference that writing makes in the life chances, personal development, intellectual growth, and spiritual well-being of our students and the difference writing makes in the work, common wisdom, and cultural cohesion

15

of communities. It is our good fortune to participate in and draw strength from this great force.

We regularly see writing to be greater than the space the academy invites it into; simultaneously, we are regularly reminded of institutional and intellectual walls that inhibit our vision and our range of action. Nonetheless, even the most straitened of visitors, entering through the most official of main doors, senses that this is far from a trivial god. So people have come to love this god even in its most orthodox emanations, with good reason.

I grew up in a household and a school system that were ever mindful of the monuments of Western culture. In the postwar New York suburbs, elite culture seemed to provide a meritocratic pathway for upward mobility for the children of Eastern European Jewish immigrants. My parents' socialist yearnings of Brooklyn in the 1930s had turned to dreams of financial success for themselves and professional achievement for their children. I was given encouragement and access to books, libraries, museums, theaters. Children's adventure stories soon turned to the hagiographies of the Landmarks of America series and of scientists' lives. I read of the personal struggle for achievement ever driving the communal journey of progress.

But history, science, and *Mad* magazine told me of complexity and critique. Steinbeck and Twain, socialist muckraking novels, and union history led me to Upton Sinclair and Bertolt Brecht as I moved through my teens. Too high-minded for early rock and roll, I tuned into lefty folk and early blues but also saturated myself with the wonderful optimism of musical comedies and the densities of classical music: Pete Seeger, Leadbelly, Mary Martin, and Dietrich Fischer-Dieskau.

I wrote and formed my consciousness in imitation of what I read and heard. In the eighth grade I wrote my history final exam imitating the rolling cadences of a film we had seen about the great Johnstown flood. I later found out it was Vachel Lindsay who inspired that exam essay. Reading Twain gave me more tools to be a cynical wise-mouth, a role I practiced in hopeless long letters to young women I met at summer arts and music camps. Brecht gave me a sharp-edged vision of life, consciousness, and the theater, which I puzzled over in many essays. After reading political philosophy in a summer program during high school, I came back with involuted considerations of fundamental principles. Four years of a citywide program for high school students being groomed for careers in science taught me not only to dwell in intolerable detail and to explain beyond the patience of all reasonable mortals but also to seek underlying principles that would lend a beautiful clarity to a vision—a vision that had to be plausibly true, empirically possible, and as close to what we can experience as possible given the limits of our means of representation. That early hands-on experience with science clued me in to how messy the process was and also how ambitious—just like writing. One could create something that would make a difference; with enough hard work and inspired thought, one could see new things about our life and world, gain evidence, understand principles, write them down, and make them visible. One could formulate statements to make sense of things.

This version of science fit well with a version of politics and social involvement I was growing up into—making the world better by understanding it better and not believing any of the pieties that we were taught to justify the naughtiness of the way things were. The civil rights movement opened up a clarity of vision that seemed to put the lie to the world we had inherited, as did the antinuclear movement. My undergraduate years coincided with the misperceptions, stupidities, and lies that led us into the waste of the Vietnam War. I remember at first thinking the government must know better, must have reasons, must have some information. But when the government mounted its best arguments and facts in a series of public white papers, it was evident that there was no more than met the eye.

I became even more stubborn about having to understand what I was being asked to believe, to be given persuasive arguments and convincing evidence. The games of the intellect, the transformation of experience into words, the arguments people made to themselves and in public—all these things were, it began to dawn on me, deathly real. We were in history; we are always in history; and words are much of what we use to create that history.

But in my own increasing stubbornness to follow only the path I came to understand, I could not align with the doctrines of the New Left that were being born on the campuses at that time. Nor could I align with another movement that by accident I came in close contact with, a movement that has since become as influential as their wildest hopes would have it. It was a movement that I came to reject early, to define myself against; but in that dialectic of argument, I was forced to contemplate my own answers to the questions they raised. During my undergraduate years at Cornell, I lived in a small scholarship house, where we were honored by the presence of resident faculty guests the likes of Madame Frances Perkins, legendary secretary of labor under Franklin Roosevelt and first woman cabinet member. Allan Bloom was another large presence in the house during my stay there. He was resident in the house for two of those years, and he developed a coterie of followers among my fellow house members—a coterie that was to form part of the core group of the neoconservatives who have had such an influence since the mid-1970s. In endless discussions over meals and late into the night, I was never quite able to accept any of the principles that seemed to drive this group of followers of Leo Strauss to believe that they were an elite of philosophers who had the right and responsibility to shape the lives of others—if only they could get their hands on the levers of power. Although I almost always wound up on the "other side" in every discussion,

I was attuned to ask fundamental questions about political and social order, the relation of culture and communication to the constitution of the state, and the ways of life possible within any regime. This perspective has helped me see the link between individual acts of communication and the various orders of society we live in, a link that I later discovered could be fruitfully explored through the social sciences.

In the prayer wheel of undergraduate majors, I spun past many of the notches—physics, math, German, government. I wound up in English. I was in part motivated by personal family issues that I was working out through the fictions of literature and the fictions of criticism (hardly an unusual motivation in literature departments, but a motivation that leads to many views with little distanced perspective and little intersubjective reliability). But I was also attracted by the powerful tools of intellectual and representational shaping I was being exposed to. I was fascinated by the structure of Shakespeare's plots and the emotional worlds created within the poetic spaces that came into being within the plot structures. I came to appreciate the large architectonic structures of Milton's writing that allowed grand visions of the workings of the world to take shape. Through drama I came to understand how each line, each utterance was embedded in layers of context and authorial structuring. I also became interested in the phenomenology and social distribution of styles that enacted different life worlds for the various characters and for the various audiences. The voices of different poems showed me different ways of being and different stances one could adopt toward the world one found oneself in.

Again my own writing imitated and drew on the resources of the writers that filled my head. As a freshman I wrote a paper on Faulkner's 1,500-word sentence that quoted internally an equally long sentence by Faulkner, and I wrote a long *Waste Land*-ish poem enacting the ditherings of my teenage love passions. (Of course I had a crush on Jean Blackall, my freshman writing professor, who allowed me such indulgences.) As a senior and then a first-year graduate student, I wrote long architectonic papers that laid out structured phenomenologies of text worlds and then Shandean papers that disrupted those orders to create small comedic spaces of sympathy. And I began to explore the romantic imagination, becoming comfortable with metaphor and synesthesia in my poetry and thought.

At the same time as I was assembling mental spaces for myself from reading and reenacting the literary tradition, I began reexamining the social spaces my own language habits were creating. I was dissatisfied with the distances I was constantly creating with others, partly from my stubbornness in working through my views, partly from the supreme confidence I had in my judgments, and partly from the language habits I had learned in my less-than-functional family. I began to observe what I said and how that influenced the unfolding of conversations and relationships. I had a long

way to go, and my personality remakes were pretty clumsy, but I did begin
to see concretely what it means to make oneself and one's relationships
through language. This predisposed me for some powerful experiences I
was to have shortly thereafter.

Before then, however, I was to experience graduate school and some
fundamental questioning about the profession I was preparing for. Although
I saw that reading of literature offered some personal pleasure and expan-
sions of my own mind, eventually those pleasures wore thin. In addition,
all the major scholarly and critical tasks (as of the late 1960s) seemed pretty
well mined out. Even if one found a "strangely neglected topic," as Amis'
Lucky Jim put it, becoming an acolyte to another's accomplishment, an
accomplishment of another place and time, struck me as a sort of weak
goal for one's life. Even more, I couldn't see that professing literature did
much for anyone else or for our society in the aggregate, despite the fact
that my graduate education was funded by a National Defense Education
Act fellowship. People on their own (with perhaps the help of a small
number of scholarly guides) could read pretty much whatever interested
them. The large industry of literary studies seemed to me only to support
class ideology, the high end of the leisure entertainment business, and the
personal indulgences of its academic employees. In short, it seemed a selfish,
and in the long run unsatisfying, kind of life, not quite appropriate for an
adult. Becoming a creative writer seemed a bit more attractive, and I began
to put more energy into my own poems and fictions. The two teachers who
meant much to me that year were the poet Howard Nemerov, who kept
alive the fire of language, and the poet and critic J. V. Cunningham, who
cut through the inflations of literary criticism by considering the material
and intellectual conditions of actual authors. Cunningham also taught me,
as he taught all of his students, the power of knowing a few well-placed
facts and the power of writing a sharply focused line.

The U.S. government, desiring from me more direct service in the national
defense, solved my dilemma by removing my student deferment, as they
did for all first-year graduate students in the spring of 1968. I did not intend,
however, to allow myself to be put in a position where I would have to kill
others out of self-defense for a cause that no one was yet able to explain
to me satisfactorily. After examining my alternatives (including an exploratory
trip across the Canadian border), I discovered that New York City was
recruiting graduate students who needed draft deferments to teach inner-city
elementary school. It seemed an honorable alternative, and I took it. We
were given the appearance of training over the summer, but I got my real
training from books like Herbert Kohl's *Thirty-Six Children.*

After Labor Day we were assigned to schools—just in time for the Ocean
Hill–Brownsville strike, where the unions were resisting community control
of the school districts. Despite my long attachment to unions, I sided with

the communities, and everything I saw about how those schools were run confirmed that the community was justified in wanting changes. My first day of teaching began with three teachers (an old-line socialist, an experienced teacher with strong ties to the community, and an untrained and overeducated college boy) and several community parents breaking the locks on PS 93K in Bedford-Stuyvesant, Brooklyn. My task that day was to keep 70 kindergartners and first-graders amused for several hours. What the day lacked as an educational experience for the students, it made up for as an educational experience for me. Events gradually became a bit less exciting, and my teaching did improve.

I came away from my 2 years of teaching first and third grade with a firm conviction that literacy was important—it made real difference in people's lives. I saw children in my classes make rapid cognitive, social, and behavioral changes as they learned to read and write, and I saw the older children in the school developing personalities, goals, and social connections depending on which side of the literacy divide they perceived themselves to be. I also learned that inner-city schools at that time, with their funding, social, political, and numerous other problems, made it nearly impossible to carry forward a progressive, student-oriented program. In order to have anything like useful reading materials for my class, for example, I had to get up at 5, write (typing a first draft directly onto Rexograph masters) a one- or two-page story about two children whose lives resembled the lives of my students, and then arrive in the school early enough to break into the basement room where the Rexograph was kept because I did not have official approval to make copies. Of course, I had to purchase the paper and the masters and smuggle them into the school, as there were no supplies.

At the same time as I was learning the deep pleasure of making a difference in other people's lives, I entered into psychotherapy with clinical psychologist Tony Gabriele. This experience is relevant here because of the nature of Tony's beliefs and the character of his therapy. He saw unhappiness and marginality in life coming from failures of social relations. Social relations, he believed, could be improved by increasing social competence, coordination, and consensuality—not to get along in a superficial way, but to build those intimacies that met our needs, allowed us to share what was important to us, and gave us space to say what we had to say to those who could listen. Furthermore, he saw the heart of competence, coordination, and consensuality in our ability to use language. His main technique of therapy was to engage in reflexive self-observations of language behaviors. That is, I had to learn to be able to look on the interactions I was part of so as to be able to monitor and examine the consequences of my own participation. Progress was made not by suppression of behaviors (quite to the contrary, he encouraged spontaneity and candor) but by coming to see the effects of various behaviors. His techniques bore some relation to the microsociology of conversational analysts and of Erving Goffman. His work is little known outside the group of people who had direct contact with him because he published little. Just before he died a few years ago, he completed a book manuscript, but it remains unpublished.

Tony provided me the key to putting together many of the themes in my own quest and then brought those themes home to the moment-by-moment experience of life. My life became something more than just a bookish life. Furthermore, what I learned from Tony about spoken language applied directly back onto the reflective production of written text, improved through inspection and revision, to achieve consequential social interactions. Tony also introduced me to and showed me the concrete value of innovative thinkers such as Harry Stack Sullivan, George Herbert Mead, and Gregory Bateson. The social sciences became really interesting.

After being fired three times by administrators and rehired twice by the community, and now having a 4F draft rating (in part ensured by the medical consequences of trying to get anything accomplished in my school), I returned to graduate school in literature. It was to be another decade before there was anything like a program in rhetoric, and I had no better idea than to complete a degree I had started. Although my strangely neglected dissertation topic, *Poems Occasioned by the Death of Queen Elizabeth I and the Accession of King James I,* seems hopelessly arcane, it actually grew out of my long-standing interest in the class distribution of styles and the relation of style to emotion, and it foreshadowed my interests in rhetorical situation and genre. The dissertation's main defining characteristic was that I could finish it fast, knowing I wanted to get out and get on with whatever was to follow. Cunningham, a writer of epigrams and other very short forms, suggested that sufficient conclusion for my dissertation would be QED (Quod erat demonstratum: "which was to be demonstrated or proved"). He was invaluable in aiding my quick getaway from graduate school before it ground me down.

What followed was the academic job market collapse of 1971. After a period of scrambling, I wound up with a full-time position at Baruch College in City University of New York (CUNY), which had recently adopted an open admissions policy. The line I was hired into was funded by an educational opportunity program, and I was told I had a particular responsibility for developmental writing. This was a job that made sense to me. In my pretenure years, I gestured toward the kinds of publications my department would recognize; I still have, sitting in my filing cabinet, the definitive readings of Nabokov's oeuvre, Ben Jonson's *Sejanus,* the grotesque in the writings of Graham Greene, and the social parameters of occasional verse in the Renaissance. My real energy, however, went into composition, as I started to figure out what was going on in my classrooms and what students would benefit from. After tenure I gave up the pretense of literary studies, leaving that to my colleagues who still harbored visions of an ivy-covered life.

Although on my campus there were few teachers who cared to do more than blame their students for their own fallen station in life, several of the campuses at CUNY were facing the task of open admissions with some energy and commitment. These were the days of Mina Shaughnessy and her group at City College, Ken Bruffee and his first exploration of peer tutoring at Brooklyn College, Sondra Perl at Hostos Community College, Harvey Wiener at LaGuardia, Bob Lyons and Don McQuade at Queens, and many others who were fully and creatively committed to basic writing. We met regularly at city and regional conferences, CUNY meetings, and our own organization, the CUNY Association of Writing Supervisors. Because of the political and institutional moment and Mina Shaughnessy's personal force, there was even for a short period universitywide administrative support for writing.

During that brief period of excitement, some campuses were able to build permanent campus commitments to writing, whereas on other campuses those interested in writing had to get by ameliorating programmatic indifference. For a number of years, I was the only member of my department's composition committee. After more than a dozen years of lobbying, the powers that be finally funded a director of freshman composition and then an English as a second language director, so that our 100 or so part-time teachers would have at least a minimum of coordination and direction. Our 30 to 40 tenure-line faculty, despite the fact that two thirds of their teaching load was in composition, were left largely to their own literary devices.

The students at Baruch were the most motivated, appreciative, and interesting with whom I have worked, although they were not uniformly well prepared nor were they necessarily interested in traditional liberal arts education. Because Baruch was located in midtown Manhattan and specialized in business degrees, we drew on all the people who inhabited the city and on immigrants from all corners of the world. Their lives were overburdened, and their personal problems were pressing. Anything teachers offered that they perceived would help them through the complications of their lives and would provide them some hope of social mobility gained their serious commitment. They knew what hard work was. On the other hand, if teachers could not demonstrate to them the value of what they were demanding, the students treated the course simply as a contract that had to be fulfilled on the way to a degree that they knew would have some exchange value.

Their need and appreciation motivated me to dig into my own privileged experience with language and familiarity with the academy to share as much as I could articulate and then to go out and investigate more how writing worked in the world. My reigning metaphors for my first years of teaching were "letting the cat out of the bag," "spilling the beans," demystifying the class secrets of language and literacy. To my mind, teaching writing was such a political act that it never needed any overt political comment or political teaching. In fact, overt politics would distract us from the task of bringing new groups and individuals into positions of economic and social power and might even undermine the motivation of the students, who for the most part were more interested in the fates of themselves and their families than in any politics. Often enough, they saw their interests tied to political positions that would not be sympathetic to the kind of social change we were enacting in the class. Baruch was a business school, and these were students who were preparing for careers in business, often with the strongest of motivations. I never quite understood my colleagues who saw the task of the humanities as to save these students from the choices they were committed to. I saw more promise in helping them become what they wanted to become.

Such concerns drove my own inquiries into what kind of writing it took to succeed in the academy and in the world, how academic and professional writing were carried out in intertextual webs of specialized communication, and how writing acted as a social force. Writing from sources, writing across the curriculum, writing in the disciplines, the rhetoric of science and technology, social studies of science, genre theory, writing and social theory, and activity theory—my developing interests in these areas is available in the open record of my publications. I do not recapitulate those pathways here except to say that textbook writing has been as much a path of discovery and contribution for me as have been research and theory writing. The payoff for our field is in the increased competence of writers as they move through their lives, and textbooks directly deliver tools for writers and teachers.

Rhetoric and composition have provided me a position from which to participate in the great drama of literacy without being encompassed, consumed, constrained, and submerged within the narrow worlds of literature, even while they have allowed me to draw on everything I have learned through my experience of literature. Rhetoric and composition have not, however, provided a way out of the institutional dominance of literature. Each of us in composition has experienced our own version of this problem; I reserve my own quaintly painful anecdotes for late nights at conference parties. I must say, however, that no English department to which I have been attached has made it easy to ply my trade or profess my profession. In each school the particulars have been different, but the forces have been the same—forces one violates only at one's own cost.

Despite the kinds of institutional struggles and punishments that seem to go with the territory, rhetoric and composition have provided satisfactions that would not have been available to me had I stayed in more traditional academic paths. Writing, this "strangely neglected topic," is sporadically studied by a few anthropologists, a few psychologists, a few historians, and a few professors of education concerned with the earliest stages of literacy. Yet modern society is deeply entangled with literacy. Literate acts underlie

modern law, government, commerce, finances, bureaucracy, scriptural re-
ligions, knowledge production and dissemination, technology, journalism,
schools and universities themselves, literary and popular literature, printing,
the Internet, and uncountable other aspects of the lives we lead. Composition, looking outward to the uses of writing in the world, is awakening to
the enormous power and ubiquity of writing. Isn't it amazing that there are
almost no university departments directly attending to this most fundamental
of human competencies and accomplishments? Isn't it amazing that the
departments we are housed in are devoted to only a very small subset of
the world's literate productions, that subset that is fictional, engaged during
moments of leisure, associated with the cultural habits of limited classes of
people, and oblivious to the sociocultural–psychological processes it is part
of? Isn't this world filled with wonders? Isn't it a wonder to look upon these
things?

Santa Barbara, California
February 12, 1997

CHAPTER FOUR

Heart of Gold

Wendy Bishop
Florida State University

You ask for a story.

I was a reentry graduate student in composition and rhetoric, beginning my doctoral studies at age 32. Twelve years later, you tell me I'm a prominent scholar and I pinch myself: papers scattered over the study floor, black dog curled up in her regular "I guess it's writing time" position near my feet, next week's single-parent kid's schedule and teaching schedule chattering through the airy reaches of my 6 a.m. Sunday-and-coffee drafting head.

As you see in what follows, I am still sometimes surprised to have laid claim to composition yet very pleased and grateful that I seem to have. Although I know such an arrival is a mixture of luck and (sometimes ridiculous-seeming-at-the-time) choices, it is also a result of finally seeing, finally naming a(n) (a)vocation and being allowed, even encouraged, to do so within a field that I have come to learn allows fairly well for last-minute decisions, that (mostly) welcomes affiliation more generously than other strands of English studies.

My story won't and can't be your story. You may find fool's gold, copper, or iron where I have found gold (and why not—there is more than one metal/metaphor that will work; in fact, I'm a collector of silver, but that is not what Neil Young's song is about).

Finding ourselves is about longing and finally meeting some of our longings face to face. For instance, most creative writers I have met secretly yearn to be (as popular as) a rock-and-roll star. Many compositionists seem to have a hidden poet or (non)fiction writer in them. And in my experience, a great number of teachers who continue as engaged teachers seem also to be lifelong learners, seekers, searchers after their own heart of gold. And what we have learned, we want to pass on ("I want to live/I want to give," croons Neil as I write this).

Today an e-mail to my Florida computer from a master's student in San Bernardino asks me about ideas for writing research, for help on his thesis project; he claims he is a fan of my work. He says, and it is generous of him, that his teachers say I am on the "cutting edge" when it comes to the intersection of composition and creative writing. Tomorrow I'll answer him as best I can—for I do love composition and creative writing, although it has been a long strange trip to this place. Right now, I am trying to share some of the much I won't be able to tell him, despite the way e-mail now speeds us toward each other, creating a sense, some days, that I finally did advertise in the *Chronicle* and raffle my Indiana University of Pennsylvania (IUP) doctorate friends and me off together as a dream English department. Penny, Kevin, and I suggested we might do this one hot humid summer morning during breakfast before our research methods class—three adults who were just refinding their teaching lives, who were enriched and completed by study in rhetoric and composition. But that moment is in this story's future.

In 1981, I return from teaching English as a second language (ESL) in Nigeria and land a job at Northern Arizona University (NAU). At 28, for the first time I'm drawing a regular salary (at least I'm drawing one in U.S. currency and not in fluctuating naira). As an instructor-adjunct, I teach four composition classes, whereas in Africa I was a creative writer teaching ESL only sometimes—that is, I would try to teach, amid war and riot, during lingering illness, in classrooms without books and with an ever-fluctuating number of chairs. Teaching was part of my writer's-life experiences.

Hiking up the hill from the lower NAU campus to the upper campus, I'm a Southern Californian, then a Sacramento Valley northern Californian ("I've been to Hollywood/ I've been to redwood")[1] for whom this is a first moment of living full time in snowy weather. San Francisco Peaks, just below the Grand Canyon, part of the Navajos' four sacred mountain boundary points, presides over the town of Flagstaff like an immense spirit guide. Soaking my shoes in slush, sliding and rebalancing, I arrive at a heated building, walk down a hall into a classroom, and through the line of desks to the front podium where I'll face class after class that term—smiling, going through an assigned textbook (which one I don't remember, but, by the time a scant 4 years later when I am teaching in Fairbanks, Alaska, I am using *Writing Brief* and thinking it is a great improvement).

Unexpectedly alone and newly arrived in this town, I am intensely lonely but accept the fact that loneliness and isolation are part of what happens to writers and that—to be honest—loneliness must happen to me because I can not keep it from happening. I have bought a lime-green Fiat—a disastrous choice—so I can drive 4 hours onto the Navajo Reservation to visit my then-husband, Brad, who applied for and took my Flagstaff office mate Susan's just-left job teaching English at Navajo Community College (and did so in our rattling-apart black Volvo sedan). This is 2 months after we've returned from Africa, 2 weeks after we married, and 1 week after we arrived in Flagstaff, we thought, to live.

I write poems on empty weekends when I can not commute to the reservation or when Brad can't make it back to Flagstaff. That is many weekends, for both the old Volvo and the new Fiat are nearly constantly broken. I inherited some agoraphobia and some Norwegian-mulish endurance from my mother, and I spend time this fall holed up in my drafty rental house trying to teach myself how to write stories—something my genre-differentiated (poetry OR fiction) master's in creative writing from University of California-Davis (UC Davis) had failed to help me learn to do in the late 1970s. Sometimes I wander to a downtown coffee shop to reread my unruly hand-typed drafts.

When I do manage to drive northeast, I find the voyage heartbreakingly beautiful and bleak. It takes me out on Route I-40. Just east of Holbrook on the road to Gallup, I turn north and travel an hour by mesa, buttes, and sky; turn right by an old piece of signage, words rubbed off by sheep and wind; whisk past hogans; stop and photograph sage clumps glistening in road clefts. I head toward Greasewood and Cornfields. Moving steadily northeast, I begin the ascent to the plateau before Chinle, see more and more pickup trucks—grandmothers, kids, babies huddled under blankets in the back—navigate the road around Canyon de Chelley in wind and storm and snow or under a stark blue sky, and crest over the rise to see Navajo Community College laid out in hogan-shaped concrete octagons, all nestled below the purple and green Chuska Mountains. The U.S. Congress provided funds for this campus and granted the tribe the land in the late 1960s. I slow and turn in at the college's entrance road; drive past the run-down rodeo ground; avoid the cattle, ponies, and three-legged dogs that wander everywhere; pass stands of pungent pinyon and ponderosa.

Sometimes, like today, I retake that drive with my eyes closed.

My in-town students write about ski trips, sports events, and parents' divorces. Of the four modes, I always skip argument. The last day of my fall classes, I read to them my first piece of nonfiction, about crossing the Sahara; somehow, I am wanting these men and women in hiking boots and backpacks to know me in a way that—in the middle of the reading aloud—I realize they can not. They listen and look at me dutifully. I can feel my voice echoing, know I am going on too long.

Over Christmas I write a short story about the person who is leaving rocks on my car on both campus parking lots—this regular, intrusive act interests, perplexes, maybe even scares me. I talk to my friend Kate in graduate school in creative writing at the University of Utah in Salt Lake City and decide to apply to her program. I am a finalist for the Walt Whitman Award, one of the more prestigious poetry manuscript contests in the United States. Because I was once told this is the way, I submit to things—contests, magazines, residencies. But I have no one, really, with whom to share my "success" (or my many failures)—Brad is a poet and a teaching assistant-trained writing teacher too, but therein resides some danger; we can not both be the best poet in the world as we had been tutored to think we should be.

I don't win the Walt Whitman award that year or any other, although I have been a several-time finalist for nearly every book contest in the country in the last 20 years of submission (there is nothing I can't tell you about poetry-book contests). If I had won that year, this might be a different story and one I can honestly say I am glad I am not telling, for I like my story; I am grateful to have it (echoing the Stephen Crane poem "In the Desert," "I like it because it is bitter and because it is mine"—though in this case I'd say bittersweet).

I am accepted into the doctoral program in creative writing in Salt Lake City but can not see my way clear to move even further away from Brad. I am lined up to walk farther into that perplexing field—creative writing—but somehow, in the next few months, I'll find I can not make myself go. There. Although I did move to Tsaile, Arizona, and into another narrative.

I start to talk to new graduate students at NAU who are being trained to teach by Sharon Crowley. This seems at the time like useless information—I am already degreed—an adjunct! Joan and Paul and I attend creative-writing readings—Leslie Silko once and then a well-known poet who hits on Joan in poet Jim Simmerman's house at the party that same evening. Just this year, the poet published a memoir about his sexual addictions, and as I flip through it in Barnes and Noble and decide not to buy it, I remember Joan edging away from him, her handsome Italian eyes rolling expressively. There is a table with food. The house is scented with pot and drunken aspirations as *Tattoo You*, the new Rolling Stones album, plays on the turntable. Isn't that just like a creative writer, I think, watching the poet move on to someone else. Rather tired of it all, and lost.

I like my students. I like to teach. I admit that I can not (creative) write all the time, although my raising-up in the creative writing world says I should—that's what writers do. (In fact, I would have to admit, my Norwegian side makes me feel impatient at such an assumption of "creative" indolence.) Anyway, it never seems as if the creative writers I know are writing all the time. Many seem quite content to smoke a cigarette, drink coffee, and gossip about people, parties, poetry prizes; what they will write if and when they have time; what they are not writing; and so on. I can soak up lots of behaviors, but how-tos that will make my Saturday mornings in front of my Smith-Corona electric typewriter more productive do not seem to be available, even for the asking.

It does not seem to matter to the "famous" creative writers, however, if my mind and attention wander. I have already learned from my master's years that taking their classes, going to conferences, sitting in bars with them is like visiting abandoned mine tailings in the California foothills above Capay Valley: rusted skeletal machinery, flywheels, and waterchutes; overgrown and boarded-over sinkholes; played-out veins of ore. Lots of fool's gold, glitter, interesting chunks of pick-axed rock, and after-the-fact history. Unmaintained national monuments, even, maybe.

My students—then, as now—want to tell stories too—I mean, really, we all do—but they want me to listen. I like this classroom's assumption of engagement. In Flagstaff, one in-my-face student claims he's the son of someone famous and I believe him for a while—naive enough to accept that Allen Ginsberg could have had him as a love child. I'm still close enough in age to my students to believe anything. To be honest, I am glad they talk to me at all. And I am glad they do not find me out—how much I do not know what I am doing, although I do it, luckily for us all, with attention and enthusiasm.

I give a young woman a D grade, and she comes to my office to complain. I am trembling mad at her and at myself when she scares me out of my own authority. I can not convince either of us why, really, one grade arrived under my pen instead of another. So I change her D grade to a C grade. True, I have something I have begun to call a *rubric*, adapted from my master's studies. ("Here, read this book—*Writing Without Teachers*," said the busy untenured program assistant at UC Davis, where in the late 1970s everyone was still suspicious of teaching, but the Bay Area Writing Project was just beginning to lay tracks inland—we were on an underground railway of teaching talk, although I didn't know that then.) I give this student a C. She has red hair. It is a sports essay—I hate sports essays, so she probably deserves a C.

I talk to my office mates—Susan, Beth, and Mary Beth—a lot—about our unfolding days of teaching. We are mostly—well, we are all—women; we have bookcases in our shared offices overflowing with complimentary copies of textbooks and a few classroom-based theories. They are, I am, very bright, but it seems to me that we have arrived in our offices and our authority more by life accident than by intention.

We are adjuncts—Susan, a bit older than I, with kids and a husband she supports and novels in her head she wants to write. Mary Beth's husband builds labor-intensive log cabins, and she is always willing to help—her husband, her students, her friends, Susan and me, the department. Beth, the most outgoing, falls in and then out of love with an improbably matched

TA. Me, I'm writing poems, feeding the woodstove aspen that burns too quickly but was easy to collect with my slowly made new friend Tom. In response to a mimeographed query, I slip into department mailboxes (how else does an introvert make friends?), Tom now plays squash with me on a campus court after telling me how to pop his wrestling-damaged knees back in should they pop out and cripple him for a moment. He will invite me to his house to watch the Academy Awards with him, his wife, and their new baby. I have never been around babies much. I do not quite see why Tom, who has a doctorate in literature and works worriedly as an adjunct writing teacher, is in Flagstaff. I do not know about the academic job market in literature. I watch the Academy Awards for the first time in my life because it is something to do in a week filled with woodstoves and student essays.

By 1982, I will live on the reservation. To be with Brad, I'll not renew my NAU job and take the only available job at Navajo Community College, directing a special services program— offering tutoring and special courses to any pre-freshman-testing Navajo students (almost half of each entering class tests this way, of course) at the 300-student (99% Navajo) college in Tsaile. The college is 4 hours from a liquor store and off-reservation town (Gallup, New Mexico, or Durango, Colorado) and 30 minutes from the nearest store at all (Chinle—where Basha's groceries serves up soft drinks and disposable diapers by the case).

I do not know yet that tutoring is teaching. I do not know that in 3 years I'll be married to someone else, have my first child, and be living in Fairbanks, Alaska, during the winter and commuting summers to Indiana, Pennsylvania, to work on a doctorate in rhetoric and linguistics. I do not know a degree like that exists—and, in fact, few degrees like this did exist then.

I am unaware that at this time the first generation of composition scholars, people I would attend my first Conference on College Composition and Communication (CCCC or 4Cs) to make "sightings of," were still making the transition from English (literature, sometimes linguistics) scholars with interesting ideas to individuals putting together a map of a new field. Eventually, I would listen with more awe to Peter Elbow, Pat Bizzell, Linda Flower, and others as they stood up to address a panel speaker than I had ever mustered in person for such writers as Ray Carver, Galway Kinnell, Gary Snyder, Herb Gold, and William Everson, who mostly baffled me as I observed them at writing conferences, unable to imagine myself translated to their place at the dinner table (and in a few cases escaping from wandering hands under a table's edge).

I did not know that compositionists—teachers of writing teachers—even existed or that these same individuals would encourage me to seek answers to questions I did not yet quite know I had.

At Navajo Community College, I am sitting at a round wooden library table in the octagonal, two-story library where my English classes meet.

After running the special services tutoring program for 2 years, I have taken a job teaching English—freshman composition—in a building 20 yards away. I learn I have skills as an administrator, but I also learn I miss plain old teaching. I continue to find I can write poems for only so many minutes and hours a day, and after that I still want to think about writing by teaching it. I am struggling to put together my ESL training and bits of past course work, my more recent composition instruction hours in Flagstaff, and my understanding of composing from an engaged writer's perspective.

I herd my students through *Evergreen*, a grammar-to-paragraph workbook—about which I can still say, years later, it was the best of its kind—but I sense this is not the best I can do. We struggle to identify verbs and subjects before we build sentences before we build paragraphs before we build (maybe if we're lucky) a five-paragraph essay in English composition that sometimes seems as strange to me as to them. Navajo rodeo, highway crashes, and grandmothers replace ski-vacation stories and basketball finals as topics. I fake it—pretend I know what a gerund or a predicate nominative or a transitive verb is, although I am relying on my native speaker's ear (my son and my daughter have learned not to trust me on elementary school grammar exercises—"You missed two," my son Tait said to me recently in a rather put-out voice).

I don't want to read about Navajo rodeos, I want to go to one. I collect names like Notah Ranger and Belinda Manygoats. I'm perplexed by my teaching—or what feels like not-teaching. Students are clean, quiet, dutiful. Lessons have a blankness of . . . well, of lessons. We all look out the glass windows of the library at the Chuska Mountains changing colors as the morning lights them up. I am learning a little about how not to teach Navajos—don't look them straight in the eye, don't demand an answer and wait, don't expect loud discussion until the students file outside and whoop and tease on the way to the cafeteria, don't expect attendance when a ceremony is taking place or grandmother's sheep have to be moved. We *beleganas* (whites) have brought our textbooks and placement tests, scoring sheets, and department goals right past the rodeo grounds and into the classrooms of this small community of first-generation college students who will mostly not go on to Years 3 and 4 in Flagstaff or Tucson or Albuquerque, although they might go hang out for a time in Los Angeles.

Luckily, English and communications, unlike math, has two Navajo teachers teaching Navajos, and I watch and learn from Della and Delilah as they go about their work while I bob on the surface of the college community: Andy Natonabah, the medicine man on staff who lives next door in the adjoining campus housing, burns a sheep skin in the backyard one week. California friends come to visit, and we take a meandering hike into the Chuskas looking for the Lost City of Lukachukai—Anasazi ruins mentioned by early archeologists. We find a place where it should have been built—a south-facing niche with a fine waterfall pouring down in front. We rest in the cave's shadow, admiring the view and the desert-lacquered cliffs of red rock.

Joan and Paul drive up from Flagstaff, then get mired in hours of mud on the way to the rodeo at the Shiprock Fair. I struggle with Gordon—the Navajo special services counselor, former member of the Native American Church—who often seems mad at me because I have such a different sense of time—still thinking semester dates are holy and academic work is the major work of the world. Jennie, my secretary, puts up with me, always visiting with various students, relatives, and friends. I listen to her bright riffs of Navajo interrupted with "Pepsi" and "Pampers" and other brand names. She tells me the horny toad I find outside the office on the walk to work is a "grandfather." Marcie, the Anglo woman who has lived there since the start of the college, is maternal and threatened by my mention of any writing instruction expertise I pretend to.

One day in the giant grocery store in Gallup, I realize I am surprised to see Anglo faces.

I send out my poems and continue to publish; but I am beginning to understand that there's something for which I am still searching, and I can not find it in the pages of my *International Directory of Small Presses and Magazines*. International? I am living overseas in the center of America

I want to be a better writing teacher. I do not need a doctorate in creative writing, I am already writing. I need something else; some "how" for the way I conduct my quiet every days—not in a classroom but around these four library tables on the second floor with the portable chalkboard, the open books, the men and women in Lee jeans with jet-black hair. I learn I want to give something back. But I don't quite know how. And I'm getting old(er).

Brad and I seem if not ill-matched, at least ill-fated, for as soon as we finally can live together at the college, we pull apart. In the overseas-yet-small-town way that Tsaile has, I connect with Marvin, who has lived here since Congressional funds moved the nascent college from Many Farms to Tsaile in the early 1970s. He is a librarian. We have a baby. But I keep thinking I need more book-learning to do this book-teaching. There seems nothing else for it—I apply to Utah again, but I am turned down. I apply to the University of Arizona, in Tucson—in, oddly, fiction writing, or in a program they want to start in creative writing. I am accepted. But Marvin won't go. With a small baby and pretty sure it really wasn't about creative writing anyway and not wanting to lose another marriage to my felt but unnamable goals, I wait, another year.

Resolution comes accidentally. Brad, who has reversed our lifelines by going to Northern Arizona University in Flagstaff to take a summer course, finds a flyer for a program in rhetoric and linguistics. And he happens to mail it to me in my new life without him on the reservation. At Indiana

University of Pennsylvania (IUP), I find I'll be able to attend in the summers, I'll be able to get a doctorate in something called rhetoric and linguistics, I'll be able to learn more about ESL instruction and how to return and teach better. I apply. I'm accepted (although I later find out the program was as worried about admitting a "poet" as this "poet" was about undertaking course work in research and linguistics). Meanwhile, we up and move to Fairbanks, Alaska.

I start graduate school.

I strike gold.

I am thirty-two. Still writing and publishing poems. Still slightly agoraphobic—terribly introverted, shy. With a 15-month-old baby. My worldly possessions are in a U-Haul Marvin is driving alone that summer to Alaska, having left me and Morgan in Indiana, Pennsylvania. I am a westerner stranded in the east. It is the summer of 1985, and I fall in love with rhetoric and composition—quickly, thoroughly, irrevocably, in 10 weeks.

Ahem. I have used up more than 4,000 of my 4,000 words, and I am only just starting my doctorate program!

* * *

Briefly, then, I was in the right place at the right time. I was ready to explore my own writing history in light of writing research. I was allowed to, although, yes, I also had to push for these privileges. I had to persist and insist by petition to take exams in writing program administration. I had to ask to write an essay exploring the connections and intersections of creative writing and composition. I also had to learn linguistics and cognitive research. I was both allowed to and was made to stretch and grow. But finally my intellectual life made sense through these groupings of investigations—into language, into the history of institutions, into research methods.

The IUP program was growing. The students were older, and most were active writing teachers wanting or needing to complete terminal degrees but with classroom experiences they could share and use to test new theories. Resistance was mediated by camaraderie. My professors—Don McAndrew, Pat Hartwell, Mike Williamson—were knowledgeable, demanding (yes, sometimes irritating), intelligent. They tried very hard to be evenhanded, and they could step out of the way. The summer sessions were like boot camp—intense, exhilarating. Best of all, the course work had a domino effect, raising questions and then suggesting answers that, when put into practice in the classroom, raised more questions. I was acquiring tools (finally I learned how to research, and luckily I attended this program just as personal computers became available, allowing me a bigger drafting breath—one that let me write as fast as I thought).

I was offered mentoring that mostly consisted of being treated as an intelligent peer (not as a poetic upstart who might try to "dethrone" the top writer or a reading drone waiting to be initiated into literature). I was allowed the experience of my time in creative writing, and it was assumed I was an intelligent reader. Because the thick skin I had acquired from years of small-poetry-press and big-poetry-prize rejections, I found it easy to submit seminar paper *drafts* (a new word to me, like *pedagogy*) to journals, where editors took the time to send my work out for review and to respond courteously to it.

It was exhausting, draining, scary—being alone with textbooks and a new baby in the dawn before the day's heat deadened the small town of Indiana, Pennsylvania. It was exhilarating to find out about process theory, basic writers, writing-aloud protocols, and collaborative learning. It felt good to debunk certain creative writing truisms and to learn to frame classroom questions. I would come back.

And I did, for three consecutive summers, teaching during the year in Alaska—running a writing center, being an irritable adjunct, being a frustrated (not-hired) full-time composition director applicant (learning does not dissolve all the disappointments of department politics—this is not a fairy tale—nor can I say it did not harm my marriage to Marvin, which dissolved some years later). Mother of a second child, I was now a happily stressed-out teacher, wife, researcher, scholar. I have a photograph of me holding Tait the dissertation baby—coding data at a table with the Alaskan snows framed in the window. I felt intensely alive. I still do today. Work in composition and rhetoric, for the most part, has remained for me both practical and exciting.

Even then, I was engaged enough to take Donald Murray to task (anonymously) in a textbook review. I corresponded with Michael Spooner, then editor at the National Council of Teachers of English (NCTE), about my dissertation turned-book-draft, and he—Norwegian-self-effacing—neglected to mention he had grown up in Fairbanks. The work was the thing. Not swapping "maybes" in coffee shops and bars but taking to heart what could be done in the writing classroom and working on it.

I was no longer an accidental adjunct. Or a wife teaching to keep the family unit whole. I found it encouraging to publish a teaching exercise in Charles Duke's *Exercise Exchange* and a teaching anecdote in Mickey Harris' *Writing Lab Newsletter*. My classes were better (and sometimes a little worse—enthusiasm has its own way of going awry). Richard Gebhardt drove me nuts asking for rewrites, and the essay never saw print in *College Composition and Communication* (*CCC*), as, in fact, no essay of mine has yet. A creative-writing-trained switch-hitter, I tried other venues, made other friends (as eventually Rick became a friend when we served on the 4Cs executive committee together).

At my first 4Cs convention in 1988, I sat nervously after arrival (no conference schema) in the echoing hotel foyer until Penny Dugan, as countless others in composition seem to do, walked by and said, "Are you alone? Me too. Let's have dinner, let's talk." (Have you noticed how all the suits at the Modern Language Association convention levitate up the escalator levels looking oh so serious?) The next day, on the streets of St. Louis, pacing along beside Don McAndrew, arguing about my most recent dissertation draft, I yell: "It's done. Leave it alone. I'm done." Friend David Wallace, who is walking with us, veers nervously off the curb. "I'm ready. I want to get going." I say. It was, and I did. And Don, bless him, understood this. He was and is a demanding professor. He was just right at that time for me. He cares about and reads and writes poetry. He cares about and reads and writes composition. He cares about teaching.

I had learned, finally, to ask for what I needed.

Since then, I have continued to search. There is no single vein that yields a heart of gold. These places I have revisited are the ghost towns, the mother lodes of my past. But that is the great thing about prospecting. There are prospects. The field of composition and rhetoric is professionalizing. Some will come to it and find it as frustrating as I found creative writing 20 years ago (I have to admit this, although I hope it is not totally true). There are claim jumpers. People who would put their thumb on the scales as they measure out the gold. But not as many, I think, as in some other spots in this boomtown we call English studies.

Metaphors are stupidly, oxymoronically, wonderful. By day, the Burkean parlor, by night, the 4Cs dance and saloon. We are a community. Access is not simple or assured. But rhetoric and composition is a pretty interesting place because in some ways it is the blue-collar, sleeves-rolled-up, why-the-hell-not frontier of English studies. It is a place where I welcome an e-mail from San Bernardino. Where I am respected for my poems and for my writing process narratives of poem-building. Such respect, in turn, completes a generous circuit—I want to teach others that process. I want others to write. As I write here, to them.

You asked me to tell you a story. You tell me I'm a prominent scholar and I pinch myself.

A secret—tomorrow's my birthday. I don't mind getting older in this field. I look forward to every word of it. In fact, by my last count, I was, as usual, over the limit—by about 1,222 words.

January 15, 1997
Tallahassee, Florida

CHAPTER FIVE

The Zen of Writing as Social/Symbolic Action

Richard M. Coe
Simon Fraser University

My dad danced for me the ways writing ability translates into real-world power and status. He had confidence in his ability to make things happen by writing and was known for his ability to produce writing that worked, even consumer-complaint letters that got defective products repaired or replaced. When I was a teenager, he helped me produce letters and resumes that got me jobs for which I was actually too young or underqualified. This ability made him special and gave him status among our family friends and in his union.

My dad later denied that he had taught me how to write, and in a sense he was correct. Aside from editing some of my school papers and application letters, thus teaching me to write tightly (*a la* Strunk and White), he did not formally teach me. But he did what we now know is the most important thing parents can do to encourage the development of children's literacy abilities—he modeled the importance and power of writing in his own life.

I love the zen of both writing and teaching. For me, both the actual process of drafting and the actual in-the-presence-of-students performance of teaching (or otherwise facilitating learning) are here-and-now alive—like making love, driving on black ice, diving to catch an overthrown football, skiing off (small) cliffs, helping my kids through their crises. With pride and pleasure, I remember 2 a.m. at the printer's, a 10-inch hole on page one, a reporter on the phone calling in facts, Mr. Barta (the compositor) yelling that, finished or not, he was going home in an hour, and me writing, in 10 minutes, 350 minimally competent journalistic words to fill that hole. Ten minutes during which I was totally engaged with that writing, undivided, conscious of nothing else, perfectly in the here and now. Zen in the art of rhetoric is its own reward.

In a more important and contrary sense, I do not love writing or teaching writing *per se*. Much as I hate to resonate to a phrase attributed to Plato, what fulfills me is "winning the soul by discourse," moving people, making good things happen by writing. Empowering students to do good in the world by helping them develop their writing abilities. That is really why I love both writing and teaching writing.

TOWARDS A BETTER LIFE

Kenneth Burke's project makes total sense to me. As I understand Burke's political motives, his lifelong project can be titled *Towards a Better Life* (as was his early novel) and can be explained something like this: There are times in history when the perspectives created by the dominant discourse become dysfunctional; at such times, the vocation of intellectuals and artists is to make clear what is wrong with the dominant discourse and to create new terms, new tropes, new narratives, new icons, new proverbs and slogans—in short, to take symbolic action to create new perspectives that, by directing and deflecting our attention differently, show us a way *Towards a Better Life*.

During the Great Depression, for instance, the dominant discourse created a perspective from which it seemed to make economic sense for people to go hungry because farmers were producing huge "surpluses" of food, for people to be unemployed because there were too many factories capable of producing "too many goods." In Burke's pragmatic rhetorical analysis, for people to go hungry, homeless, and jobless because of a crisis of *over*-production—when there was no actual shortage of food or homes or work that needed doing—meant that there was something wrong with the orientation and perspectives created by the socially dominant discourse. People going hungry because crops fail is terrible but natural; people going hungry because there is too much grain in the granaries signified to Burke something profoundly wrong with the economic system of distribution. For this to seem to make "common sense" was surely a form of social insanity. And so Burke set out, in tandem with other progressive intellectuals and artists, to critique and replace crucial aspects of the dominant discourse.

After World War II generated enough economic activity to "bootstrap" us out of the Great Depression, Burke saw Cold War "common sense" (e.g., strategic policies like *MAD*, mutually assured destruction) endangering the very survival of life, certainly human life, on this planet. Though he certainly took the long way round (which was generally his preferred way of avoiding reductionism), the motivoruum project that produced *A Grammar of Motives*, *A Rhetoric of Motives*, and most of the essays collected in *Language as Symbolic Action* was written to further the cause of world peace.

Even in my undergraduate papers, I can now read a focal concern with the rhetoric of form and genre. Both my thesis and my dissertation treated representative anecdotes of this rhetoric, a core aspect of Burke's agency–act ratio, showing how form motivates both substance and response. In the early 1970s, before I had ever heard the phrase *epistemic rhetoric* or read Burke, I became convinced that teaching writing is teaching ways of perceiving and thinking—and that outmoded and dysfunctional modes of perception and thought were built into traditional composition instruction. My first significant academic publication, "Rhetoric 2001," asserted that what we taught students about process and cause-to-effect development encouraged ways of thinking that led predictably to misunderstandings of human motives, of social processes, and especially of ecology (see also Coe, "An Apology"). It offered alternatives that formally embodied more contextual modes of investigation and explanation that would direct students' attention to complexities and contextual factors from which their attention was deflected by traditional linear forms. (Ed Corbett and Mina Shaughnessy voted to give that essay a prize; the third judge demurred, arguing that the essay, however intriguing, was not really about teaching writing.)

Similarly, I have taught and written a fair bit about Rogerian persuasion (Coe, "Classical Rogerian") and am now teaching and preparing to write about consensual strategies that work better than argument in political briefs. I see this as offering student writers effective strategies for changing minds and motivating people, for "winning the soul by discourse." By offering alternatives to traditional *agonistic* argument and debate, moreover, this approach validates traditionally feminine modes of persuasion, thus making a small contribution to gender role liberation. To use such persuasion strategies effectively requires empathy and an ability to perceive multiple perspectives, thus making a small contribution to world and local peace. (If these claims seem extreme, please emphasize the "small.")

Helping individual students succeed gives me great satisfaction. In the end, however, if a student achieves "upward mobility" and gets a good job because I taught well, that usually means someone else is losing out. In many cases, my good teaching may help individuals without doing any net good socially. From a broader perspective, I fear helping individual students achieve success may reconstitute the existing society, probably without decreasing the unemployment rate or moving us *Towards a Better World.*

THE RHETORIC OF "GOOD SENTENCES"

From time to time, especially when I have had extended opportunities to revise, I am praised for my "good sentences." Reviewing my textbook, Richard Marius even granted the accolade "graceful." Tossing modesty to the wind, I conclude that I sometimes produce "style"—yet I almost never think about style when I write.

Though I have no desire to produce admirable sentences, I do strongly desire to influence readers. When I write, I think very little about style and a great deal about readers, especially about directing and easing their understanding (and sparing, insofar as possible, the exercise of their short-term memories). I often see a contradiction between complexities I wish to communicate and readers' desire for ease and clarity. My struggle, always, is to fulfill their desire without oversimplifying my subject. I believe I can, with craft, write long sentences, using enough clauses and phrases to convey complexity, without contradicting easy reading. Thus I am heartened by Hemingway's invisibly long sentences. What I learned from transformational grammarians about syntax, ambiguity, and short-term memory, along with what I learned from Francis Christensen about free modifiers, led me to ways of revising that sometimes produce "good sentences." It is probably significant that these stylish sentences come about because I am concerned not with sentences but with readers.

In this I am a New Rhetorician, following Burke and the I. A. Richards of *The Philosophy of Rhetoric*, both of whom were strongly influenced by Bronislaw Malinowski's phrase *symbolic action*. For Burke and for Richards (and for me), this means thinking of writing first and foremost in terms of what it *does*, thinking about what it *says* only within the frame established by that action. This always reminds me of Augustine, who, following his newfound god and Cicero, insisted that it is not enough to teach (i.e., to convey knowledge) or even to convince; the crux of rhetorical success lies in motivating (in Latin, *movere*) listeners/readers. In teaching writing, this distinction between *doing* and *saying* turns out to be a totally radical move, especially when the focus shifts away from school writing (i.e., away from writing motivated by teachers and grades). Asked what they are trying to *do* (as distinct from what they are trying to *say*), students often discover a whole new perspective from which all sorts of writing moves and conventions start to make sense.

Perhaps this is why I cringe, albeit silently, when I hear my colleagues at the Conference on College Composition and Communication talk about "opportunities for publication." Nominalization aside, the phrase is crucially arhetorical, like writing just for a grade, just to advance an individual's career, not as social/symbolic action. Although I certainly am familiar with the temptation, I have rarely written just to get a publication on my CV—not so much because I am unselfish as because I have always had great difficulty motivating myself to do that. Publication is a byproduct of attempting to help students *Towards a Better Life* by influencing how and what their teachers teach.

This chapter was submitted 5 months late because, shortly before the deadline, I hit the longest writer's block of my life. Why? Because I had lost faith in my ability to influence what and how students learn by writing for their teachers. It was a great relief finally to complete the chapter in May 1997 because that act of completion hints that I may have found a way back to the faith that gives meaning to my scholarly work in composition.

Vancouver, British Columbia
May 15, 1997

WORKS CITED

Burke, Kenneth. *Towards a Better Life: Being a Series of Epistles, or Declamations.* 1932. Berkeley: U of California P, 1966.

Burke, Kenneth. *A Grammar of Motives.* 1945. Berkeley: U of California P, 1969.

Burke, Kenneth. *A Rhetoric of Motives.* 1950. Berkeley: U of California P, 1969.

Burke, Kenneth. *Language as Symbolic Action.* 1966. Berkeley: U of California P, 1966.

Christensen, Francis, and Bonnijean Christensen. *The Christensen Rhetoric Program.* New York: Harper, 1968.

Christensen, Francis, and Bonnijean Christensen. *Notes Toward a New Rhetoric: 9 Essays for Teachers.* New York: Harper, 1978.

Coe, Richard M. "An Apology for Form; or, Who Took the Form Out of the Process." *College English* 49 (1987): 13-28.

Coe, Richard M. "Classical and Rogerian Persuasion: An Archeological/Ecological Explication." *Rogerian Perspectives: Collaborative Rhetoric for Oral and Written Communication.* Ed. Nathaniel Teich. Norwood, NJ: Ablex (1992): 83-108.

Coe, Richard M. "Rhetoric 2001." *Freshman English News* 3.1 (1974): 1-13.

Malinowski, Bronislaw. "The Problem of Meaning in Primitive Languages." Supplement 1 in C. K. Ogden and I. A. Richards, *The Meaning of Meaning.* London: Kegan Paul (1923): 296-336.

Richards, I. A. *The Philosophy of Rhetoric.* London: Oxford, 1936.

CHAPTER SIX

Truth or Consequences

William A. Covino
University of Illinois at Chicago

For a time when I was a beginning teacher, composition pedagogy went psychedelic. In the wake of the 1960 Dartmouth conference, which initiated intense work on the importance of self-expression and self-realization in the composition classroom, and the Vietnam War era, which activated student and faculty interest in alternatives to "establishment" practices in general, a number of composition textbooks in the 1960s and 1970s looked like a cross between McLuhan's *Medium is the Massage* and Rowan and Martin's *Laugh-In*. They emphasized self-expression, word games, associative thinking, meditation, and prerational, antiestablishment, highly visual imagination, all pursued in an atmosphere of discovery and play; and they discouraged conventional ideas, conventional forms, and the equation of good writing with correct writing.

Two of the most widely adopted texts of this kind were *Montage: Investigations in Language* (1970) by William Sparke and Clark McKowen and McKowen's solo sequel, *Image: Reflections on Language* (1973). *Image* is a grab bag of games, koans, essays, and poems, all focusing on imagination and creativity (many by canonical figures such as Eliot and Coleridge, many by early New Agers such as Carlos Castaneda and the San Francisco Bay Area mystic Alan Watts), and colored pages (bright orange, red, green, blue) full of cryptic juxtapositions of pictures, epigrams, excerpts, and quasi-mystical prompts ("Which is narrower, a fact or an idea?" "Which is angrier, your kitchen or your living room?"). Altogether, *Image* stresses the value and mystery of a sympathetic universe full of untapped associations and discoveries. A typical instance of advice for writers is Edward Lueders' 1969 "Your Poem, Man":

> unless there's one thing seen
> suddenly against another—a parsnip
> sprouting for a President, or
> hailstones melting in an ashtray—
> nothing really happens. It takes
> surprise and wild connections,
> doesn't it? A walrus chewing
> on a ballpoint pen. Two blue tail-
> lights on Tyrannosaurus Rex. Green
> cheese teeth. Maybe what we wanted
> least. Or most. Some unexpected
> pleats. Words that never knew
> each other till right now. Plug us
> into the wrong socket and see
> what blows—or what lights up.
> Try
>   untried
>   circuitry,
> new
>   fuses.
> Tell it like it never really was,
> man,
> and maybe we can see it
> like it is. (25)

Image was the textbook I assigned through my whole teaching assistant (TA) career, from 1973 to 1981, my graduate work broken up by a 1975–1976 stint at Diablo Valley College in Pleasant Hill, California, where my senior colleague was McKowen himself. These years also framed my developing commitment to rhetoric and composition; in 1981 I completed a doctorate in English in the rhetoric–linguistics–literature program that Ross Winterowd created at the University of Southern California (USC). Before my year with McKowen and my USC experience, however, I was a TA (pursuing a master's degree in English literature) at California State University-Northridge. Untrained in composition and rhetoric, I found myself presented one June day in 1973 with three textbooks that had been approved for use in the Northridge program where I would begin teaching that fall: McCrimmon's *Writing With a Purpose*; McKowen's *Image*; and, I believe, *The Norton Guide to Writing*. I flipped the pages of all three and noted that *Image* had no table of contents and no teacher's manual but was colorful and crowded, with a strange cover (an x-ray of teeth on a black background). It looked like fun. I chose it and was the only one among the 12 new TAs to do so.

And that choice, I see now, was the nexus of my personal past and my professional future, a consequence of my adolescent obsessions and aspirations, and an announcement of the direction of my teaching, my research, and in fact my whole professional life. That said, let me begin nearer to the beginning.

BOB BARKER IN PERSON

I always wanted to be a game-show host. At least ever since my family moved from Stamford, Connecticut, to California's San Fernando Valley in 1964 when I was 13. It was there and then that a neighbor took me to a taping of *Truth or Consequences* at the NBC Studios in Burbank, and I saw Bob Barker in person. There he was, with gleaming teeth, spotlighted in his impeccably tailored dark blue suit, leading contestants through embarrassing antics with unflappable wit and suave presence. And for this, he was fawned over again and again by an excited studio audience that reacted automatically but (to my mind) passionately whenever the applause sign flashed.

What a life. You get to dress up, guide people through fun and games, and get adored, day after day. Glamorized play: I could do that, I thought. Bob Barker—and then Gene Rayburn and Wink Martindale and Peter Marshall—made up a sort of pantheon for me, and although they were not exactly role models, neither was anyone else. I meandered through junior high and high school, getting A's in everything but gym, with no real ambitions except to be witty and entertaining.

To that end, I played the accordion. I had begun lessons in the 1950s, a time when lots of kids were strapping on accordions, their parents excited by the popularity of virtuosos like Dick Contino and performances on *Ted Mack's Original Amateur Hour* by teenagers who could play "Lady of Spain" blindfolded. I was trotted out at every holiday family gathering, to play marches and polkas and tarantellas, even then—at age 9 or so—relishing my celebrity. In the 1960s, kids playing accordions were replaced by kids strumming guitars, but I stuck with the squeeze box. I had by then determined that I was odd, staying inside and reading books (mainly biographies of American heroes and the lives of saints) while the other boys played ball in the street; watching old movies and practicing impressions of James Cagney and Cary Grant and the rest in front of the mirror (and for any of my uncles and aunts who would tolerate such silliness); and—especially after my day with Bob Barker—gluing myself to game shows. I was a student of celebrity, not starstruck so much as apprenticed to the craft. And, as you might expect, I was overweight: fed on spaghetti and meatballs and whole milk and chocolate cake most days and awfully sedentary, effectively "marginalized" from the athletic body culture of my peers and driven, through my own habits and obsessions, to make myself in rhetoric.

Celebrity, I noticed, required a certain impeccable literacy. It was, in terms of the professional lexicon I would later acquire, all a matter of *kairos*: the right words with the right timing. Apart from trying to remember jokes I had heard on *The Ed Sullivan Show* and deliver them like the pros for the kids in the school lunch yard, I began to discover that giving the right answer to a teacher's question could effect a kind of *kairic* moment. "What kind of person is Falstaff?" asked Mrs. Fleming, my ninth-grade English teacher. "A pathetic buffoon," I said, drawing my vocabulary from one of those remarkably literate exchanges I had found in an old movie (probably something Katharine Hepburn said to Spencer Tracy) and betting that the very audacity of my phrasing would get me points. Mrs. Fleming smiled and winked at me and said "very good" quietly, almost too quietly for the class to hear (I always sat in front), we were, as Aristotle might observe, sharing an enthymeme. And the *kairos* of my utterance was not lost on the rest of the class, who—I could tell—knew that I had said something smart and raised the stock of my ethos. In a sense, the ingredients for my "conversion" to rhetoric and composition and my career as a teacher were in place by my early teens. With a penchant for celebrity, gamesmanship, intellectual play, oratory, wit, and audience manipulation, I was an incipient sophist.

My celebrity ambitions were fueled by a particularly encouraging accordion teacher, Fred Scordino, who convinced me—when I was about 15—that I could have fun and make money in quasi-Bob Barker-like fashion by becoming a band leader. By the time I was 20, my trio—souped-up accordion, drums, and sax—was busy every weekend with wedding receptions, bowling banquets, bar mitzvahs. I liked getting people to dance. And sometimes I could do this by just giving orders: "Everyone form a circle on the dance floor," I would say, getting ready to take them through the Hokey Pokey. And sure enough, dozens of the guests got up and obeyed. There was something proximate here to being Bob Barker: I was dressed up (even better than Barker, in a tux), supervising the antics of the crowd with a combination of directives and clever remarks, and getting applause. Far from an accomplished musician, I was a talented facilitator.

But band leaders were a dime a dozen in southern California. I declared an English major at the University of California-Los Angeles in the early 1970s with some vague sense that I was pursuing a respectable career but mainly because English was my best subject. Fascination with celebrity trailed me through my classes, and I began to notice that my professors stood in a kind of spotlight, defined by the penetration of their intellect and the ease and wit with which they entertained complex and erudite subjects. I often sat rapt as one or another of these brains, dressed in the 1970s uniform of tweeds and corduroys, rhapsodized about, for instance, the relevance of

Coleridge's Ancient Mariner to Vietnam-era problems of moral conscience. With much the same eagerness that had attended my response to Bob Barker, I decided that I wanted to be a professor, to have an audience, a rhapsodic space, and an elevated ethos. By my senior year in college, then, I had decided that teaching was for me—not in high school, where having to act *in loco parentis* robs the job of glamor, but in college, where I could really work the crowd. A beginning TA at Cal State-Northridge, I found myself adopting McKowen's *Image* and beginning to construct my own.

BOB BARKER GETS PHILOSOPHY

My adolescent reminiscence has gone on long enough to make its point, that the desire to teach, and the intellectual facility to pursue English studies, can arise from a fascination with the cultural coin of personal power. But fortunately, once I found myself actually responsible for the lives of students, I began to worry about my motives and their consequences. With no directive TA training program in place at Northridge, I was free to leaf through *Image* over the summer and figure out how to be a Bob Barker who did not merely work the crowd but taught them something.

The book seemed to understand my dilemma, interspersing classroom games with very philosophical views of language, selfhood, and education by William Wordsworth, Robert Frost, W. B. Yeats, Carl Jung, Ernst Cassirer, Noam Chomsky, Lev Vygotsky, William James, Jean Piaget, Fritz Perls, Hermann Hesse, Buckminster Fuller, Carlos Castaneda, Malcolm X, and McKowen himself. Most of these statements struck me as too difficult for my first-year students, but as I began to figure out how to teach, they served as guideposts for me, a built-in teacher's manual. Here was Jung saying that "if [people] are enabled to develop into more spacious personalities, [their] neurosis generally disappears" (155); Vygotsky saying that "the measure of generality determines not only the equivalence of concepts but also all of the intellectual operations possible with a given concept" (292); and McKowen insisting that "to give a pupil new concepts deliberately is as impossible and futile as teaching someone to ride a unicycle by the laws of equilibrium" (223). Reading these folks, I concluded that play—set apart from the mere activity of celebrity and audience manipulation—could be a very serious enterprise, one that created a psychophysical space in which discovery and change are possible; and furthermore, that direct instruction (like a lecture on thesis sentences or subordinate clauses) was inimical to concept formation. My guiding statement was written by McKowen, as a follow-up to a "matchstick game" that was proffered on page 10 of *Image*. To play the game, one arranges four matches and a paper clip like this:

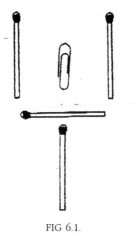

FIG 6.1.

Imagine that the matches form a "cocktail glass," and the paper clip is the "olive." Then, by moving two matches one time only, you must end up with the cocktail glass shape intact, but with the "olive" outside it.

For me, the matchstick game and activities like it initially promised considerable classroom liveliness, an atmosphere that was both entertaining and conducive to intellectual discovery. For McKowen, the matchstick game represents the complex of attitudes, efforts, presuppositions, and abilities that inform or discourage learning in general:

> The way people play the matchstick game represents their approaches to life in general. In any group there is virtually the full array: Those who don't try at all—because they know they can't do it, because they had planned on something else, because they don't want to risk ego deflation, and so forth. Those who try a little and then give up. Those who want hints. Those who try to follow someone else's lead, the imitators. Those who want to be given the answer. And those who struggle with it and solve it. . . . The game is a metaphor for learning processes and attitudes and is also an analogy for attitudes toward language. We see that language is a mind-set, the parameter of our conscious world—language plus all the nonverbal symbols that connect with it. Language gives us a sense of stability in the world, but it also gives us a tendency toward blindness to alternatives. . . . We become set in our ways and approach problems along narrow channels though there are infinite possible choices and channels. Trying to solve the matchstick game reveals how our habits of language can prevent us from seeing in new ways. The game shows us how we can break through our regular habits of seeing, how we can loosen up our discovery processes to find solutions to our life problems. (203)

Admittedly, this is an essentially Romantic view of learning as some sort of willed spontaneous combustion (McKowen says elsewhere in this passage,

"Those who solve the puzzle experience at the instant of discovery the thrill of living poetically") and of failure to learn as a consequence of fear or laziness. Its sentiments maintained great appeal for me at the time, though, and ultimately fueled my initial excitement about the field of rhetoric, as I explain later. But at this point, I want to stress that McKowen's views—along with remarks like those from Jung and Vygotsky—began to come together for me as a philosophy of composition, one that gave purpose to what I call my sophistic propensities and a semblance of ethical substance to my vocation as a celebrated facilitator. Here are the principles I began to believe:

1. Language acquisition is a kind of game.
2. Play motivates fluency.
3. Coherence and closure are vices.
4. Open-mindedness is a virtue best cultivated in nonthreatening situations.
5. Associational fluency (becoming a more "spacious personality") is central to intellectual, and even psychological, health.
6. The teacher's job is to lead the students in activities that will bring them heightened awareness, new concepts, and a vital, participatory attitude toward language and learning.

Given my personal identity as it had developed from *Truth or Consequences* on, these principles were a mode of validating my own way of being in the world. And they also corresponded with the kinds of activities I enacted well in the classroom. The students and I would spend whole class meetings inventing associations among the excerpts and pictures and questions scattered across a page of *Image* or explicating one of the book's brief prompts ("True or false: All moods are punishment for one's self or for others") into a life philosophy or playing language games such as the "simile game," in which, for instance, the phrase "fuzzy as a _____" was to be completed with far-fetched but justifiable words ("fuzzy as a tequila sunrise"). I egged them on. Awash in play and spacey concepts, class meetings were full of energy. And so was the students' writing: in tune with the "freewriting" focus of 1970s composition instruction and with the generally disparaging view of formal academic themes that was advanced by *Image*, I assigned informal journal writing, lots of it. Students were asked to go home each day and "reflect" in writing on what had happened in class. I read journals by the stack; they were always interesting, often exciting.

A year at Cal State-Northridge completing a master's degree and teaching composition—in a departmental atmosphere that pretty much left composition TAs to themselves—left me sure that I had found my calling. And then I was recruited by McKowen himself for a 1-year position at Diablo Valley College (DVC) in the San Francisco Bay Area. It was an idyllic year.

Trailing McKowen, disciple-like, left me even more convinced that there was something healthfully eccentric and true about my pedagogy. The students were eager and attentive; McKowen was relaxed, receptive, and wise.

But what I was committed to, I see now, was a pedagogical mood that could not last. The autonomy I had been afforded at Northridge and DVC was a lucky break; this was confirmed in a series of community-college job interviews after my McKowen year, where I was typically handed a set of regulations governing the composition program that exuded dreariness ("Students will practice the formation of clear thesis sentences, and should by the end of the term be able to produce coherent paragraphs that contain compound/complex sentences and concrete examples") and that required very formulary textbooks. College English departments were very alert to the "back to basics" movement that took hold in the late 1970s, and when I began talking about language games and journal writing and an atmosphere of discovery, they tended to stop listening. So as the never-very-bright psychedelic glow of antiestablishment pedagogy began to fade, I maintained stubborn enthusiasm for the sort of classroom *Image* allowed; but I had neither the disciplinary authority nor the academic qualifications to take it very far. Apart from picking up a section of composition here and there, there was no work for me, mainly because the market was bad for masters of arts in English, but also—to my mind—because I was something of a rebel. "You need a PhD," a friend told me.

THE MOMENT OF TRUTH:
WINTEROWD AS BOB BARKER

Back to graduate school then. I had heard of a program at USC that turned out rhetoric and composition specialists; I applied and was accepted, a TA again carting *Image* into my 1977 composition classes. My first USC teacher was Ross Winterowd, who gave a remarkable course introducing students to the field of rhetoric, notable initially for the range of its reading list: Hazard Adams, *Critical Theory Since Plato*; Wayne Booth, *Modern Dogma and the Rhetoric of Assent*; Robert Pirsig, *Zen and the Art of Motorcycle Maintenance*; Cooper and Odell, *The Nature and Measurement of Competency in English*; Kenneth Burke, *Counter-Statement*; Chaim Perelman, *The New Rhetoric*; Francis Christensen, *Notes Toward a New Rhetoric*; Winterowd, *Contemporary Rhetoric*; E. D. Hirsch, *The Philosophy of Composition*; Janet Emig, *The Composing Processes of Twelfth Graders*; Mina Shaughnessy, *Errors and Expectations*; Susanne Langer, *Philosophy in a New Key*; Richard Young, Alton Becker, and Kenneth Pike, *Rhetoric: Discovery and Change*; Peter Elbow, *Writing Without Teachers*; J. L. Austin, *How To Do Things With*

Words; Frank O'Hare, *Sentence Combining*; James Kinneavy, *A Theory of Discourse.*

"What is rhetoric?" was the first question Winterowd addressed. I had entered this doctoral program—titled "Rhetoric, Linguistics, and Literature"—with foundations in literature and literary criticism and some scant knowledge of linguistics but no formal idea of what was meant by rhetoric (except that it was sometimes used in conjunction with or as a substitute for "composition"). But the title of the program had suggested to me a certain interdisciplinary, associative energy that might license the sort of exploratory scope I tried to create in the classroom, and as Winterowd began his lecture, I sensed that some new clarity was at hand.

He drew a diagram on the board (taken from Roman Jakobson):

	Context	
	Message	
Addresser		Addressee
	Contact	
	Code	

FIG. 6.2.

Winterowd explained that this diagram illustrated a transaction between addresser and addressee in which an intention evokes a response, within a context of information that constitutes "reality," through a structure (message) and style (code) in a medium (contact).[1] He then explained that literary criticism has defined its schools in terms of these categories, locating those stressing artistic intention under "Addresser," those interested in reception under "Addressee," the New Critics allied with "Message" and "Code," the neo-Aristotelians under "Context" (given their focus on how literature imitates reality), and the linguistic critics under "Contact."[2] Isolated as these schools may sometimes be from one another, he told us, taken together they define criticism (that is, reading) as a global, transactive process. "What is the name for that process?" he asked, then drew a large chalk circle around the whole thing, and wrote on the outside in capital letters: "RHETORIC."

So that's it, I thought, rhetoric is *everything*. Whereas scholarly specialists are working within their limited domains, rhetoricians stand outside and watch, no feature of discourse irrelevant to their attention. I readily acceded to this heady, global conception (the rhetorician like Joyce's artist paring

---

[1]This diagram and its explication appear in Winterowd's (1986) "From Process to Transaction."

[2]Realize that these critical categories were preferred just before any of us, including Winterowd (who later wrote at length about the "wrongheadedness" of Derrida), knew that postmodernism had arrived and all categorical illumination was suspect.

his fingernails), mainly because it fueled my own need for intellectual authority and disciplinary power. I concluded that as a composition teacher informed by rhetoric, I would be licensed to play, my scope of instruction no
less than the universe of discourse. Rhetoric became for me, in the course
of that semester, the ultimate game show, and Winterowd the arch-example
of the eclectic as rhetorician, blustering through that rangy reading list of
his and connecting the dots on the intellectual landscape. He was audacious
and exuberant, well aware of the spaciousness of his illustration of rhetoric,
and persistent through sheer force of attitude, in demonstration of one of
his favorite quotations from Kenneth Burke:

> An *attitude* toward a body of topics has a unifying force. In effect its unitary
> nature as a response "sums up" the conglomerate of particulars towards which
> the attitude is directed. ("The Anaesthetic Revelation of Herone Liddell," qtd.
> in Winterowd, 1986, ix)

Here then was the intellectual's Bob Barker, calling on the audience to
participate in the synthesis of pedagogy, theory, and history. In the course
of filling in and connecting more securely the parts of the diagram he drew
on that first day (by lecturing on the course readings), Winterowd proposed
much about the nature of rhetoric as a field and pedagogy as a scholarly
focus that complemented the principles I had been developing on my own:
I learned that rhetorical invention was a crucial intellectual activity just beginning to get scholarly attention, that language acquisition did not result
from deliberate instruction and did not take place in a threatening evaluative
atmosphere, that sentence play increased syntactic fluency, that "quality" in
writing was an eternal question, that "correct" form was indeterminate, and
that rhetoric, poetics, and philosophy had long been in conversation with
one another.

I was prepared, then, by winter 1977 to begin calling myself a rhetorician,
realizing that rhetoric was a fitting designation for the holism that *Image*
and I had been professing. Rhetoric was, in effect, the game I had been
trying to play all along, as I sought vitality in literacy and as I resisted the
compartmentalization of composition into academic skills. My 1977 identi-
fication with rhetoric was, I realize now, essentially romantic: the rhetor as
Walt Whitman, declaring, "I am large. I contain multitudes."[3] The rhetor as
the giant self. The rhetor as multivocal. The ultimate game-show host playing
the ultimate game, hearing his own echo in Cicero's *On Oratory and Orators*:

---

[3] This is not Winterowd's conception of rhetoric; rather it is my appropriation of the materials
and synthesis he offered. Winterowd has written against Romantic rhetoric in several places
(e.g., Winterowd, 1981).

The real power of eloquence is such that it embraces the origin, the influence, the changes of all things in the world, all virtues, duties, and all nature, so far as it affects the manners, minds, and lives of mankind. (3.20)

FACING THE CONSEQUENCES: BOB BARKER GROWS UP

There are problems with my 1977 conception of rhetoric. To the extent that it is aligned with McKowen's tone in his celebration of the matchstick game, it tends to idealize language teaching and learning and give the teacher-rhetor the corner on insight. As I have found out over the years, the multivocality that rhetoric accords and encourages—that is, its essentially dialogical character (manifest on the pages of *Image* and on Winterowd's blackboard)—provides less for the aggrandizement or therapeutic explication of the self than for an ongoing social critique (voices in contention with one another), as Kenneth Burke pointed out:

> A rhetorician, I take it, is like one voice in a dialogue. Put several such voices together, with each voicing its own special assertion, let them act upon one another in co-operative competition, and you get a dialectic that, properly developed, can lead to the views transcending the limitations of each. ("Rhetoric—Old and New," qtd. in Steinmann, 1967, 63)

In other words, the play of rhetoric is one of correctives that both supplement and check each other. It does not allow for the completion of the giant self; rather, rhetoric is a process of unsettling disruption.

But this view, essentially a dialogical/dialectical ethics of rhetoric, did not motivate my work until some time after that day in Winterowd's class when I realized that rhetoric was for me. The child of Bob Barker, I was initially taken in by the legitimation of play and the celebrity of intellectual scope. Correcting my motives has been, truly, the work of the last 15 years, leading through more and more refined and qualified conceptions of intellectual play (Covino 1988, 1994)—my own substitution for *Image*, which puts dialogical literacy ahead of the individual imagination (Covino 1990), and my recent dismissal of the "giant self" as an emblem of elitism (Covino 1996). And my teaching, too, has changed; still putting invention and play at the center of composition teaching and learning, I am inclined to view formal institutional conventions (like the thesis sentence) ironically rather than dismissively and to understand my penchant for classroom performance as an affectation rather than a service. All this is to say that in 1977, at the age of 26, the aspiring game-show host found rhetoric, and I have been making up for it ever since.

Chicago, Illinois
January 6, 1997

WORKS CITED

Cicero. *On Oratory and Orators (De Oratore)*. Trans. J. S. Watson. Carbondale: Southern Illinois UP, 1970.

Covino, William A. *The Art of Wondering: A Revisionist Return to the History of Rhetoric.* Portsmouth, NH: Heinemann-Boynton/Cook, 1988.

Covino, William A. *Forms of Wondering: A Dialogue on Writing, for Writers.* Portsmouth, NH: Heinemann-Boynton/Cook, 1990.

Covino, William A. *Magic, Rhetoric, and Literacy: An Eccentric History of the Composing Imagination.* Albany: SUNY P, 1994.

Covino, William A. "Grammars of Transgression: Golems, Cyborgs, Mutants." *Rhetoric Review* 14.2 (1996): 355-73.

McCrimmon, James M. *Writing With a Purpose.* Boston: Houghton, 1972.

McKowen, Clark. *Image: Reflections on Language.* New York: Macmillan, 1973.

McLuhan, Marshall and Quentin Fiore. *The Medium is the Massage.* New York: Bantam, 1967.

Sparke, William, and Clark McKowen. *Montage: Investigations in Language.* New York: Macmillan, 1970.

Steinmann, Martin, ed. *New Rhetorics.* New York: Scribner's, 1967.

Winterowd, W. Ross. "A Philosophy of Composition." *Rhetoric Review* 9 (1981): 340-48.

Winterowd, W. Ross. *Composition/Rhetoric: A Synthesis.* Carbondale: Southern Illinois UP, 1986.

CHAPTER SEVEN

In Search of the American Dream

Frank J. D'Angelo
Arizona State University

I have always been fascinated by language. My sisters tell me that before I was 3 years old, I would stand on a chair, put an Italian record on the phonograph, and sing along with the music. I am not suggesting that this love of language was the immediate cause of my deciding to study and to teach rhetoric and composition, but it was a proximate cause.

I grew up in a rich linguistic environment. I was born and raised in New Orleans, the son of immigrant parents, Francesco D'Angelo and Mariana Grisaffi. My parents spoke four languages—English, Italian, a Sicilian dialect, and Italglish. I do not know who coined the term *Italglish*, but this combination of clipping and compounding perfectly describes the idiom my parents used as a medium of communication among Italians and between Italians and English-speaking New Orleanians. My mother spoke excellent English, but she would occasionally blend English and Italian morphemes if there were no Italian or Sicilian equivalents for a concept in English. My father, however, would "fracture" the language (so I thought in my ignorance). Call his attention to what you thought was a grammatical or lexical error, and he would deliberately mispronounce a known word or coin a nonsense word.

I had no idea that my father was intuitively using Italglish as a *lingua franca*, sometimes making use of Italian syntax, incorporating English words, transforming their sounds to make them correspond to the sounds of Italian (e.g., *stritto carro*, for *streetcar*), other times using English syntax, incorporating Italian or Sicilian words, blending Italian and English lexicons. Our

55

immediate neighbors spoke French, Cajun French, English, Spanish, and German.

My parents had a limited formal education but a wealth of practical experience. My mother taught her children by example (she lived an exemplary life), by wise sayings (*Nenti dire ca nenti si sapi*, she would intone; "Say nothing when you know nothing"), and by traditional storytelling (she would recount tales of personal experiences, tales of the old country, folktales, and stories about saints). My mother believed that if you knew the Italian or Sicilian proverb or story, you would know how to act in the appropriate situation. She used maxims, proverbs, and aphorisms to comment on people's behavior and to give advice.

When my father was not working, he usually went to the Italian Hall in New Orleans, where he read Italian newspapers, acted in plays performed in Italian (the plays were usually set in the remote past and had melodramatic plots), and played the drums in a marching band. The band called itself the Roma Band, and it frequently participated in the Mardi Gras parades. When my father was studying for a part in a play, he would ask me to help him memorize his lines. The dialogue was in Italian, and even though I did not understand most of the words, I took great pleasure in trying to pronounce them. I would take the part of one of the characters in the play, and my recitation would prompt my father to remember his lines. Through constant repetition, I learned the lines by rote, and to this day I can recite some of them, although I do not know what they mean.

Besides playing the drums in a marching band, my father played the guitar and the mandolin. My mother also played the mandolin, and occasionally they would play and sing Sicilian folksongs like "E la Luna Mezzu Mari" (remember the wedding scene in *The Godfather*?), songs with general Italian-American appeal (e.g., "Santa Lucia," "O Sole Mio," "Mama," and "Come Back to Sorrento"), and bits and pieces from Italian operas (e.g., "La donna è mobile" and "Vesti la giubba"). I got my love of music from my parents, but in those early days Mario Lanza, Frank Sinatra, Vic Damone, and Louis Prima were more to my liking.

You cannot grow up in New Orleans without music and song being a part of your linguistic heritage. When I was quite young, I would awaken to the sounds of street vendors peddling their wares, crying, "Watermelon, lady! Red to the rind. Get your red, ripe watermelon, lady!" Then the vendor selling crawfish would sing out, "Crawfish! Get your red hot crawfish!" Because (according to musicologists), the first music was vocal, I consider the cries of street vendors, the counting-out rhymes we used as children to determine who was "it" when playing Fate ("Ipsi dipsi soda cracker/Does your father chew tobacco?") and the work songs ("Where do you work-a, John? On the Delaware Lack-a-wan"), a part of my musical and linguistic heritage. I progressed in my informal musical education from the cries of street vendors to the sounds of the military marches played by bands in the Mardi Gras parades to the blues, New Orleans jazz, rhythm and blues, swing, bop, and progressive jazz.

Although my parents had little formal education, they encouraged their children to read, to get the best education possible, and to follow the American dream. When I was in the sixth grade, I came home from school one day to find that my mother had purchased (on the installment plan) an entire shelf of books that included an inexpensive set of encyclopedias, an atlas, *Bulfinch's Mythology*, and the complete works of Mark Twain (an odd assortment of books). Somehow a door-to-door salesman had convinced my immigrant mother that these were the kinds of books every educated American child should have. I read those books (in whole and in part), together with many other books by writers good and bad (comic books, books by Zane Grey, Edgar Rice Burroughs, Sir Rider Haggard, and books written by writers whose names I have forgotten).

I was always a good student, highly motivated, inquisitive, interested in learning. As a child I attended Sacred Heart parochial school. My best subjects were reading, spelling, grammar, geography, and penmanship. I loved to fill up tablets with the letters of the alphabet, using the form of script prescribed by the Palmer penmanship method. I took almost an aesthetic delight in forming the letters. I was an excellent "speller," often winning spelling contests. But after grading thousands of student compositions over the years, I am less confident about my spelling today, and occasionally I have to consult a dictionary about words that I should know how to spell.

I entered high school when I was 12, going on 13. I got an academic scholarship to Jesuit High School in New Orleans, at that time one of the best schools in the city. My father owned a small grocery store before I was born, but he lost everything in the depression, so he wouldn't have been able to send me to a Catholic school had I not received a scholarship. Jesuit High was strictly college preparatory—4 years of English, 4 years of Latin, 4 years of public speaking, 4 years of religious education, 4 years of math, 2 years of a foreign language, 2 years of science, 2 years of history.

I loved every minute of my high school education. My classes were very competitive. The Jesuits made learning into a game and into a competition. I excelled in English and public speaking, did very well in Latin and history, and got good grades in subjects I liked less well because I spent more time on them. I liked all of the things about school that generations of school kids hated—conjugating verbs, declining nouns, diagramming sentences, parsing English and Latin sentences, translating from Latin into English and from English into Latin, tracing etymologies, memorizing poems and patriotic American speeches, delivering extemporaneous speeches, reading and discussing poems, essays, and short fiction, composing themes. I had no idea at that time that I might later become a teacher of English.

My father died when I was a junior in high school, so I had dim prospects of going to college. My oldest sister, Veronica, was still living at home. After my father died, she was the sole support of my mother, a younger brother, and me. She was engaged to be married, but the weight of responsibility hung heavily on her shoulders. When I was a senior in high school, she encouraged me to take a civil service test for a position with the federal government. I took the test, passed it, and after I graduated, I went to work with the Veterans Administration. My sister got married and moved to New York, and I took over the responsibility of supporting my mother and my younger brother.

For the next 6 years, I worked at that job and several others until I was drafted into the army, despite being the sole support of my mother and brother. I served for almost 2 years in Korea. When I first entered the army, because of high test scores, I was stationed for 6 months in Fort Sam Houston, Texas, where I helped to administer tests to incoming soldiers. There I met three inductees (one from New Orleans) who had been high school English teachers. We became friends, and even though I was fascinated by their discussions of their experiences in teaching high school, I gave little thought to becoming an English teacher at that time.

When I returned home after my tour of duty, few people (except for my family) even knew I had been gone, and few even understood what the Korean War was all about. (The press labeled it "a police action.") I went back to work for the federal government, this time for an agency called Commodity Credit. A year later I got married. My mother and brother lived alone for a time, then went to live with my sister, who had returned to New Orleans. I decided then to go to college. Because I had been to Korea, I took advantage of the GI Bill. My wife, Sylvia, was very supportive, but because we started having a family of our own, I kept my full-time job and took most of my classes at night and on Saturdays. Because I was working in a large office of the federal government and because I had responsibilities, I decided to take a business degree, with a concentration in accounting. I attended Loyola University of the South, a Jesuit institution in New Orleans. Even though I was studying for a business degree, I still had to take a full range of required liberal arts courses—12 hours of English, 15 hours of scholastic philosophy, 6 hours of speech, 12 hours of history, and so forth. Needless to say, I did better in these courses than in the business courses because I was more interested in the liberal arts and the humanities. Then, after 2 years of study, for no seeming conscious reason (other than boredom with my job and with the business courses), I decided to switch majors and become a high school English teacher. I made that decision, I am convinced, not merely because I had met English teachers when I was in the army but also because I had developed a lifetime love of reading and learning and language. "I am a part of all that I have met," declaims Ulysses in Tennyson's well-known poem. I became a part of all that I had read and studied and experienced.

I continued to work full time for the federal government while I completed my studies. In my last semester, my wife went to work for the federal government so that I could do my practice teaching. Like my sister who had put off her marriage to support a family, my wife made a similar sacrifice to enable me to finish college. My mother lived to see the first of her children graduate from college. I graduated with honors, and I took a position as an English teacher at De La Salle High School in New Orleans.

My first teaching semester was a disaster. I tried to be too friendly with my students, and they took advantage of my friendliness and lack of teaching experience. My students paid me no mind, talked constantly, and had a great time at my expense. The next semester I was determined to get some measure of control in my classes and went to the other extreme. I was so strict that my students were afraid to flinch. I was constantly sending students to the prefect of discipline for any transgression, real or imagined. The following year I struck a happy balance between autonomy and authority, relaxation and restraint.

After a year or two of teaching, I began to read the professional journals (particularly *The English Journal* and *College Composition and Communication*) to help me to improve my teaching. My colleagues were conscientious teachers who, like me, were burdened with teaching five classes of almost 175 students a semester, but they had little time for professional development. However, I was highly motivated to learn more about what I was doing, and in the early 1960s I attended my first National Council of Teachers of English (NCTE) meeting in San Francisco. The keynote speaker was William Golding, the English novelist whose first published novel was *Lord of the Flies*. I enjoyed what he had to say because I had been impressed by his reputation as a highly original writer of moral allegories.

When I got back from the conference, I became eager for more learning and decided to work for an advanced degree in English at Tulane University. My favorite writers were Gerard Manley Hopkins (for his linguistic innovations and poetic technique), Emily Dickinson (for her terse, aphoristic style), Ralph Waldo Emerson (for his epigrammatic sentences), and Henry David Thoreau (for his acute observations and interesting prose style). I was surprised (but delighted) that in many of my classes at Tulane I had to memorize lines from poetry and prose. I had thought only high school teachers made students memorize lines. Because of my Jesuit training, I had already developed a facility for memorizing poems and speeches, and this kind of training was to prove invaluable when I later became a professor of English. For my master's thesis, I did a genre study of Hopkins' long poem, "The Wreck of the Deutschland."

I thought my master's degree would be a terminal degree, because my family was expanding, and I had a basic responsibility to support my children as best I could on a high school teacher's salary. But in the summer of 1966, I participated in an 8-week National Defense Education Act (NDEA) Summer Institute for high school teachers at the University of Nebraska at Lincoln, and subsequently, in 1966 and 1967, in a full-year Experienced Teachers Fellowship Program in English at the University of Illinois under the auspices of Title V of the Higher Education Act of 1965. Both programs provided advanced study in linguistics, rhetoric and composition, and literary theory. The purpose of these programs was to qualify high school teachers for positions of greater responsibility in the schools. Nick Hook directed the program at Illinois, and he encouraged us to attend the NCTE convention in Houston, where we were introduced to professional leaders, poets, and other professional writers. We also visited schools and listened to and talked with experienced department heads. Both at Nebraska and Illinois, I studied structural and transformational linguistics, the criticism of Northrop Frye, folklore, film studies, recent developments in scholarship in British and American literature, the characteristics of British schools, the learning process, and so on. Under Nick Hook's guidance, the 17 members of the program elected an editorial committee consisting of Charles Suhor, John Mayher, and me, and we put together a book of essays on the teaching of English, titled *The Growing Edges of Secondary English*, which was subsequently published by NCTE.

Although both these programs were designed to make us better teachers and administrators on the high school level, they inspired at least three of our number to become college English teachers. As a result of participating in the Nebraska Institute the previous summer, the University of Nebraska offered me a teaching assistant (TA) position to work on a doctorate in English the following year. But I could not support a family on a TA's salary. So Dudley Bailey, who was the department chair at that time, offered me a position as an instructor, teaching 12 hours a semester (plus summer school). I accepted the offer, took a full range of graduate courses, and got my degree in 3 years.

Although my first love was literature, I got interested in rhetoric and composition at the University of Illinois and at the University of Nebraska as a result of the courses I took in the summer institute and in the Experienced Teachers Fellowship Program. Les Whipp taught the summer institute course in rhetoric and composition at Nebraska, and he had invited Ed Corbett, who at that time was teaching at Creighton University in Omaha, to give a few guest lectures. In addition, Dudley Bailey had previously edited a collection of essays on classical rhetoric. So my course was set. I decided to develop an area of expertise in rhetoric and composition, even though in my degree program I had to take the full range of courses in British and American literature and take the comprehensive exams in seven areas of literature.

I was fortunate to be at both the University of Illinois and the University of Nebraska when both of those universities were developing curriculum programs in rhetoric, composition, linguistics, and literature from kindergarten through Grade 12. The idea was to get high school teachers and university professors to develop an integrated curriculum by drawing on the practical experience of high school teachers and the educational expertise of the university professors. As best I can recall, the literature program developed at Nebraska was based on the ideas of Bruner and Northrop Frye. In *The Process of Education,* Jerome Bruner had argued that you can teach any subject to any student on any level provided that you break it down into manageable units. Using Frye's concept of archetypes as the basic unit, the curriculum makers devised a literature program from kindergarten through Grade 12, beginning with fables, folktales, and etiological tales, moving through adventure stories, comedy, and tragedy, and ending with the epic and satire. The composition program moved from narrative to exposition (with a heavy dose of Francis Christensen) to argument (using ideas from Corbett's *Classical Rhetoric for the Modern Student,* the first edition of which had been published in 1965).

The freshman English course I taught at Nebraska used Corbett's *Classical Rhetoric for the Modern Student* in the second semester of a two-semester required course. I was barely conversant with classical rhetoric, although I got bits and pieces of the rhetorical tradition in my courses in public speaking, logic, ethics, and faculty psychology as an undergraduate student at Loyola University in New Orleans. Nevertheless, I managed to get through the course, putting too much emphasis on the enthymeme, logic, and the square of opposition and not enough emphasis on the rhetorical situation. However, I probably learned more about classical rhetoric in teaching that course than did my students.

As a result of my educational experiences at Illinois and Nebraska, I decided that the emerging field of rhetoric and composition interested me most, and after I got my doctorate, I entered the job market, interviewing for a number of positions at the Modern Language Association (MLA) meeting in Denver in 1970. That was a dismal year for jobs in literature, but because of my diversified background, which included not only the standard courses in British and American literature but also courses in rhetoric, composition, linguistics, psycholinguistics, literary theory, folklore, and film studies, I had 11 job interviews at the MLA meeting. I was most impressed with the people from Arizona State University who interviewed me that year. Both Jerry Archer, the department chair, and Bill Ferrell, the assistant chair, had been long-standing members of the NCTE and the Conference on College Composition and Communication (CCCC) and knew Nick Hook. In addition, all the members of the interviewing team had deep tans in the middle of the cold Nebraska winter, an observation that impressed me. I was born and raised in New Orleans but lived 4 years in the midwest, so when a position in a warm climate was subsequently offered to me, my wife and I packed up our belongings, put the children in the station wagon, and off we went to Arizona and to my first official teaching position as an assistant professor of English.

Because of my experience as a high school English teacher and my wide experience in educational and curricular issues at the University of Illinois and the University of Nebraska, Jerry Archer asked me to assist Bob Schafer, who directed our English education program, in supervising student teachers that first year. I visited prospective high school English teachers in the schools and taught a range of undergraduate English courses in composition, English prose style, transformational grammar, and the short story. The next year, 1971, Del Kehl, who directed the composition program, decided to return to teaching American literature full time. Bill Ferrell, the assistant chair, remembering my background and interest in rhetoric and composition, asked me if I would be interested in directing the composition program. I eagerly assented, and the next year both Archer and Ferrell encouraged me to attend the CCCC program in Boston. I accepted a role as a recorder, mostly to find out what was going on and to learn how to conduct myself as a professional. In 1973, I gave my first paper at the CCCC meeting in New Orleans. I also published my first professional essay (an article entitled "Imitation and Style") in *College Composition and Communication* in the same year.

The following year I attended my first Rhetoric Society of America meeting at Ross Winterowd's house in Huntington Beach, California. This meeting was held in conjunction with the annual meeting of the CCCC in Anaheim. That meeting deepened my interest in classical rhetoric and the history of rhetoric and put me in touch with scholars from other disciplines with similar interests. From that year until my recent retirement, I felt I had a direction and a goal, and I continued to develop my professional interests in rhetoric and composition. In 1976 I was elected to the executive committee of the CCCC. In 1980 I became chair of the CCCC. That same year I served on the executive committee of the NCTE. I chaired the MLA Writing Division in 1985 and was elected to the board of directors of the Rhetoric Society of America in 1986.

At Arizona State University, I continued to teach a range of undergraduate courses in rhetoric, composition, linguistics, and literature. But the English department was slow in developing a graduate program in rhetoric and composition. However, in 1978, John Gage and I put together a modest program consisting of a sequence of four courses in rhetoric and composition that was subsequently approved by the department after much debate. Students in that program had to take the prescribed courses in British and American literature, but they were allowed to develop a specialized area in rhetoric and composition.

I continued to publish articles in rhetoric and composition over the years, although for me, as for others, the boundaries between rhetoric and composition were not too clear. Almost all of my publications in rhetoric and composition were influenced in some way by classical traditions. Early on, for example, I connected the classical *topoi* to the 19-century methods of developing paragraphs, to the Kinneavian concept of the modes of discourse, to schema theory, to literary structuralism, and thence to methods of organizing texts. Later, my interest shifted from the *topoi* to the four master tropes of Giambattista Vico and Hayden White, and I tried to develop a rhetoric of tropes using the four master tropes as a conceptual framework for producing texts.

As my interests changed, I began to call myself a rhetorician rather than a teacher of writing, not out of any perceived or imagined difference about the superiority of the one over the other but because I was beginning to have different perceptions about the role of rhetoric and composition in English studies. I was becoming more and more convinced that it was merely a historical accident that writing was taught in English departments. I concluded that writing, as a medium of communication and instruction rather than as a discipline, should be taught in all colleges and departments in the university (not as writing across the curriculum, in which faculty in English serve as facilitators, but as a medium used by scholars in other disciplines for their own purposes). But rhetoric (by which I mean the art of persuasion in ancient Greece and Rome, Kenneth Burke's theory of dramatism, rhetorics of inquiry, and rhetorical criticism, broadly conceived—to give but a few examples) should be taught in English departments in conjunction with poetics, as part of a long, time-honored humanistic tradition.

Toward that end, I began to develop and to teach courses connecting classical rhetoric (and rhetoric in the classical tradition) to literary theory, cultural studies, rhetorical criticism, and so forth. I also began to publish in these areas. And, although earlier in my career I had argued vehemently to graduate students that imaginative literature should not be used in the composition classroom to teach writing, I now argue that literature can be used to teach writing effectively, provided that it be taught rhetorically, as it was in antiquity.

I realize that I am not the first to argue that composition as it is traditionally taught ought to be abolished in favor of teaching some form of rhetoric or rhetorical criticism. Years ago, Richard Lanham argued that freshman English ought to be abolished because it has no content and because all too often it is concerned with a narrowly defined usefulness. In addition, Lanham contended that composition is not in tune with itself or with literary studies and postmodernism.

As a teacher and scholar who has devoted most of his career to the study and teaching of rhetoric and composition, I want to add my voice to the voices of others who want to restore rhetoric to its former central role in education, to connect it again to literature, art, history, philosophy, and especially to public discourse, in order to produce a community of shared values, to train the literary and moral imagination, and to provide foundations for thought and action. In his book *Cultural Literacy*, E. D. Hirsch claims that American schools have failed to impart a common heritage of cultural information necessary for those who must function in a democratic society. I believe that American schools have failed to impart a common heritage of rhetorical skills and knowledge necessary for those who must function in a democratic society.

At the beginning of my narrative, I mentioned that early in my upbringing my parents encouraged me to get the best education possible and to follow the American dream. For my parents, the American dream consisted of a decent job, bread on the table, clothes on the back, a roof over the head, and a happy family. For me, the American dream consisted of discovering my talent and my goals and of helping others to develop their talents and to achieve their goals. As a teacher of rhetoric and composition, I see my main task as imparting a common heritage of rhetorical skills and knowledge to enable others to participate fully in a democratic society.

Tempe, Arizona
February 24, 1997

WORKS CITED

Burke, Kenneth. *A Rhetoric of Motives.* Berkeley, U of California P, 1969.

Christensen, Francis. *Notes Toward a New Rhetoric: Six Essays for Teachers.* New York: Harper & Row, 1978.

Kinneavy, James L. *A Theory of Discourse.* Englewood Cliffs, NJ: Prentice-Hall, 1971.

Lanham, Richard A. *Literacy and the Survival of Humanism.* New Haven: Yale UP, 1983.

Suhor, Charles, John Sawyer Mayher, and Frank J. D'Angelo, eds. *The Growing Edges of Secondary English.* Champaign, IL: NCTE, 1968.

Vico, Giambattista. *On the Most Ancient Wisdom of the Italians.* Ithaca, NY: Cornell UP, 1988.

White, Hayden. *Tropics of Discourse.* Baltimore: Johns Hopkins UP, 1978.

CHAPTER EIGHT

The Curious Case of
Harry Caplan's Hat, or,
How I Fell in Love With Rhetoric

Richard Leo Enos
Texas Christian University

If there is a "moment" when one falls in love with rhetoric, I know just when that moment happened to me. I took my first course in classical rhetoric as an undergraduate with Hal Barrett at California State University-Hayward in 1968. I fell in love with rhetoric right then—even before it was fashionable—and have continued this love affair, without interruption, since that moment. I remember, even back then, how comforting it was to study rhetoric. In fact, I was so taken with rhetoric that I found myself bringing George Kennedy's *The Art of Persuasion in Greece*—at the time a very new and unique book—to my draft physical during the Vietnam War era. On all other occasions, I read Kennedy's book for the direct purpose of learning classical rhetoric; on that occasion, however, I took the book for the more indirect purpose of having something close to me that was a source of appreciation and refuge, more as a source of comfort to relieve anxiety than to learn. I found in rhetoric a safe harbor from the tumultuous sea of events that I was immersed in three decades ago. I suppose I can say that rhetoric has served that dual role for me down through the present.

Graduate students sometimes ask me if I prefer teaching rhetoric or doing research in rhetoric. I tell them both: Rhetoric is a subject that continues to fascinate me in any aspect. I demonstrate this belief when I remind students to study their rhetoric by saying, "Remember, a day without rhetoric is a day wasted!" I am familiar with the normal response of eyes rolling back and eyebrows raising, but, after the joking has stopped, students know that there is a kernel of truth in that expression. I would like to think that my love for rhetoric resonates. I am happiest when students evaluate my classes and speak of my "enthusiasm" for rhetoric. To articulate an accurate view of how I fell in love with rhetoric, however, I must qualify my first statement. Although it is true that there was a moment when I fell in love with rhetoric, it is better to say that there is a moment when I *knew* that it was rhetoric that I had fallen in love with. In short, "rhetoric" gave a name to what I had been experiencing since my childhood—I just did not have a name for it yet. To appreciate how that moment came, it is essential to see how my upbringing reveals interests that coalesced in the study of rhetoric. Understanding these events will help explain how at the moment that Harry Caplan, one of this century's preeminent scholars of rhetoric, lost his hat, I discovered that I had fallen in love with rhetoric.

ORALITY AND LITERACY IN
AN ITALIAN NEIGHBORHOOD

Long before Harry Caplan misplaced his hat, there were three factors that contributed greatly to my falling in love with rhetoric: my early years growing up in an Italian neighborhood, the Catholic Church, and the scholastic education I received through high school. Normally, when I meet undergraduates for the first day of their first class in rhetoric, I begin by telling a story of my immigrant grandparents. I tell them that many people who came to the United States at the turn of the century could not speak, let alone write, English. When individuals do not have the power of orality or literacy in a country's primary language—I explain to my wide-eyed students—the land of opportunity becomes far less opportune. I ask these beginning students to consider what jobs do not require proficiency in language. The students soon begin to list jobs that have a craft skill—bricklayers, cooks, cobblers— along with other jobs that require backbreaking manual labor. I cannot think of a more dramatic illustration of the power of discourse (oral and literate) for these new students, but I know that to them this is only a hypothetical illustration. For me it was a reality, sometimes a rather painful reality.

It may be odd for some readers to think that someone can grow up in America and not know English, but that was exactly the case with my mother when the time came to start school. My parents learned in brutal fashion how "inappropriate" it was not to be fluent in English. It might have been because of these experiences that my parents always encouraged us to read, to write, and to study. Shortly after my grandparents came over to America from Italy, my grandfather, an iron worker, was injured in a work accident and, after a few years of convalescence, passed away. My grandmother, who spoke to me in both her dialect and in broken English, had to work as a cleaning lady and in a cannery in order to raise her three children.

These jobs take work and discipline but little proficiency in literacy. The great hope of all immigrant parents is that their hard work will be rewarded by a better life for their children. Unfortunately, the American dream was not realized by my parents, primarily because the Depression and World War II provided no opportunity for them to go on to college. My father, a welder, could read and write but (because of the Depression) had little chance to develop his literate skills, having to leave school for work at an early age. My mother, as mentioned earlier, started school as a native Californian who could not speak English. Although she became an honor student in high school—I wear her honor pins on my academic robes to this day—she had to work after high school to support my grandmother and her younger brother and sister. Needless to say, my parents were convinced, I tell my students, that I was to have a better opportunity in life. My father would not permit me to become a welder; my vocation must come through school.

At home my parents broke the traditional patterns of childrearing. In our neighborhood, questioning adults was a sign of disrespect, and answering back to parents was a sure sign that the family was not doing its job of raising children properly! "Children should be seen and not heard," was a commonplace in my childhood, but my parents in an effort to develop our language skills broke with tradition and convention by encouraging us to speak out and give voice to our opinions. The family dinner table became a forum for lively exchange where I was actually permitted to do the un-thinkable—to "argue" with my parents. I know that many relatives disap-proved, but it became common practice in our family for the children to debate topical issues with our parents, as long as we were polite. I soon learned that the route to success in life was through effective expression. I do not know if I ever appreciated how helpful the liberal temperament of my parents was, but I do know that the experience was invaluable. I was groping toward rhetoric but did not yet have a label for it.

RHETORIC AND THE LAST
OF THE LATIN-SPEAKING ALTAR BOYS

Another factor that directed my path toward rhetoric was the Catholic Church. At that time, the official language of the Church was Latin, as it is today. Given the supremacy of English, it may seem odd for younger readers to understand, but for me the standard for education was not English. As a Roman Catholic in an Italian neighborhood, I learned that the true standard of literacy was not English but Latin. English was certainly what we "used" to be functional and to access most of our education, but undoubtedly the standard of excellence was Latin. When I was growing up, all Masses were in Latin, and it was a given that boys in Catholic grammar schools would become altar boys, which meant learning Latin. Latin was learned by altar boys not so much to be read but to be pronounced aloud. We were told that one of the primary functions of an altar boy, in addition to assisting the priest by serving the Mass, was to say aloud the responses so that we became the voice of the congregation. Because we studied Latin not to be read but to be expressed, oral Latin was primary over written Latin. In a true oral tradition, altar boys did not "study" Latin but rather memorized the Latin responses and would say the Latin on cue from the priest's dialogue. It didn't take long, however, to memorize the Latin, nor very long to learn the ritual movements and cues for serving the Mass. Because I soon could serve the Mass without concentrating, my mind would wander, and I began deciphering Latin during the Mass by comparing it with the transliterated English. I suspect that these skills helped not only in learning Latin but in memory training and comparative linguistics from the saddle! In effect, I was learning Latin without grammar and rhetoric; indirectly, I was learning how to decipher texts. Off and on, I remained an altar boy through my junior year in high school at Saint Mary's College Preparatory High School in Berkeley, California. Little did I know that these skills would prove invaluable when I began to study classical rhetoric and especially when I began deciphering Greek epigraphical sources on classical rhetoric in the mid-1970s.

RHETORIC IN THE SCHOLASTIC TRADITION

The final factor that led me to rhetoric was my early education. Of course I didn't know it at the time, but rhetoric would be a natural fit with my scholastic training. Attending Catholic schools from kindergarten through high school meant two things. First, as indicated above, the highest form of language was Latin, the language of the Church. We practiced Latin orally in class. We memorized Latin for the Mass. We read Latin during the Mass, which often was part of the school week. Second, the emphasis on orality at home and at Mass was reinforced at school. Although it was true that most children were not encouraged to debate at home, we were all encouraged to argue at school. The scholastic education of the 1950s was overwhelmingly oral and argumentative. In grammar school, the Sisters of the Holy Names made us memorize (word for word) the exact answers to catechism questions. An inaccurate preposition was enough to make the entire answer wrong! These responses to catechism questions were to be prepared for oral recitation before the entire class and, on occasion, the priest who would come to visit. In a spirit not unlike Roman declamation, Monday morning was devoted to writing down the sermon that the priest gave at the 9 a.m. Sunday Mass—the Mass that we were required to attend.

We then discussed the theme and turned in the composition. As arduous as this training was, I now see its benefits. Over the years I learned to argue publicly, to use the ability to memorize massive amounts of material to make new arguments, and indirectly began to study the workings of languages other than English. At this young age, however, I had not realized that these heuristics were endemic to the study and practice of rhetoric. Needless to say, however, when I teach graduate students about the study of rhetoric in Jesuit educational systems of the Renaissance, I am at no loss for personal examples.

Although it was during my high school years that the Roman Catholic Church decided to replace Latin with local vernaculars, the scholastic mode of education remained in full force at Saint Mary's under the watchful eyes of the Christian Brothers. People sometimes wonder why Catholic school students do so well in high school debate and forensics. It's no secret. As part of the scholastic method—from grammar school through high school—we debated about the relative merits of topics in every class. Brother Hubert, I recall, told us that since we would speak far more than we would write, we needed to be proficient in expression. Teachers, in fact, saw a strong relationship between oral and written expression. I can recall how in the ninth grade I not only had to engage in a formal debate over the relative merits of the generalship of Alexander the Great but also discovered that my paper (with accompanying illustrations) approached 40 pages—quite a length for a 14-year-old. As I mentioned earlier, if this curriculum sounds to rhetoricians like the residue of declamation, I can answer in the affirmative. But as I tell my rhetoric students, declamation is an effective preparation for critical thinking and spontaneous creativity. It will go without saying that the Christian Brothers, first and foremost, taught self-discipline through example and corporal punishment—both of which I experienced. In retrospect, I see my upbringing in an Italian community, my Latin in the Church, and my scholastic education as providing indirect heuristics. That is, these experiences and ways of thinking gave me a strong value system, a respect for history, a love of language, and an appreciation for the relationship of oral and written expression. There is little wonder why, when I entered college, I was ready to discover, and to fall in love with, rhetoric. I only needed to find Harry Caplan's hat!

I should not leave these early years without discussing one final, but important, factor. My father died of cancer when I was 12, and, by Italian custom, I became the "man of the house." In today's culture this gender role would not be emphasized, nor would a child be asked to assume such responsibility at such an age. It was clear before I was a teenager, however, that finances would be tight to the extent that my mother would take in neighbors' laundry and that I would assume responsibility for my own education. I was able to remain in a Catholic high school, but my mother made it clear that her work schedule meant that much of what I had to do in high school was done on my own and that I would have to compete directly with boys who had far more resources than I had. I think, however, that this early preparation was invaluable, and I firmly believe that whatever merits I have as a researcher are credited to the support of my parents, the compassion of my teachers, and my arduous upbringing. Italian children are taught that doing well in school brings honor to the family; in fact, much of the motivation for performing well centers on the gratification of the people you love most. My proudest moments came when my mother told me that I had "made the family proud" by doing well in school. It soon became apparent to the family that "Richard" would go to college and, perhaps, fulfill a family dream . . . be the first member ever to graduate from college. I have always been grateful for the support of my relatives, and in truth, my mother did help me greatly, even into graduate school. Yet I also realized how important it was to be self-sufficient and to be prepared to work alone. I preach that doctrine to my graduate students to this day, that the training that they receive is intended to make them independent scholars and to collaborate, when they wish, from a position of strength and not dependency.

RHETORIC AND HARRY CAPLAN'S MISPLACED HAT

My love for oral argument led me to speech communication classes in college. I entered California State College (now University) at Hayward in 1965. At the time, Cal State was overwhelmingly undergraduate, and professors emphasized teaching. My love for rhetoric and composition grew out of speech communication. In the 1960s English equaled literature, and writing was taught through models of literary masterpieces. Writing in English was adjudicated by aesthetic features. Writing in speech communication was adjudicated by clarity and reasoning. I found the orientation of writing in speech communication much more compatible to my interests. Writing in speech communication was often done to case-build; students argued for a thesis and valued the coherence of the material and the validity of claims. In these speech communication classes, clear, direct expression was emphasized, both in speaking and in the substantial amount of writing that was expected, especially by Bruce Loebs, one of the best professors I have ever had. I soon found that the principles of effective speech, especially in argument and organization, were very helpful in my English composition and literature classes.

What I also learned as an undergraduate was that the principles of effective communication were based on a long history of theory and research, which came under the heading of "rhetoric." I was very much impressed when I realized that the teaching of effective communication in speech departments was based on research and theory, that the directives of the teachers were not idiosyncratic but principled. In short, much of the teaching of writing in English at the time was arhetorical, whereas in speech the tenets were based on scholarly principles. Finally, I was impressed by how important effective writing was to the professors of speech communication. Many of my professors encouraged us to write papers in the mode of potential journal articles. By my senior year in college, I was submitting for publication. Each year, Cal State hosted its Conference in Rhetorical Criticism. Hal Barrett, who coordinated the conference for over 30 years, always—as discussed later—had distinguished keynote speakers. The best students in rhetorical criticism came from the western states, and meeting them introduced me to the world of graduate education in rhetoric.

As I indicated at the beginning of this chapter, I feel that my falling in love with rhetoric can be pinned directly to my senior year in college. I had the good fortune of taking classical rhetoric from Hal Barrett in 1968. In that class I saw the coalescence of much of what had influenced me in my life. My love of history, my respect for Latin, my passion for oral and written expression, and my attraction to history and theory—all these came together in classical rhetoric with Dr. Barrett. From that point on, much of my planning for graduate school was in preparation for the study of rhetoric. I began to buy books on rhetoric on my own, and I studied Cicero to the degree that my mother bought me the letters of Cicero for Christmas. With the help of another Cal State professor, John Hammerback, I selected Indiana University as my top choice for graduate education. I was fortunate enough to receive an NDEA (National Defense Education Act) Title IV fellowship, which paid for 3 years of graduate education. I should say, at this point, that I realized that the only way I could afford to go to graduate school was with a fellowship, so I had built-in motivation for my classes.

In the spring of my senior year, I had an epiphany that solidified my love of classical rhetoric. In fact, if I ever write an autobiography, I will have a chapter titled, "Harry Caplan's Hat." Everett Lee Hunt, the great Swarthmore professor of classical rhetoric and a major figure in the Cornell School of Rhetoric, was invited to speak at Cal State at the Conference in Rhetorical Criticism. Dean Hunt's dear friend Harry Caplan, the translator of the *Rhetorica ad Herennium* and one of this century's preeminent scholars in medieval rhetoric, was visiting at Stanford University from Cornell and came to hear Hunt speak. At the end of his keynote address, Hunt had made the "mistake" of saying that he would stay after to answer any questions; I kept poor old Dean Hunt up for hours talking about classical rhetoric. A few days later, Hal Barrett mentioned that Harry Caplan had left his hat and asked if a friend and I would mind running it over to Stanford. I eagerly accepted the invitation and had a fascinating conversation with Professor

Caplan. I corresponded with Hunt and Caplan all the remaining years of their lives. I also began a long association with Wilbur Samuel Howell, who paid me the great honor of nominating me for his position at Princeton when he retired. In some ways I feel that I became a junior member of the Cornell School of Rhetoric. Returning Harry Caplan's lost hat had helped me to recognize that I had fallen in love with rhetoric.

THE TRIVIUM IS ALIVE AND WELL IN THE LAND
OF THE HOOSIERS

I think having all but locked in my interest in classical rhetoric before graduate school gave me a real advantage in planning my program. Professor Michael Prosser, my first advisor, was invaluable in helping me chart out my years at Indiana. We began by asking what was the best way to prepare for a career in classical rhetoric and then began preparing from that perspective. At the time, the English department offered no rhetoric courses. I took all rhetoric courses in speech communication, classical studies, and history. Dr. Prosser had me taking so many courses in classical studies and ancient and medieval history that I declared both as graduate minors. I can say that without question the preparation I received at Indiana University was better than I could ever have expected. My principal professors were both kind and enthusiastic. J. Jeffery Auer, Robert Gunderson, Raymond Smith, Dennis Gouran, and James Andrews all taught different subjects, but all stressed writing and analysis. At Indiana I began in earnest to prepare for a career in rhetoric.

My opportunities to study rhetoric at Indiana were complemented by the continuing support I received at home. My work in rhetoric at Indiana had given me a strong background in rhetoric, Latin, and Roman history. I felt, however, that an appreciation for classical rhetoric must be experienced as directly as possible, which meant studying in Italy. My mother had, as is the custom in old Italian families, taken out a life insurance policy on me when I was young, and it matured (as planned) when I turned 21. My mother asked what I wanted to do with the policy, and, naturally, I said, "Cash it in and study rhetoric in Italy." Through her gift I was able to study in the summer study program in southern Italy at the Vergilian Society. Ironically, that life insurance gift marked the beginning of the end of my mother's life. She died of cancer near the completion of my doctoral dissertation. I was able to bring to her hospital bed, however, a reprint of my first article, a translation of Suetonius's treatise on rhetoric at Rome. As an adult, I realize how such support had enabled me to have the opportunity to fall in love with rhetoric, and I dedicated my dissertation to my parents.

I was fortunate enough to teach at the University of Michigan for my first position (as visiting assistant professor) and to teach graduate courses in rhetoric in my very first semester. In fact, I taught my first graduate course in rhetoric at the age of 25. In truth, I was so eager to teach the course that I wasn't even nervous, even though I was close to being the youngest one in the class. As an assistant professor at Michigan, I decided to take advantage of the opportunity of being surrounded by great scholars. Although I taught three courses a semester for 6 years, I always tried to sit in on Greek classes and felt that I had a second education after my doctorate. Having a paycheck and realizing how helpful study programs can be, I again decided to attend a study program. I spent the first summer after my rookie year as an assistant professor at the American School of Classical Studies at Athens; I was later told that my application fascinated them because I was the first person who had ever applied to study in Greece who had an interest in rhetoric. I have returned to Greece several times on research projects, and I correspond frequently with the American School, whose associates always have been immeasurably supportive of my research.

A DREAM COMES TRUE: A RHETORIC DOCTORATE IN AN ENGLISH DEPARTMENT

There is little doubt, however, that the fruits of my love of rhetoric were harvested when I first met my old colleague, Richard Young, at Michigan. We became instant and deep friends. I left Michigan to help Richard Young plan a doctoral program in rhetoric at Carnegie Mellon, and the success that that program enjoyed is known to the extent that it need not be repeated here. Wilbur Samuel Howell once told me that he believed that his purpose was to reinstate rhetoric in English departments, for that was (he felt) its natural home. In a real sense, that is what happened to me as a person. I became a professor of English through rhetoric and have been able to continue to work on writing through my interests in not only classical rhetoric but also the relationship between orality and literacy that has existed all my life. I will just say that Richard Young and I were academic colleagues in the best imaginable sense, and I would not have had the opportunity to have accepted the Radford Chair at Texas Christian University in 1995 had it not been for his initial confidence in my potential to contribute to English as a discipline through rhetoric.

Much of what I could say at this point would be a statement on the present and my views of the future—certainly topics that would extend well beyond the design of this volume. If, as the saying goes, past is prologue, I can see that much of what will be in store for me in rhetoric has already been established on a solid foundation. I tell my students at Texas Christian that what motivates us to learn is natural eagerness and the satisfaction of discovering knowledge. Falling in love with rhetoric has been an enriching experience both personally and in my quest to understand the relationship between thought and expression that has fascinated me as long as I can remember. Rhetoric is a discipline that for whatever reason attracts congenial people. Rhetoric is a discipline with a rich and distinguished history. Rhetoric is a discipline that has immediate pragmatic value but is also rich in its potential for scholarly inquiry. I have found that rhetoric is a discipline that attracts excellent students who quickly evolve into colleagues. To have all this is more than one could ask. Yes, I have always been grateful that Harry Caplan lost his hat.

Fort Worth, Texas
February 7, 1997

CHAPTER NINE

Road Rhetoric—Recollecting, Recomposing, Remaneuvering

Theresa Enos
University of Arizona

At milepost 2, still at the canyon base, I see the first road sign, "Rumble Strips Ahead." I am riding with my road club, the DooDahs ("We brake for bagels"), but the first rolling hill and headwinds have separated the pack. I am never with the group, either between two clusters or trailing behind, the maverick I am. Forget about the goddamn hill; I can begin re-collecting my own life and education to join the others in this volume.

Memory is history. It is both our history and our received wisdom. And this thought takes me back to a slender little book by Ray Bradbury. I think more than any other book, *Dandelion Wine* captures growing up, shows us the process of recollecting and recomposing. It's about a boy's summer and its ending at a time when the world was simpler, or seemed so. The boy had helped his grandfather harvest dandelions to be made into wine, which they stored away in the cellar against the winter's chill. The very words *dandelion wine* become "summer on the tongue," and some of his "new knowledge," "some of this special vintage day would be sealed away for opening" on a winter day, when some of the miracle, by then forgotten, would be in need of renewal. "Hold summer in your hand, pour summer in a glass . . ." (9, 10).

So I too find myself communing with a last touch of a calendar long departed—yes, memory is history. Although I have become a desert creature, I can still unbottle the embers of summer in Texas, Fort Worth to be exact. So let me situate myself near the wine press of memory. I've never tasted dandelion wine, but I know what Bradbury's book means, what it is like to have memories of the summer of childhood glowing golden somewhere and consciously try to retrace how youthful rites and revelations led to my being seduced by the power of language and then by rhetoric. And of course it is language that allows me to create order out of all those sensations of childhood's summer, to bottle and store them for later recollection.

> *I am far behind the pack now. I can beat any of them, though younger than I, when it comes to endurance (what is that old saying, that although men can lift a heavier load off the ground, women can carry it longer?), but I am all slow motion when it comes to steep grades. "Defacing rocks unlawful," the sign greets me in advance of the hoodoos, those bizarre pillars of rock developed by differential weathering and erosion. The hoodoos tower above the road and march down the mountainside. They're inscrutable, ancient—make me think of the pyramids.*

I was a notch baby, some calling my generation the "sandwiched generation." In the U.S. population pyramid there is a notch indicating the decrease in births during and right after the Great Depression that interrupted the otherwise increasing generational growth. We notch babies seem always to be between significant shifts in anything. We're not unlike what today is called the 1.5 generation, children of immigrant parents who hold fast to the old ways and who still speak a different language, somehow stuck or feeling divided between the "old" and the "new," never quite belonging to either world.

I'm a one-point-fiver in rhetoric, too. I came along right between the real pioneers like Ed Corbett and Janice Lauer and the first replications of those who created the second wave, the real crest, of doctoral programs in rhetoric and composition. But I am getting ahead of myself. Let me go back and recollect more of a blue-eyed, cotton-headed little Danish/English girl who found it so difficult to cross generational borders.

Like Douglas Spaulding, the boy in *Dandelion Wine*, I remember summers more than winters—they were a time for reading, or being read to. We were a family of females—three little women and our mother, who had had to quit her job as a primary grade teacher for a civil service job with the Quartermaster Depot. She barely made enough to support us—had been divorced from our father since I was just a few months old. (I would be 8 before I would meet him.) Genteel poverty.

During the summers, my older sister Bettye would take care of Margye, the middle sister, and me while Mother worked at her government job. Every 2 weeks in the mornings, we sisters would walk downtown (about 2 miles) to the old Carnegie public library and check out our limit, 10 books each. I couldn't read, but I would pretend to. When we would get back to the house, I would sprawl on my stomach on the hardwood floor, absorbed in one of my library books, looking just like Margye and Bettye, so I hoped, even though my book more than likely would be upside down. Then I would go outside to play, the front door screen tapping behind me, until twilight. I was fiercely competitive and, if I could help it, never let a boy beat me at anything. Occasionally, I would play jacks with a neighborhood girl, but mostly I joined the boys in kick-the-can and tag football. Then the magic moment when the streetlights came on all at once: I would join Mother on the front porch swing, each with our Mason jar of "ice tea."

Then a little later, inside, Bettye would read to us—I hung on every word—from the books many of you grew up with, too, Louisa May Alcott's *Little Women*, Laura Ingalls Wilder's prairie books, and *The Jungle Book*. (What do you think of the new "simplified" version of *Little Women* published after the 1994 movie, "easier reading" because young people found Alcott's book too hard?)

Even then I knew I wanted to make my life out of words. Reading— knowing how to read—was magic to me. How strange, I rethink now, that when I was learning to read, I was punished for my passion—another chunk of memory. In my second-grade class, we were not allowed to take our readers home. I don't remember being given a reason for this rule, but I disobeyed it as often as I could, several times a week, hiding a book under my coat and taking it home to read that same night. I had to read, you see, and going to the library was for summers. I got caught—of course. Each day I was usually at school before anyone else. I had special permission to come early because my mother worked, a situation that was unusual in those days. But one morning, so early it was still winter dark when I got to my second-grade room, my teacher (her name is blocked from my memory), raspy-voiced from laryngitis I remember, was already there. I tried to slip in and put the book back, but she glimpsed the half-concealed book under my coat, snatched it out, shook me so violently that my head whipped back and forth, and yelled in that scratchy whisper what a bad girl I was to take home books for reading.

Being punished for loving to read, and that was what I thought I had done that was wrong—loving to read—had a not minor effect on me for the next 2 years. I was labeled "bad," thought myself so, and withdrew from trying to make magic out of words, that is, to use language as a way out of a world, the culture around me, into which I did not fit.

But when I got to the fourth grade, Miss Bates (see, I remember *her* name) had us not only read a lot but also memorize poems and passages from literature (why do we no longer have our students memorize?) and *write*. This was to me both discovery and revelation, for I was named a writer and thought of myself as a writer from that time on. Odd that it all began with a little essay Miss Bates had assigned us to write, choosing a topic from several readings. One of those readings was about Balboa and his discovering the Pacific Ocean, and I knew I wanted to write about travel, exploration, discovery. In writing that piece—and it just came out whole, as if I had poured it from a bottle—I imagined how the explorer felt when the great expanse revealed itself to him. When I got the paper back, Miss Bates had written on it that I was a Writer. And she told me to read Keats' "On First Looking Into Chapman's Homer" and to notice some of the similarities in theme and imagery. And she promised me a future; she told me she knew I would be rewarded for my writing. Well, I know I will never discover a Pacific Ocean or write an ode or sonnet. But I reflect that a teacher had lowered a beautiful burden onto me—an invitation to see myself in a different way when she named me in a way I had not been named before. So language, for me, was a way out, has been a way out, is my way out—as well as my way in.

> *Now in a rage to reach some goal, I feel I am getting nowhere although I am churning the pedals. Why does the road sign say "Blowing Dust Area"? That message should greet Interstate 10 automobiles on the flat terrain from Tucson to Phoenix or back, where the road mostly follows the course of the Santa Cruz river, dry most of the time, on the way to Picacho Basin and Casa Grande Valley where the Hohokam people lived long ago. I begin to count the revolutions as if this will tell me I'm making progress up the hill.*

I guess the rage to be reachable describes my life through the 1960s. None of it is academic, but like many women now in their 40s and 50s, I was in that space between careers that characterizes so many of us who have had nontraditional careers and, fittingly enough, find rhetoric. But I like to think rhetoric finds us.

This was my period of conformity, of sorts. I guess everyone in the 1950s "fit"—what else was there to do? I graduated from high school and married—almost at the same time. How horrible that I must say this. It is true, though. I had to get married—no, no, not that—it is just that "back then" that was what a girl was supposed to do. How strange that the convention was not questioned or tested much. I married my school sweetheart, now a U.S. Marine, traveled from base to base—California, Florida, North Carolina—had the "required" two children, a boy and a girl. I still read every day, mostly those romantic historical novels, but I really got into biographies, too. I was pretty domestic and became a first-class cook, winning several contests and having my 15 minutes of fame in the local newspaper food column.

Then came my move back to Fort Worth, divorce, and a secretarial job with a major defense contractor. I was good, known for my efficiency, organizational skills, typing, grammar. I advanced as far as I could go, to administrative assistant (meaning, back then, executive secretary).

The spreading liberalism throughout our nation in the 1960s did not affect my life much. Reich's Consciousness II and III meant nothing to me; I was far too busy trying to please my boss and attending PTA. Then I married again (an Air Force officer, yes, I know—didn't I have any sense?), resigned my position at General Dynamics, and moved to North Little Rock, where my husband was stationed. I had another son. I loved homemaking.

Arkansas seemed almost untouched by the 1960s. The boys were not interested in long hair; their only observance of the hippie movement was to wear Bass Weejuns with no socks. The girls did not even shorten their skirts, but they did begin to buy Beatle records. I began to perceive my growing restlessness, a restlessness apart from any social movement. I felt stultified; why not go to college? A state college was waiting for me 30 miles down Interstate 30, and tuition was only $110, full time.

> *I will never learn to zoom up hills like my cyclist buddies—where are they now? At the top, of course. But hills are the cyclists' bane, except for those who readily go on the twice-weekly "testosterone rides," as they are called. My road rhetoric is "head down, eyes always fixed a few yards ahead—don't even look for the top of the hill. Do, however, keep its image sharp in your mind." Eyes progress before your pedaling feet, charting direction a little at a time. I see the next road sign, "Maintain Safe Distance Between Vehicles."*

I majored in business. "You should be an English major," my English profs told me, while I was taking a minor in English. I commuted 30 miles twice a day, had a 1-year-old child, two by-now-rebellious preteenagers, and a husband who would wag his finger in my face and remind me that my foremost responsibility was home and family, not college. Somehow I maintained balance—and a safe distance.

I worked hard for grades, maintaining a 4.0. Recognition from home was harder. No encouragement or support. I saved enough for tuition by craftily raiding from the food budget, by working summers as a Kelly Girl, and, once, "borrowing" $60 from my younger son's Pinocchio bank (I paid it back).

I was a senior when we moved back to Fort Worth after my husband's retirement from the Air Force. I again took an administrative position with General Dynamics. I also took one or two evening courses every semester. No turning back now. I had gone into Consciousness II without ever having heard about Reich's *The Greening of America*. I was no longer satisfied by pleasing others—boss, husband, kids—at the expense of my own self.

So it was time to do what I wanted, what I really wanted. I switched from business to English—as a senior, for god's sake! I had had only 18 hours of English. Thrust into upper level classes with both articulate undergraduate and graduate English majors, I was intimidated—but not so much that it prevented me from asking questions that still make me cringe when

I think about it. Here I am in a 400/500-level English lit course—most of the students being graduates—and, after the professor spends at least 15 minutes making references, I ask, "Who is Ovid?" I caught up, however, reading and studying all the time. My grades remained high, but I knew I was an imposter. I knew I was not thinking for myself. Talk about the banking concept of education! I depended almost entirely on secondary sources. After all, I couldn't possibly have any authority for knowledge-making. I finished my bachelor's—got Phi Beta Kappa—and still did not know anything really, I thought.

When my husband got accepted to Baylor Law School in Waco, I followed and began my master's work in literature in central Texas.

> *Tracking the white shoulder line when there is no bike lane (and there usually is not even though Tucson has just about more bike lanes than any other city) can be dangerous. Ride to the right and there is so much debris kicked off the road by cars that it is surely a flat tire for you. Ride too close to the left and—well, there are those unexpected right-side mirrors that will swipe you silly. And the sign coming up on my right says it all: "Soft Shoulders." Go too far right without angling off the lane and you are down.*

Many of us women writing teachers were first placed at the margins of the profession by graduate school experiences, too near treacherous fall-off. I can trace my perspective back to the 1970s when I was working on my master's in central Texas. Already different from my fellow students at that time—older, married, with children—I began what I now call my first academic misadventure. I was studying literature (there were perhaps only three rhetoric and composition programs in the United States then), and all of the literature professors were men. The department was housed in an impressive marble edifice that was also a research center for Victorian literature. Each professor's office opened into his very own classroom.

I was in my first year as a teaching assistant (TA), not only teaching writing but also liking it and talking about it, which moved me even more to the margins. We TAs were housed in a dark, run-down building 2 blocks away from the English department, along with the full-time lecturers (all female, all writing teachers). But there was one lone male in that old building: the director of composition, ruling over his harem. There was no mentoring, unless one could make the case for the most rigid form of imitation, the traditional master/apprentice model.

When I took my master's orals, I was "examined" by my jury of 12 White men. Sitting six to a side at a long table (I was sitting far down at the other end), they began the formalities. As each professor, in strict turn, asked his question so that I might perform for them, all of the 12, in unison, would lean forward and turn toward me, staring down at me where I sat, diminished. I performed poorly, although I "passed" the trial.

I had not been prepared at all for the experience. I had assumed that the questions would focus on my thesis topic (Bernard Malamud), but I was questioned from Beowulf to Bellow. In the 2 years of my studies there, not one action—advising, supporting, mentoring—had been initiated by even one of the professors to help graduate students—at least none of the female ones—prepare for the oral exam, to even know what to expect behind those chamber doors.

But I loved teaching—finally, this was what I was meant to do. To be. Given no formal TA training, I was assigned a "buddy," who counseled me and helped me on matters of grading in particular. (I still did not know what a comma splice was. I knew how to use semicolons; I just didn't explicitly know the logic or rules underlying sentence structure and how words, phrases, dependent clauses, and independent clauses work together.) The grading system there: two sentence fragments—F; three misspelled words—F; two comma splices—F. I graded for correctness—and, for a while, stayed in my appointed below-the-salt place.

I still have moments of shame about that first semester of teaching. I know that somewhere in the country, there are 26 absolute failures in life because Enos taught them a textbook, line by line, paragraph by paragraph—even the chapter-end exercises, for God's sake. They did not write; they learned to demonstrate formulas.

When I finished my master's in 1975, there were no jobs. (This was during the time that everyone had heard about doctorates in English driving cabs.) I wanted to come home to Fort Worth, so we did. We built a home within 10 miles of the Texas Christian University campus, pretty convenient to work on my doctorate—and teach. No jobs anyway. That was really why I began my doctoral work.

I told Peter Elbow a few years back that it was because of him I got into rhetoric and composition. The director of composition at TCU required all first-year TAs to take a "teaching of composition course," each one of us reporting on an important book on "process" (I was right in the middle of the big paradigm shift), as well as reading lots of journal articles from *CCC* (*College Composition and Communication*) and *CE* (*College English*). It was pretty heady stuff: Ohmann's "In Lieu of a New Rhetoric," Dudley Bailey's "A Plea for a Modern Set of *Topoi*," Wayne Booth's "The Rhetorical Stance," Janet Emig's "Writing as a Mode of Learning," James Kinneavy's "The Basic Aims of Discourse," Paul Bryant's "A Brand New World Every Morning"—I could go on. We even had a visit by Ed Corbett, Edward P. J. Corbett to us then.

For my report in the teaching of comp class, I was assigned Peter Elbow's *Writing Without Teachers*. When I read it, I shouted, "Yes! Yes!" I felt I had discovered the world, not just the Pacific Ocean. I had never heard of such a concept, but I knew it was the way I wanted to teach. So I had my students free write, every class period. Of course, I really didn't know yet why I was having them free write—I hadn't yet connected with the rich theory behind Elbow's method—but I was a firm believer in the "cooking" metaphor for invention. Thus began my interest and sustained research into voice and ethos.

Elbow was all it took; I began to read everything I could lay my hands on. I read only rhetoric. Gone were my former dreams of being a Keats scholar. Oh, for a while I tried to do Keats and rhetoric, but it didn't really work out, although I still growled every time I heard someone say there was no Romantic rhetoric.

I became a maverick; I had my own unorthodoxy. I *would* stray from the herd, I *would* wander off, I would not get branded. This all sounds pretty tame, as I think most people who discover rhetoric and composition aren't really of the herd mentality anyway. But being a maverick comes at great cost.

First of all, I was angry because, even in the late 1970s, I knew it was not right that as a doctoral student I had no mentor. I was angry that all my professors in rhet/comp were male. I felt patronized; either the implication was that married women did not need doctorates or the impression was that no one had time for you unless you were one of the chosen few—read "male." Same as with the master's: I had no help with my dissertation, and I was not prepared in any way for the oral. I had no positive role models, and, besides, by now I was too much of a maverick to "master worship" and play the apprentice to the master. I was on my own—I would just go to hell, like Huck. (You can tell I still harbor hostility.)

But in the end I decided to complete the doctorate even if there were no jobs because I needed to do this for myself. This was 1980, still a very depressed academic job market for English majors.

When I accepted my first full-time ("tenure-track") position as an instructor at a southwestern university, I had a doctorate in English with a concentration in rhetoric, a little unusual then. (They offered me $10,000; I got them up to $12,000 and felt proud. I didn't have to make the house payments anyway—I had a rich lawyer spouse.) In fact, in that English department, I was the first person with a doctorate hired to teach writing. In retrospect, I know that I should have paid more attention to the circumstances surrounding the hiring of a rhet/comp person (a former colleague of mine with whom I had gone to graduate school) several years before who had since left. Although she had completed her doctorate, she was told by the department chair that she could not hire on with a doctorate, that if she wanted the job, she would have to delay the "official" granting of her doctorate degree until after her hire date, which she did. For some reason, I was not asked to join the department under such subterfuge. In this department in the early 1980s were 22 to 25 instructors, all but two female—who taught only freshman writing. We were housed, of course, in basement cubicles—the "sad women in the basement" in today's terminology. Of the literature faculty—who had individual offices upstairs, of course—all but two of the assistant professors were women, all but one of the associate professors were male, and all of the full professors were male.

At this southwestern 4-year university, I taught four sections of freshman English each semester. (During my last 2 years there, my schedule changed to one section of technical writing and three freshman writing sections.) For 7 years, I was the only ranked instructor who was publishing in rhetoric and composition journals. I also published more than the literature faculty (save one), participated in more conferences than any of the English department faculty, and founded *Rhetoric Review.*

I crest the hill; looking back swiftly, I see it rolling back down from me. Pretty satisfied with myself, I switch to #3 on my big gear and #7 on my right and enjoy for a few moments the death-defying descent. The road flattens out—uh, oh, I knew it. I read "Dangerous Crosswinds." Nothing is ever easy for long.

My first book (*A Sourcebook for Basic Writing Teachers*) came out of my despair when, as a brand-new faculty, I was given a basic writing course. I had not a clue. My doctoral work had not prepared me for basic writers. Teaching basic writing was exhilarating (frustrating, too), and I was learning so much about writing. When the book came out, I was considered a basic writing "expert." I was not, but I was determined no one else would have to teach basic writing without resource to the ideas and strategies of the best people in the field.

Same with *Rhetoric Review* (*RR*). The winds of change had brought us cognitive rhetoric and quantitative analysis in the 1980s. *College Composition and Communication* (*CCC*) was full of it; there seemed no place to submit or read other kinds of theory or, especially, history. Not really aware of what I was getting into, I decided to start a journal. It is kind of funny now, but I think in part that it was my idealism and some ignorance that helped make *RR* a success so soon, becoming self-supported in its second year, which is almost unheard of in scholarly journal publishing, especially for an independent journal. So my maverick and impulsive strain paid off in bringing me some recognition in the field. But editing a scholarly journal cost me plenty in my long struggle for promotion and tenure. Like writing program administration in so many places now, scholarly editing is considered by most P&T committees and upper administrators to be "service."

I have written elsewhere about my and others' struggles with the tenure process, so I will not spend much time on it, although the struggle took up a large part of my career (see *Gender Roles and Faculty Lives in Rhetoric and Composition*). Anyway, I did not get tenure at that southwestern university; now I wonder how I possibly could have thought that such a traditional English department would tenure me. At that time I thought that if one did her job well (I was honored by students with a university teaching award) and met the "official" criteria for promotion and tenure, promotion and tenure would follow. I did not know that there were two different standards applied to the tenure track. If one were a rhet/comp person, one simply did not get tenure in this department. There was enough fear and envy felt toward rhetoric and composition in the mid-1980s that such stories were pretty common; English departments all over the country were denying tenure to rhetoric and composition faculty.

It was 1987; I had lost my job, my marriage, and my home. I moved to Arizona, having been recruited by the University of Arizona—the best thing I ever did, although for a couple of years I was in a daze much of the time. I had "experienced" life's three biggies—and all in one year. At the University of Arizona, my work was respected, even if it was not always understood. My colleagues and I built a solid doctoral program in rhetoric and composition. For the first time, I was teaching graduate courses along with an occasional undergraduate course. As associate composition director, I worked with TAs in a year-long preceptorship on the teaching of composition. Life was good.

The department wanted to put me up for tenure. At long last everything seemed right. But we had a new dean, who "dismissed" my years of administrative work. In her damn-with-faint-praise letter during my tenure process, she termed all the work I had done as "quasi-administrative." Although I did not have the "official position" with the "real title" that sometimes validates administrative work, I was in charge of curriculum, TA orientation and training (year-long preceptorship and colloquia), and teacher evaluation. My *work* was not "quasi"—but my title was.

Although my own department and college supported me when I stood for tenure in my fourth year (it really was not "early" tenure because I had come with 7 years of full-time experience from my former university), the dean did not support me, although she professed to have done so. The department vote was unanimous in my favor; the college committee vote was unanimous in my favor. Yet the university committee reversed, I found out later, because of a negative letter by the dean that was forwarded to the university committee but not part of my official tenure dossier.

This dean invited me to dinner at an elegant restaurant one evening shortly after I had heard the negative decision from the provost. Over a meal in this lovely setting, a meal I cannot even remember, she asked me how I planned to change my area of research in light of the negative decision. I told her I had no plans to change my area; I had been "doing" rhetoric and composition for 14 years and would continue in the area that most interested me and in which I had gained some recognition from my peers. She "implored" me to really think about this decision. She "implored" (she used that word often in the conversation) me to go out on a mountaintop and meditate for 1 or 2 days, to find something fresh and new that had never been done before—as she had done in writing about woman and landscape, scholarship that brought her fame. What she was telling me was to give up my research interests in rhetoric, find a "narrow" topic, write a "real" book on it. Do literature—and get tenure. I told her no. She then said, "You poor thing, as an editor, you help others get tenure, and you sacrifice your own chances."

I waited till my sixth year, came up for tenure again, and was successful this time.

"New Traffic Patterns Ahead"—well, indeed. I have done my 30 miles today. Next week I will try another route, but I will never find one without hills. But do I want to? The whole idea behind these Saturday maneuvers and remaneuvers is to build strength and endurance. Like all workouts, you enjoy them only when they are over.

As I was composing my own history in rhetoric and composition for this volume, I also was preparing to go through the promotion process for full professor. I worked at churning the machine, but it was hard to tell if there was much progress. Once again I had to argue, first, that work in rhet/comp is intellectual work, that what we do is a perfect example of Ernest Boyer's scholarship mosaic of discovery, integration, application, and teaching. I had to argue, first, that the 19th-century German pure research model with the subsequent separate categories of research, teaching, and service adopted by U.S. universities is not working. Especially in rhet/comp, the activities do not work as categories but as perspectives for seeing, for instance, how teaching informs and is informed by both research and administration. Only after "legitimatizing" what it is we do in rhetoric and comp could I then write the three statements about why my research, teaching, and service credential me for promotion. (Spring 1998: I have been promoted to a full professor.)

Of course, both my academic adventures and misadventures have buffeted me enough to make me chart, if not a new course, at least a tangential one. For the last 6 or 7 years particularly, I have become quite involved in the politics of the profession, especially gender-related issues.

I sometimes for a while give in to the common characteristic of always trying to be the things you were, instead of the person you are. It won't work, as Bradbury shows us in *Dandelion Wine*. No matter how hard you try to be what you once were, you can only be what you are here and now. Time hypnotizes. I may be caught in a present, but there is no other now to be seen. Yes, time is strange—but life is twice as strange. Here I am—cogs miss, the wheels turn. I like where I am at this moment.

Now words! I enter worlds made real to me through the power of language, hurrying through domestic chores, the necessity of buying bagels, pulling a dandelion here and a dallis clump there, responding to my students' writing, politicizing both gender and disciplinary bias—to the larger necessity of picking up my books, my papers, my pen, my writing—my world.

Tucson, Arizona
April 29, 1997

WORKS CITED

Bailey, Dudley. "A Plea for a Modern Set of *Topoi.*" *College English* 26 (1964): 111-16.

Booth, Wayne. "The Rhetorical Stance." *College Composition and Communication* 14 (1963): 139-45.

Bradbury, Ray. *Dandelion Wine.* New York: Doubleday, 1957.

Bryant, Paul T. "A Brand New World Every Morning." *College Composition and Communication* 25 (1974). 30-33.

Elbow, Peter. *Writing Without Teachers.* New York: Oxford UP, 1973.

Emig, Janet. "Writing as a Mode of Learning." *College Composition and Communication* 28 (1977): 122–28.

Enos, Theresa. *A Sourcebook for Basic Writing Teachers.* New York: Random, 1987.

Enos, Theresa. *Gender Roles and Faculty Lives in Rhetoric and Composition.* Carbondale: Southern Illinois UP, 1996.

Kinneavy, James L. "The Basic Aims of Discourse." *College Composition and Communication* 20 (1969): 297-313.

Ohmann, Richard. "In Lieu of a New Rhetoric." *College English* 26 (1964): 17-22.

CHAPTER TEN

How Way Leads on to Way

Richard Fulkerson
Texas A&M University-Commerce

It's still hard for me to have a clear mind thinking on it. But it's the truth even if it didn't happen.

—Chief Broom

PART I: EARLY MEMORIES OF LITERACY

At age 4, I sit on my father's lap in the front room, with his arms around me, holding his ancient wooden clipboard and his green- and black-streaked Esterbrook fountain pen, filled I know with permanent blue-black ink out of the Schaeffer Scrip bottle with the little glass reservoir on the side. My father writes basic arithmetic problems for me to solve and write the answers with his pen. So it is that I learn to add, subtract, multiply, and divide—and to write numerals—long before I learn to read and write letters.

The pen and clipboard become talismans for me, representing the life of the mind and my father's values: mathematics, problem solving, and precision. I still have the clipboard, and I have become a collector of pens, both contemporary and antique. Esterbrooks are not much valued by collectors; they were efficient, middle-class pens with replaceable steel nibs, not the valued work of superior craftsmen, like Parkers and Watermans.

In school, "writing" was first the painful act of printing letters over and over on wide-lined paper with a dotted line running between the bolder lines. Later it became copying a passage of several sentences that the teacher

87

had carefully printed on the board. In third grade, the letters changed to cursive, and in fifth grade, these confusing cursive squiggles were to be done in ink and in rhythm as Ms. Entsminger counted out the strokes each letter was supposed to require. My handwriting was ugly and never matched her counting, but at least I had my own Esterbrook now. I can recall no original composition before the eighth grade.

My father had grown up poor in rural Illinois. The only one of his family who had gone to school, he became the teacher and janitor for his own one-room schoolhouse at age 18. By the time I was born, the last of six children, he had become a highly successful high school principal, and before I reached junior high, he would be a university math professor. He had taught everything from algebra to Latin and had learned to speak an overprecise English with neither usage errors nor the standard southern Illinois twang.

My father is seated at his big desk in his study and overhears me talking to a friend. He is perturbed at my slovenly pronunciation of get. *He lectures me from his desk with a twinkle in his eye: "Son, the word is* get. *It rhymes with* bet. *If you cannot say* get *properly, then say* obtain." *I respond, "I'm going to* obtain *the heck out of here." I suspect his reaction is despair over teenage manners mixed with pleasure at his son's wordplay.*

In my father's house, middle-class literacy and a respect for education were automatic.

PART II: HIGH SCHOOL

I considered Southern Illinois University High School to be an ordinary school. We had 4 years of math, 2 years of Latin, Spanish, and German—all taught by the same teacher. My father thought that standards had declined significantly when I wasn't able to take solid geometry but instead had a mixture of modern mathematics. In chemistry and physics, I learned how to write clear definitions and good essay test responses from Dr. Gross. Speech was a required course, and Dr. Buys talked me into joining the debate team for 2 years. Most of my teachers were men, with doctorates.

In English I read traditional stuff traditionally: *Silas Marner, The Scarlet Letter, Julius Caesar*. But life became more interesting my senior year, when young Mr. Ostrander supplemented our survey of British literature with the paperback *Eight Great Tragedies*. We read Aristotle on tragedy, then argued for the rest of the year over whether and how each play was or was not tragic. We also read a lot of poetry, memorizing authors and titles and literary periods. True to the mathematician within, I came to regard a poem as a problem to be solved by paying close attention to the "givens" and what they added up to. Writing was a cross between a geometry proof and a debate case, with a point to be proven, based on careful reasoning from starting data. The unfortunate difference was that you always knew when a geometry proof was correct and complete; writing never shared that sort of certitude.

I am a junior taking American history. I have written a research paper, typed, complete with footnotes and bibliography. It is four pages long. The topic is World War II. The teacher's note at the top says, "This is good. Why didn't you write more?" I get an A−.

PART III: COLLEGE

In 1959, I crossed the street to attend Southern Illinois University, the same college from which my father and all of his five brothers and sisters had graduated. I promised the state of Illinois that I would pursue a teaching certificate, and the state rewarded me with a full scholarship. Naturally, I majored in mathematics.

Because of high test scores I am in the A level of English 101. It meets only 3 days a week. The professor is Dr. Staton. We have a handbook, a collection of essays, and McCrimmon for textbooks.

Dr. Staton is returning a set of papers on his assigned topic, "Your first day in school." The only directions were to be very specific, to use details. I couldn't remember my first day in school and thought it was a dumb assignment. I had eventually finessed the topic by writing about a day I had spent in my father's science classes before I was old enough to go to school.

Dr. Staton reads my paper aloud and asks the class for comments. Someone points out that I have indeed used some details that help make the writing effective. I learn a lesson that stays with me. But someone else points out that it takes almost half the paper to get to the topic. I learn a second, less-pleasant, lesson.

The teacher of my third-quarter required composition course is Dr. Georgia Winn, a slender, elderly woman with twinkling eyes and a melodic but raspy voice. Getting in her section is an accident. I do not know that she is an old friend of the family. It is a literature-based writing course, and Dr. Winn pushes us to read critically by giving us impossible true–false tests about modern plays, over which we argue in class. The answers tend to be debatable, but the approach fits with my view of literature as a puzzle to be solved.

She also requires that we write five-paragraph essays about the literature. More, the opening paragraph must have a thesis enclosed in square brackets, and each body paragraph must have a topic sentence underlined. This is a new and enlightening format for me. For the first time, I learn that one can design paragraphs rather than writing a paper and hunting for them later. Dr. Winn is flexible: We don't have to add the fifth paragraph if we feel we can adequately close the paper at the end of the third main point.

Later I will take advanced electives from her, courses in which she blind-grades all the papers. She tells me that in my case it does no good, for she recognizes my writing from the first paragraph onward. "You write like a math major," she says.

Because I liked to read, English was my minor, and I took extra English electives because they were more fun than math. Beyond the requirements for a minor, I chose classes based on what my favorite teachers were teaching. That meant I never studied *Beowulf* or Milton, but I took Modern British Poetry, Restoration and Eighteenth-Century Drama, and Modern Continental Drama (although when I signed up I didn't know what "modern" meant and had no idea what "continent" was involved).

And then there was college debate. I met the new coach, M. Jack Parker, at a freshman extracurricular night, and he flattered me into coming to a meeting. I cannot say I took it very seriously, and I was not very good at it that first year. But I enjoyed the problem-solving research in the university library, the same library I had used in high school. And Parker was a teaching coach. He had a formula for every debate argument, a formula that was drummed into my head at least twice a week: name, explain, support, conclude. It soon became my formula for writing paragraphs.

Sharon was a year ahead of me in school, already on one of the varsity teams when I arrived, and in the spring of her sophomore year she was the Illinois extemporaneous-speaking champion. As she and I traveled to tournaments together, we flirted occasionally. In the fall of my sophomore year, a group of us were driving back to Carbondale on a Saturday afternoon after a successful tournament in midstate. Sharon and I were in the front seat of a crowded station wagon. Trying to be offhand and cool, not easy at 18, I said something like "maybe we should go see a movie tonight to celebrate." She said okay.

We went out again the next week, and I gave her a ride to the train station for Thanksgiving break. When she came back on Sunday, I was waiting for her—and she seemed pleased. In December she accepted my high school ring, and by the following fall we had drifted into being engaged.

In her senior year we badgered Parker to let us debate together. He refused, saying he didn't want to destroy a perfectly good romance. Finally, in February, he broke down and agreed to let us try one competition at Northwestern University. I can still replay many of the rounds—we won six of the eight prelims, enough to get into the sudden-death elimination rounds. We won again in octafinals, quarterfinals, and semifinals. Suddenly, we were in the final round, one of the top 2 teams out of more than 100 that had begun. We lost a split decision.

Now Parker had a problem. He had expected us to be merely adequate; in my third year, I still was not even a varsity debater. Sharon was to rejoin her regular partner for the Dartmouth tournament the next weekend, and I was to go back to classes. But we had turned in the best performance of any Southern Illinois University team for the year. He had to put us together again and find out if our performance was a fluke. It was not. We went on to become the top team and to win our way to the National Championship at West Point.

Meanwhile, I had decided not to teach after all. Following in my brother's footsteps, I would go to graduate school, then become a research mathematician.

Sharon and I are parked in my '58 Chevy outside her dormitory about an hour before the 10:30 curfew. We are alternately talking and making out, and the car windows are steamed in the cold winter air, providing as much privacy as necessary. I'm telling her about my decision and my doubts. My brother makes really good money at his job at the Rand Corporation, doing I'm not sure what as a research mathematician. And I have grown up in a family full of public school teachers; I know about the salaries and working conditions, the long hours and petty politics and unruly students.

Displaying her usual insight, Sharon asks, "If salary didn't matter, if money were completely out of the picture, which would you rather do, teach math or do research." The answer comes instantly: "Oh, I'd rather teach." So it is decided. I am going to teach but probably go to graduate school first anyway. And whether I will teach college or high school is an open question.

I did my student teaching my junior year, and I was good at it. I could explain concepts clearly and systematically, I could lead a student by questioning to see an approach to a problem, and my debate experience made me comfortable in front of a roomful of students.

I am taking a course in Methods of Teaching Mathematics. It does not live down to the stereotype of "education" courses. We read a book called How to Solve It *by Polya. And I learn the word and the concept,* heuristic.

The final examination consists of one essay question: "Explain how you would lead a student to solve the problem of calculating the three-dimensional diagonal of a room, given that he already knows the Pythagorean Theorem."

In the spring before graduation, an opening came up for a senior assistant to teach trigonometry in a vocational division of the university, and I was hired for the job. I got to teach from the same textbook I had studied in high school. (I suspect I am one of the few English professors ever to have taught college math.) It was satisfying work. I saw my students progress. By the end of the term, because of my tutelage, they could do things none could do when we began.

It was a good term all around. I was debating with one of the guys Sharon and I had displaced the year before, and we were tearing up the circuit. I had been named the top debater in a string of national tournaments. I did not even seriously mind that I gave up a letter in tennis to concentrate on debate and a return to West Point. I would never again be this good at anything.

PART IV: GRADUATE SCHOOL

Meanwhile, I had consulted my brother about the best graduate schools in mathematics, and I had applied to 10 of them. Sharon had applied for assistantships in speech at most of the same schools. We were planning to marry after graduation, my bachelor's and her master's, and we would go to graduate school together. If we had to, we knew that we could both have assistantships at SIU, but we did not really want to stay in the department that she already had two degrees from or to live in my hometown.

I had amassed a lot of hours in English, nearly as many as I had in math. And my English grades were actually better than my math ones. Mostly as a matter of ego, I wondered if any graduate school would want me in English, so just for fun I applied to two in English, Northwestern and Ohio State, schools I knew from debate visits.

Northwestern did not want me, although they offered Sharon an assistantship. A school in Colorado wanted me to come study math, but it had no doctorate in speech. Then I received two letters from Ohio State, one offering me an assistantship in math, the other one in English, and Sharon had been offered an assistantship there, too.

So Ohio State was the school, but which field? In one sense, it didn't seem that big a deal; teaching was teaching, and I wasn't wedded to a field. I chose English. And I can't explain the decision to this day. The English teaching assistant (TA) position paid somewhat better. I hope that wasn't the reason.

Sometimes I think that what it took to earn a graduate degree in math scared me off: You have to solve an original problem, one nobody has solved before. I had never been much good at that sort of math; in fact, I wasn't very good at solving problems I had not seen models of before. I could see myself unable to get a degree at all. In English, I figured if I stayed with it, persistence would pay off. I had already decided that I was going to get my doctorate; after all, Sharon would be working on hers.

I am meeting with a young assistant professor, Wally Maurer, who is having to do the grunt work of advising new TAs about their fall schedules. He says, "I assume you had an undergraduate course in Shakespeare." I answer in the negative, and he says, "Chaucer then?" When I say not that either, he remarks, "Well, maybe we better see what you have had," and opens a folder with my college transcript in it. Looking at the peculiar spread of courses, he seems perplexed and shuffles through the folder. "Well, there's no green form here indicating that you were admitted provisionally." I sign up for Renaissance Poetry and Prose and Medieval and Renaissance Drama. Several years later, I learn that in order to teach three courses each to all 10,000 freshmen, the OSU English department must sometimes hire less-than-outstanding TAs. With enough hours in English, and a 4.8 GPA (on a five-point scale) I am more than qualified.

In fall 1963, with good grades and a mathematics major, plus some scattered literature courses (but no advanced composition), I was to teach my first two sections of English 416, freshman composition, at Ohio State University, complete with an office on the fifth floor of Denney Hall (I did not know until 30 years later that the building was named for the famous Joseph Villiers Denney, who had coauthored groundbreaking composition textbooks with Fred Newton Scott around the turn of the century). And Sharon was across the street in Derby Hall, teaching Introductory Speech and studying Aristotelian rhetoric and Kenneth Burke, topics I had never heard of.

I enjoyed teaching writing, just as I had enjoyed teaching trigonometry, even though the results weren't so evident. I taught my students to write much as I had been taught, stressing the importance of a clear thesis and thorough proof. I especially liked the second-quarter course that emphasized argumentation, logic, and the research paper, even though my own freshman research paper had been a disaster. I had actually learned the syllogism pretty well from some handouts Sharon had been given in a speech course, and I had taken logic as an elective. Between that course and debate, I had a practitioner's knowledge of fallacies, evidence, induction, deduction, and refutation, and I subjected my students to all of it. The spring course was more problematic because it focused on literary genres and used literary texts, including a novel, but was—we TAs were constantly reminded—*not* a literature course. We were not to assign interpretive writing as though our students were beginning English majors. Most of the TAs were baffled at what we were supposed to be doing, but we liked getting to teach some literature, and students consistently liked this course better than its precursors.

I taught freshman writing for 2 years, then requested and got some sections of Advanced Composition, required for all noneducation majors, as well as a promotion to teaching associate (teaching 8 or 9 hours a quarter). Advanced Comp was a 5-hour course, and most sections were taught by a schedule that involved the teacher meeting with some students all 5 days, although the entire class met only on Mondays and Fridays. On the other days, groups of eight met, with one or two selected for peer review of their papers. It was my first (and perhaps still my best) experience with collaborative response groups.

My 7 years in graduate school run together. I confidently told the adviser that I intended to go straight through for my doctorate, not knowing that the department used the master's degree to weed some folks out of its programs.

I had vaguely planned to focus on dramatic literature because that was what I liked as an undergraduate. But the English department had only two drama courses, Medieval and Renaissance drama and Shakespeare. After taking them in my first two quarters, I had to find something else. I had read some Dickens and liked it, and an accidental graduate course in Victorian fiction was interesting, so I gravitated in that direction and to the redoubtable R. D. Altick as an adviser.

I was not, and would never be, a good literary critic—even in those simple days before High Theory became de rigeur. But I assumed that clear and thorough scholarship would make up for my lack of literary insight. Besides, literature was still something you studied to relax from calculus—not that big a deal. And my goal was to teach it, not write about it.

Monday, February 5, 1968. I have an appointment with Dr. Altick at 9 a.m. to discuss my written examinations, which start on the following Monday. I teach on Tuesday and Thursday and have scheduled the exams on Monday, Wednesday, and Friday so that I won't miss classes.

But at 9 a.m. I phone Dr. Altick from a waiting room at the university hospital. Six weeks before our second baby is due, he is suffering from Rh-factor incompatibility. Sharon has been having regular amniocentesis, and the doctor has told us it's dangerous for the baby to wait any longer. So he will be delivered by Caesarean today, then undergo a complete blood exchange. I tell Dr. Altick that I won't be in this morning because we are having a baby, but I assure him that I'll go ahead and write my exams the next week.

The exams covered all the literature written in England or the United States. Altick had told me to list everything I had ever read. The list still did not include *Beowulf* or Chaucer. Then he had added to it everything else he thought I needed, and I had read for 18 months. Altick had already made me take a practice examination lasting 8 hours, and although the real exam was much longer, it wasn't nearly so threatening. And my speaking skills stood me in good stead when I met the committee for my oral follow-up.

One member of the committee was the new director of Freshman English and assistant department head, E. P. J. Corbett. He represented British Literature of the 18th century.

So 5 years into graduate school, I had a dissertation to write. In the symbolism of TA rank, I had worked myself down from the large shared office on the fifth floor to an office with two others on the fourth floor, and the next fall I was promoted to the third floor with only one office mate.

I was put on the freshman English committee, chaired by Dr. Corbett. We were to select a set of textbooks for the three-quarter sequence, an adoption that would mean 10,000 copies of any book we chose. In 5 years I had taught from a variety of texts: handbooks, thematic anthologies, argument anthologies, "snippet" anthologies with selections averaging three paragraphs, current–traditional rhetorics, and even a text based on modern logic. But the freshman committee assignment was the first time I had thought seriously about the variety of approaches to first-year writing. The committee fell into camps with allegiances to certain books and determination to defend them to the death. The "light-their-fire" camp wanted books to excite students and motivate them to let out their naturally inspired honest voices; the "they don't have any experiences worth writing about; they're only 18" camp allied with the "freshman composition has to have some sort of content" camp, although the latter fragmented into platoons, one favoring more literature and one wanting linguistics/semantics. In working through the allegiances, we were forced to articulate both methods and goals for teaching first-year writing. These were early versions of arguments I have heard a hundred times since, but they were stunningly new and important to us. I suspect Ed Corbett had heard them all before also, but he entered the fray with gusto.

I learned a lot and expected to teach composition throughout my career, but I was not a convert. I was busy writing a dissertation about the London stage versions of the novels of Charles Dickens performed between 1838 and 1870, all 150 of them. Heady stuff.

PART V: THE JOB HUNT—THE MARKET
COLLAPSE 1970 STYLE

I planned to graduate in the spring of 1970, which meant attending the Modern Language Association (MLA) convention in Denver just after Christmas. What I didn't know was that the job market for doctorates in English had fallen apart. I had read Don Cameron Allen's 1968 report sponsored by the MLA, *The Ph.D. in English and American Literature* (New York: Holt). Allen spent most of chapter 2 lamenting the terrible shortage of college English teachers and bemoaning the fact that there was no possibility of producing enough English doctorates to satisfy demand in the foreseeable future: "Everything has seemed to grow in measure with everything else except trained faculty and the means of training them" (18). I think I had five interviews at MLA, only one from a school with any prestige, and those were the result of 400 application letters hand-typed by Sharon. The letters had gone out in three waves, my skills becoming more sweeping and less specialized with each one.

Of course, it was a different world then. No MLA job list guided candidates to possible openings. The *Chronicle of Higher Education* didn't exist. And research universities, unaware of the impending market crisis, weren't giving advice about how to network, how to build a vita, how to select a dissertation topic that would sell, how to interview, what to look for. I recall having a single meeting with other graduating students and the department chair. The most significant point was that he gave us permission to use departmental letterhead for our application letters.

In a hotel in Denver, I am in a large room seated across a card table from an elderly white-haired gentleman with a walrus mustache, Dr. Thomas Perry. He is the department head at somewhere called East Texas State University. In the same room are about 40 other department heads, also at card tables, each with sets of credential files, seated opposite hopeful job candidates. Dr. Perry at first has trouble matching me up with the files he is carrying.

I explain my dissertation and assure him that I really will finish in the spring. He has noticed that I had been on the composition committee. He asks how I might respond to a departmental attempt to quantify the grading of freshman papers, either with so many points off for each error or with a list of errors that would lead to certain grades. It's December 28, and I am still confident of getting a job at a major university north of the Mason-Dixon line, so I am blunt. I know enough from our arguments on the freshman committee to realize that no good could come of such a procedure. I tell him so and add, "If I were in a department that tried to do such a thing, I would fight as hard as possible to prevent it."

By mid-March, late in those days, I had two job offers. One came from a branch of a midwestern university, a branch that had mostly night students and only five members of the English department. I would be the second doctorate. I had spent an enjoyable 2 days there, staying the night in the chairman's house. The other offer came by phone, as the result of the MLA interview with Dr. Perry.

When I got the phone call, I was within 12 hours of taking the branch position in the midwest. I asked the head to send me more information about East Texas State University and the small town of Commerce. If I took the job, it would be sight unseen. The English department had a graduate program and 25 professors, and that seemed like a better place to be *from* than my other offer. Sharon and I knew we weren't going to be staying, so as easily as I had chosen English over math, we chose to go to Texas. The $10,500 salary I received seemed like a fortune, and the house payments would be no problem.

PART VI: THE TRACK OF TENURE AND BEYOND

I was, of course, hired as a British-literature specialist, but everyone in the department also taught composition as part of a 12-hour load each semester, no sabbaticals. And I guess the head liked my answer about quantifying the grading of papers, because I found myself immediately a member of the freshman composition committee.

I sometimes ask myself how it happened that I never left the job I had meant to keep only 3 years. I did not change my mind and fall in love with Texas. I still refer to Texans as "they" and am constantly astonished at how "they" think. Partly, I was too busy to leave. Leaving would have meant a conscious focus on making myself an attractive hire to some larger department, and as I vaguely knew, that would mean publication. But teaching four courses a semester, along with extra work in the summers, and taking the teaching seriously did not allow much time for worrying about publication. I kept telling myself that I would "soon" get around to publishing and that obviously the place to start was with parts of my dissertation, dull as it was.

I did eventually get around to doing that. But rereading my own vita tells me that my first three "publications" dealt with composition, followed by three in literature. I had been made secretary of the freshman committee and decided to do a quick survey of other Texas English departments to see what their requirements were, what books they used, what they did with the research paper, and so forth. Gary Tate at Texas Christian University got the survey and asked me to write it up briefly for his new publication, the *Freshman English News*. As I recall, the "article" ran to two paragraphs— all the space Tate would give me. It isn't even listed in my vita any longer. There followed two short pieces about using full-length books as the readings for a freshman writing course, something I had experimented with in Advanced Composition in Ohio and then used with an honors section of English 102 my second year at East Texas.

As I look back at carbon copies of my vita from those days, I also find carbons of earnest but fruitless letters of application, five of them in 1972, before I had published anything, another in 1975 when I had two literary journal articles to my credit, as well as the notes about composition.

But besides being busy, I found life pretty pleasant. ETSU even gave me credit toward tenure for my associateship in Ohio, so after 3 years, I got tenure. After 5 I became an associate professor.

I had been teaching honors sections of English for several years and began working with honors colloquia. I had taught senior-level surveys of British literature, junior Shakespeare, and eventually graduate courses in Development of the Novel and Carlyle and Arnold. I was elected to the faculty senate, and largely as a matter of rotation became chair of the freshman English committee in 1977. Life, although not perfect, was good, with tenure, raises, teaching awards, respect, and good friends among other young faculty. In short, I was a big success on my campus. And I failed to realize that local success does not equal "professional" success, at least not the kind that leads to other job offers. Local success does not a vita make.

I did publish three articles from my dissertation and one on Anthony Burgess.

As I look back, two events signaled that I had indeed shifted into composition without planning it.

In trying to make sense of the arguments I heard about composition, the same ones I had heard at Ohio State, I one day fell back on M. H. Abrams' *The Mirror and the Lamp*, a book that had helped me understand British literature for my exams. Abrams argued that at different times different features of the discourse "triangle" had been stressed and that this accounted for the revolution from the Neoclassic "mirror" to the Romantic "lamp." I began playing with the same notion (four elements in the "triangle" and the possibility of foregrounding any one) as it might apply to composition.

I recall eating lunch at the Roundtable, our local greasy burger joint, and explaining my just-forming viewpoint to Brenda, one of my colleagues and closest friends. She remarked, as supportive friends are wont to do, that the idea sounded like something I might publish.

I wrote a grant proposal to our local committee; I had been on it since my second year and knew how to write a grant that would sell. It paid for some free time for the project in the summer of 1976. Another colleague said that I should propose it for a Natonal Council of Teachers of English (NCTE) conference.

Kansas City, November 1978. I am to read my paper. I have never been to a conference before, but I'm not nervous. It isn't like giving a debate speech. This time all I have to do is read—rapidly—from a typewritten text. I have about 10 copies of the longer final report I have sent to the university grants committee, in case anyone is really interested or wants proof that I have actually done my homework.

However, my confidence has been a bit shaken from learning I am to appear with Don Stewart and Frank D'Angelo. They are big-name scholars—in fact, both are treated in my paper as exemplifying certain viewpoints about composition. I am determined not to be in awe of them, and fortunately my paper doesn't criticize either one. Okay, I can do this. Then I learn that NCTE wants to tape record our session and make copies available for sale later. More pressure, yet being on a tape with D'Angelo and Stewart would be pretty cool.

But I am not prepared to walk into a room and find an audience of about 200, obviously drawn by the fame of my fellow panelists. I had been warned to expect 15. D'Angelo's and Stewart's presentations are complex, historical, and erudite, although I am too nervous to listen carefully. I take comfort in the conventional wisdom that some degree of stage fright is both natural and enabling. My paper will be simple by comparison.

When it is my turn to read, I pretty much go on automatic pilot, hoping that the practice I had done ahead of time will make the piece under-

standable and bring it in close to the time allotted. I finish with a moving anecdote about a teacher's dishonesty with his students, which illustrates my major point about philosophic inconsistency. There is loud and sustained applause. An experience I have not had again.

There are even several thoughtful quetions from the audience, most of them directed to me. Fortunately, I have read widely for the grant and can answer most of them. Afterward, my copies of the report are snatched up. From the back of the room comes Ed Corbett, now editor of College Composition and Communication (CCC). *He wants to publish the paper.*

Probably my fate was sealed that day, but I continued doing double duty as a compositionist and literary scholar. The next year, the article was published in *CCC*, a rhetorical analysis of King's "Letter From Birmingham Jail" came out in the *Quarterly Journal of Speech*, and an article on Hemingway appeared in *Studies in Short Fiction*, my final publication about literature. A good year.

We had recently hired a young professor who had promised that he could write a grant to bring us a site from the National Writing Project (NWP). I had never heard of the NWP, but as the freshman composition director with a couple of "publications" in composition, I was the closest thing to another comp person in the department, and he needed someone to list as associate director on the grant. I said okay. I don't think I understood that if this worked out, I was actually going to be involved, up to my ears, in studying composition and working with public school teachers. The grant did come through, and he and I became the teachers of record for the first Northeast Texas Writing Project. We had been forced to run it through a regional service center of the Texas Education Agency in order to get the guarantee of cooperation from school districts. It meant unusual red tape, and it meant we had to drive 180 miles to the center every day. Driving was my major contribution. Because I did not know much about public schools, I was mainly an observer as Glenn and the others did their presentations and a series of guest speakers came in. It was eye-opening.

Two other departmental peculiarities encouraged my transition.

Part of what had attracted me to East Texas State was the graduate program. It turned out to include an ordinary master's degree and a strange doctorate, a doctorate of education in the college teaching of English, the result of an equally strange political compromise between a state agency that had wanted to cancel doctorates at regional institutions and a local congressman with enough clout to prevent it. The unique feature of the doctorate in education was that all graduate students had to serve as teaching interns and take courses in pedagogy; that meant students working in literature had to study composition because that was virtually the only subject they would get to teach during the degree. So the curriculum included teaching colloquia, a course in composition theory, and an independent pedagogical research project. The only person prepared to teach these courses was a woman hired a couple of years after me as the director of graduate studies. Because she couldn't teach them all, my service as freshman director for several years, along with my few publications, "qualified" me to begin teaching the colloquium—essentially a weekly staff meeting of the first-year teaching assistants. We would discuss their courses, grading, assignments, classroom management, and so forth. And I would observe each of them as they taught and write reports for their files. I was not qualified to play this role, but I didn't realize it. At the time I thought I knew both how to teach writing and what good teaching looked like.

In addition, ours was a mixed department, including both foreign languages and a smattering of philosophy courses. Introduction to Logic, Philosophy 251, was taught by the German professor. He found out that I had studied patches of logic, so when he needed to be gone, I would substitute, which always meant my reading a chapter of Copi's textbook and trying to help students understand what I had "mastered" the night before. Eventually, the German professor left our department for computer science, and the head asked me if I could teach the logic course. I guess my idea of building a vita included seeing how many different courses I could put on it, and it sounded like fun anyway. I also admitted that it would be a break from grading freshman papers.

The chance to teach logic itself, to study logic textbooks, and to compare them to composition textbooks about argument, a topic that had always interested me, led to frequent frustration, frustration I took out in a series of articles about composition, logic, argumentation, Toulmin, and, most recently, feminism. Because our graduate students frequently seemed at sea when asked to teach argumentative writing, I seized the chance to revise one of the internship courses and created a course in Teaching Argumentative Writing. At first I taught it mostly by having students read articles and examine the available textbooks. Eventually I found the articles and handouts inefficient. So when Sharon and I bought our first computer, I decided I would learn to use it by writing a manuscript for the course, pulling together what I knew about argument and what I thought graduate students teaching English 102 needed to know. I revised that manuscript as I taught the course, over the next 12 years, until it became a slim volume published by NCTE that I tend not quite to think of as "my book," *Teaching the Argument in Writing.*

When I got my doctorate in 1970, I expected to go to a major research university in the midwest where I would have to struggle for tenure and eventual promotion as a Victorian scholar and would be low man on the totem pole for a long time but with a light teaching load. Instead, I went to a struggling regional university in the Bible Belt with a relaxed and flexible department that would let me do pretty much what I wanted to. I just had to figure out what that was.

A couple of us managed to create some graduate composition courses in addition to the internship. Eventually, we had enough that a student could concentrate in them, and when we requested that composition dissertations be allowed as well, no one objected. Now I am director of English graduate studies, as well as assistant head and composition coordinator, and our doctorate has two equivalent tracks, including one called Theory and Practice of Written Discourse.

I sit in my study, as always, trying to dream up a pungent conclusion to this piece. My gaze wanders to the books above the computer screen, four 6-foot shelves of nonfiction. Among books on race, science, ethics, depression, and education are some incongruous leftovers: a 1963 edition of Perrine's *Sound and Sense*, flanked by four Norton anthologies. The shelves to my left show an even more curious mix. My Dickens scholarship used to be part of the grand sweep of British literature; now it's stuck between 8 feet of mystery novels and 5 feet of books on feminism. On the rear wall are my "serious" novels, from Sherwood Anderson to Yevgeny Zamyatin, including complete sets of Dickens and Conan Doyle, but I know a deep layer of dust lies atop them. The debate and tennis trophies are tarnished and out of place, but the wedding picture of my daughter, holding her 3-year-old granddaughter, fits right in. I would never have predicted it, any more than a shelf on feminism or the complete works of Chaim Perelman.

Commerce, Texas
January 31, 1997

CHAPTER ELEVEN

A Backward Look at 55 Years
of Teaching Writing: 1941–1996

James L. Kinneavy
University of Texas, Austin

In one sense I have a modest agenda in this chapter; I would like to show you what it has been like, from a theoretical perspective, to teach writing for more than a half century in this country. I started teaching in 1941 in the elementary grades, and I taught fourth, fifth, and sixth grades in a small public school in New Mexico. I also taught 7 years of high school in four cities in Louisiana, from 1945 to 1949 and from 1953 to 1957. I have taught college for 44 years in two private and five public institutions in four states and the District of Columbia.

I have generally tried to keep up with intellectual trends, and, when possible, have tried to accommodate them to my profession as a writing teacher. Consequently, it might be useful to participate in a travelogue through these different venues, partly because many others have taken similar trips in the past 55 years and partly because I believe that such a travelogue in the next 50 years looks to be much more varied and promising. The theoretical travelogue and its pedagogical practices, are, however, only a part of the general picture. I had originally hoped also to address professional status, but publishing restraints have forced me to eliminate this dimension of the issue.

There was no course offered to prepare someone to teach writing, regardless of level—elementary school, high school, or college—when I went to college.

Consequently, most of us at the time simply took our freshman writing course (if we had one) and transferred it to the level we were assigned to teach. I remember rather vividly my freshman writing course in 1938. We had a text that provided paraliterary models, mostly 19th-century writers such as Matthew Arnold, John Ruskin, and John Henry Newman from England or Washington Irving, Henry David Thoreau, and Ralph Waldo Emerson from American literature. We would take, for example, Irving's descriptions of the Catskills and transform them into descriptions of the Rockies in New Mexico, where we were living.

Descriptive paragraphs were frequent in the texts of the day, but there were also narrative paragraphs, expository paragraphs, persuasive paragraphs, and poetry. These were usually called the forms of discourse—later the modes of discourse—and that formulation stretched back to Alexander Bain in the 19th century.

So, when I took my first job in a public school in Bernalillo, New Mexico, in 1941, I took descriptive, narrative, expository, and persuasive paragraphs and had the students read them. We then discussed the features that I wanted the students to embody in their imitations. The discussion usually centered on sentence structure, sometimes on figurative language, and often on paragraph structure. Then the students wrote their imitations, nearly always on a subject suggested by the teacher. For description, we often had students read a simplified passage from Washington Irving and then describe the nearby mountain called Sandia (meaning "watermelon" in Spanish). There was not much process intervention, and there was usually only one draft. This persisted throughout the 1940s, first for 3 years in elementary school and then for 5 years in high school in three schools in Louisiana.

NEW CRITICISM AND CLASSICAL RHETORIC

In 1949, I went to graduate school at Catholic University in Washington, DC. There I was introduced to two different theoretical influences that curiously supplemented each other, and both transcended the boundary of imitation. The first was what we now call New Criticism, as championed by people like Cleanth Brooks and Robert Penn Warren and several of my major mentors at Catholic University. This was a theory of how to read a literary text, but some of us interested in writing, such as myself and Ed Corbett, enlarged its terrain by extending its method of careful analysis into methods of reading other kinds of texts, such as expository or persuasive writings.

This has been a very fertile expansion, one of the many by-products of New Criticism.

The second major theoretical influence that I encountered at Catholic University was classical rhetoric. I took several courses in classical rhetoric dealing with Plato, Isocrates, Aristotle, and Cicero. Classical rhetoric was concerned with persuasive texts of different types and supplied methodologies to produce, as well as analyze, such texts. These methodologies were easily adapted to the careful reading techniques of New Criticism.

At Catholic University, classical rhetoric courses were paralleled by courses in classical poetics, and we studied such theorists and practitioners as Plato, Aristotle, Horace, and Longinus, who were given a heavy New Critical spin at the time.

Historically, rhetoric and poetics were a part of the general language arts trivium of grammar, rhetoric, and logic or grammar, rhetoric, and dialectic that dominated the educational curriculum of Europe from the fourth century B.C.E. until the end of the Renaissance. Grammar was concerned with the study of literary texts, rhetoric with the study of persuasive texts, logic with the study of scientific texts, and dialectic with the study of exploratory texts.

Consequently, this historical framework provided a map of different kinds of texts on which to project the careful reading techniques of New Criticism, and it also helped to supply different reading—and eventually writing—methodologies.

When I returned to high school teaching after my 4 years of graduate school, I immediately applied these two major influences. Other teachers were undertaking similar applications.

A third influence I encountered in graduate school was the literary theory of expressionism. Joel Spingarn, in an essay published in 1917, "The New Criticism" had introduced an expressive-based theory of literature, called at the time "the New Criticism" or "creative criticism"; it was derived from Italian theorists like Benedetto Croce and came originally from Hegel. I also encountered an expressive theory of literature in M. H. Abrams' *The Mirror and the Lamp*, published in 1953. Finally, I encountered many expressive practitioners of the lyric (mostly French) while working on my dissertation, which was on lyric theory. But despite these converging streams, this influence did not extend to my composition theory until much later. For the time being, it was dormant.

New Criticism and classical rhetoric both influenced pedagogy in the classroom. First, classical rhetoric, in Isocrates, Plato, and Aristotle, reinforced the pedagogical practice of imitation that we had inherited from the traditional rhetorics of the 19th century and the first half of this century. Second, the close reading of texts coming out of New Criticism, extended to other kinds of writing, initially to persuasive techniques, and accompanied by the methodologies coming from classical rhetoric—such as the ethical, pathetic, and logical arguments and the stylistic figures of speech—created a quite different pedagogical working practice. There was much more careful reading and analysis of the texts that were to be imitated preparatory to making the assignment, which was still very product-oriented and usually entailed only the final version.

This concludes the second stage of this history. For me, it took place between 1949 and 1953, my graduate student tenure, and during the sub-

sequent application of New Criticism and classical rhetoric in my own practice at the high school level and at the college level from 1953 to 1957.

SEPARATION OF MODES FROM AIMS

In 1957, I took a job at Western State College in Gunnison, Colorado. Two
forces at the time helped to form my developing theory. The first is closely
related to the Conference on College Composition and Communication
(CCCC). One of the motivations behind the CCCC, which first met in 1949,
was to consider the relationship of writing (composition) to the other communication arts: speaking, listening, and reading. These communication arts
were called the language arts in elementary and secondary school curricula.
Because I was very aware of this, coming from an elementary and secondary
teaching situation into the college situation, I was very interested in the
relationships among these various "arts." Clearly, the word *arts* was being
used in a different sense than that attributed to it in the history of the
so-called liberal arts of grammar, rhetoric, logic, or dialectic to which I have
previously referred.

I had never seriously thought about the distinctions involved in thinking
about writing problems as distinct from speaking or reading or listening
problems, aside from problems of literature, persuasion, exploration, or
scientific proof. I then began to read about listening and about how much time
we devoted in our lives to writing, reading, speaking, and listening. Statistical
studies at the time showed that about 50% of our communication life is devoted
to listening, about 30% to speaking, about 12% to reading, and about 8% to
writing (if we are college freshmen). So at this time I forced myself to address
the particular problems involved at the communication arts level, and I
incorporated these distinctions in my general theory.

The second issue that came to the fore during my teaching career at
Western State College had to do with the modes of discourse. Unlike the
previous issue of the arts, which received little or no publicity, the modes
issue has been given a good deal of publicity. Bob Connors has written
about this in a major article; so have James Britton and James Moffett. Given
the resurrected importance attached to the liberal arts, which I called attention to previously, the question arose, What do we do with the forms of
discourse that were taught in the current traditional texts (description, narration, exposition, persuasion, and poetry)?

Clearly, there was some overlap with the liberal arts. But neither Bain
nor anyone else had provided a clear rationale for distinguishing the modes
from one another or from the other arts of the liberal arts tradition, logic
and dialectic. I discussed the modes at some length with Bob Anderson,
one of my colleagues in philosophy at Western State. I was aware that in

classical rhetoric there had been a long tradition by which its status paralleled that of the liberal arts. The status, or issues, in Cicero and others were broken down into matters of fact, matters of definition, and matters of value. If one further divided matters of fact into descriptive or narrative fact, then one could talk about description, narration, classification and definition, and value as being the issues, or status. A solid philosophical grounding could be given to such a breakdown of the modes. So I proposed such a breakdown and suggested that the modes run parallel with the aims of discourse, just as the status had run parallel with the liberal arts. I also gave priority to the aims over the modes, but I have never approved of getting rid of them, as some have suggested.

In 1963, I moved to the University of Texas at Austin, mainly because I couldn't get anyone to publish *A Theory of Discourse* since, publishers argued, no one had ever heard of Western State College of Colorado. As far as my development in rhetorical theory was concerned, the 1960s and 1970s were the decades of existentialism and structuralism; this was also true of quite a few others in the discipline. Again, rhetoricians emigrated to other boundaries.

EXISTENTIALISM AND STRUCTURALISM: THE 1960s AND 1970s

Both philosophically and socially, in America the 1960s could be called the decade of individualism. I had tried to read Sartre's *Being and Nothingness* in French as a graduate student in the early 1950s, but it was too formidable for me. So I waited for the English translation and systematically read it in the early 1960s. At the time, I also read Merleau-Ponty, Gusdorf, and Camus. In the early 1960s, however, I did not read Heidegger. I was quite impressed with French existentialism, and it quickly influenced my philosophy of composition.

When I arrived at Texas in 1963, I taught part time in education and part time in the English department. One of my education colleagues, who was an ardent follower of Dewey, called my attention to the fact that self-expression was not a part of my writing theory in any of its dimensions. I told her that I had encountered self-expression among French writers who published lyric poetry and that there were some Italian critics, such as Croce, who were concerned even more generally with self-expression in all of literature.

Consequently, my attention was alerted to this aspect of language as I undertook my readings in existentialism. It was soon quite clear to me that self-expression, especially emotional self-expression, was at the core of existentialism and that several of the existentialists, especially Georges Gusdorf, had paid considerable attention to some of the language corollaries of this position. None of this had been applied to rhetorical or composition theory at the time. Eventually, I saw some major philosophic similarities between Sartre's position and Ernst Cassirer's work on symbolic forms. They provided me with the philosophic basis that I attempted to provide for self-expression in *A Theory of Discourse*.

Structuralism, both in linguistics and in literary theory, was also a part of the scene in the 1960s. What both linguists and rhetoricians took from structuralism was the ability of a system to take a core theory, such as the communication triangle, and to give it different interpretations at different parts of the system. This is sometimes called *model theory*. At any rate, once I discovered it, I started to triangulate everything, much as the logician Charles Peirce had tried in his work. Peirce even called himself a "triadomaniac." Anyone who has read my work knows that I have used the basic communication triangle at many critical places in my own system. So maybe Peirce and I share a mild form of borderline insanity—speaking of boundaries.

HERMENEUTICS, *KAIROS*, ETHICS:
THE 1980s AND 1990s

In the 1970s, for several reasons, I turned to hermeneutics, which had been a major trend in this country since its German version was introduced by E. D. Hirsch in 1960. I read several hermeneuts but ultimately ended up studying Heidegger quite thoroughly in 1975. I discovered, incidentally, that much of what I had admired in Sartre's existentialism was derived from Heidegger, and, ultimately, from Hegel. But Heidegger's hermeneutic principles in *Being and Time* represented a significant general advance in the field originally dominated by specialists in law, theology, and the humanities. Heidegger's philosophic hermeneutics had universal applications.

One area of rhetoric in which I could see an important application was what scholars in composition were calling the process of writing. I felt that Heidegger's theory of forestructure in interpretation theory provided a philosophical background for understanding the nature of rhetorical invention because invention in rhetoric is a kind of interpretation and interpretation is a kind of invention. Although I did much of my hermeneutic reading in the 1970s, I didn't get around to publishing on it until I wrote an article on the topic for the *Journal of Advanced Composition* in 1987.

Heidegger's theory is closely related to what I have for some time, following anthropologists, called the situational context of a communication, as distinct from the more general cultural context of the period. Rhetoricians in speech communication call the situational context the rhetorical context, and it has been important in their field since Lloyd Bitzer's article on the subject in the first issue of *Philosophy and Rhetoric* in 1968. The juncture of hermeneutics with anthropology and speech communication and theology (especially in Paul Tillich) interested me, and, in 1983, I gave a talk in Washington, DC, resurrecting the classical concept of *kairos* (timeliness and good measure), which was the notion the Greeks used for something like situational context. It is a very rich concept, with ethical, aesthetic, and educational connotations. Since that time, I have written three articles on the subject, and others have joined in using the concept.

Another movement emphasizing situational context is postmodernism, as articulated, for example, by Jean-François Lyotard. Particularly when used in a computer classroom situation that emphasizes the individual student rather than the teacher-dominated situation of traditional rhetoric, this represents a move in postmodernism that I have supported. Indeed, I have written an article in *Focuses* that explores the possibilities of exploratory discourse.

A good number of people in the discipline, including myself, Linda Brodkey, and James Porter, are currently concerned with writing about ethical issues in English composition classes. Thus we are being forced to turn to philosophy, anthropology, psychology, and theology in areas that we have not previously examined.

Thus the past 55 years have been and continue to be a continual foraging into alien territories for ideas and then applying these ideas to the business of teaching writing in the English department. What does this suggest for the future? Given the current rapidity of change and projecting this into the future, I would say that the travels of rhetoricians in the next 50 years will be more frequent, more dramatic, and more frighteningly exciting than those I have outlined from the last half of this century.

Austin, Texas
March 26, 1997

WORKS CITED

Abrams, H. H. *The Mirror and the Lamp: Romantic Theory and the Classical Tradition.* New York: Oxford UP, 1953.

Bain, Alexander. *English Composition and Rhetoric.* New York: Appleton, 1867.

Bitzer, Lloyd. "The Rhetorical Situation." *Philosophy and Rhetoric,* 1 (Winter, 1968), 1-14.

Britton, James N., et al. *The Development of Writing Abilities (11–18).* London: Macmillan, 1975.

Brooks, Cleanth, and Robert Penn Warren, eds. *Understanding Fiction.* 3rd ed. Englewood Cliffs, NJ: Prentice-Hall, 1979.

Brooks, Cleanth, and Robert Penn Warren, Eds. *Understanding Poetry.* 3rd ed. New York: Holt, Rinehart & Winston, 1960.

Camus, Albert. *The Rebel: An Essay on Man in Revolt.* Trans. Anthony Bower. Foreword by Sir Hubert Read. New York: A. Knopf, 1956.

Cassirer, Ernst. *The Philosophy of Symbolic Forms.* Trans. Ralph Manheim. Preface and introduction by Charles W. Hendel. New Haven, CT, Yale UP, 1953.

Connors, Robert J. "The Rise and Fall of the Modes of Discourse." *College Composition and Communication* 23, 4 (1981): 444-55.

Corbett, Edward P. J. *Classical Rhetoric for the Modern Student.* New York: Oxford UP, 1965.

Dewey, John. *Democracy and Education: An Introduction to the Philosophy of Education.* New York: Macmillan, 1944.

Gusdorf, Georges. *Speaking (La Parole).* Trans. Paul Brockelman. Evanston, IL: Northwestern UP, 1965.

Heidegger, Martin. *Being and Time.* Trans. John Macquarrie and Edward Robinson. New York: Harper & Row, Publishers, 1962.

Hirsch E. D., Jr., *The Philosophy of Composition.* Chicago: U of Chicago P, 1977.

Kinneavy, James L. "The Electronic Discourse Community: God, meet Donald Duck." *Focuses* 4, 2 (Winter, 1991): 91-108.

Kinneavy, James L. "*Kairos*: A Neglected Concept in Classical Rhetoric." In *Rhetoric and Praxis: The Contribution of Classical Rhetoric to Practical Reason.* Ed. Jean Dietz Moss. Washington, DC: The Catholic University of America Press (1986): 79-105.

Kinneavy, James L. "The Process of Writing: A Philosophic Basis in Hermeneutics." *Journal of Advanced Composition* 7, 1 (1987): 1-9.

Kinneavy, James L. *A Theory of Discourse.* New York: W. W. Norton, 1980.

Lyotard, Jean-Francois. *The Postmodern Condition.* Trans. J. Bennington and Brian Massumi. Minneapolis: U of Minnesota P, 1984.

Merleau-Ponty, Maurice. *Phenomenology of Perception.* Trans. Colin Smith. New York: Humanities Press, 1962.

Moffett, James. *Teaching the Universe of Discourse.* Boston: Houghton Mifflin, 1968.

Peirce, Charles Sanders. *Chance, Love, and Logic: Philosophical Essays.* Ed. Morris R. Cohen. New York: Harcourt, Brace and Company, 1923.

Sartre, Jean-Paul. *Being and Nothingness: An Essay in Phenomenological Ontology.* Trans. with an introduction by Hazel E. Barnes. New York: Citadel Press, 1956.

Spingarn, Joel Elias. *Creative Criticism and Other Essays.* New York: Harcourt, Brace & Company, 1931.

Tillich, Paul. "Kairos and Logos." In *The Interpretation of History.* Trans. N. A. Rasetzki and Elsa Talmey. New York: Scribner's, 1936.

CHAPTER TWELVE

Doing as One Likes

Richard Lloyd-Jones
University of Iowa

I was too sick to be sent back to duty, the doctors said, and too well to stay in bed, so I spent my time in the library of the regional hospital at Fort McClellan. I read omnivorously, as I always had, without much regard for genre or subject. I read what struck my fancy, and one of the books was Bertrand Russell's *A History of Western Philosophy.*

I decided that I would become a philosopher. Russell wrote clearly of people who asked interesting questions about human existence, probably just the ticket for a person with whom the army doctors did not know what to do. Eventually, a brand-new doctor who had just graduated from Johns Hopkins found that I (and a flock of others) had bronchiectasis, and that was that.

The army sent me to the Veterans Administration (VA) to be "rehabilitated" under Public Law 16. The VA people asked me what I wanted to become, and I said, "Either a philosopher or a poet." I had written a good bit of poetry in high school. Their counselor opined that there was not much market for either, so why didn't I become a teacher of English? Indeed, why not? Perhaps this is not an ideal example of academic planning, but it will serve to illustrate the force of unintended consequences.

I was sent to a warm, dry climate—the University of New Mexico—to major in English. I did that, but I immediately took a course in philosophy, got myself exempted from first-semester English, and volunteered for the debate team. I was eventually to collect three majors, not because I was crazy to fulfill requirements but because each area had courses I wanted to

111

take just for fun, not for the purpose of becoming anything in particular. So much for the prudent seeking of credentials!

Philosophy was best, mostly because of Hubert G. Alexander, who was chair of a two-person department. In his introductory class, I met Plato, phrase by phrase, teasing out the implications. Then, in his two-semester history course, I met the pre-Socratics and Aristotle, Locke and Hume, the German Idealists, and a great many others who probably did not impress me as much at the time. Alexander had worked with Native American languages, especially Navajo, so his incidental comments were laced with examples of how language controlled thought. I went on to take his Philosophy of Language course, using Charles Morris' *Signs, Language, and Behavior* as the main text, and then a course in aesthetics, which enlarged on the nature of meaning and symbol. I did not assume that the VA was wrong about practical vocations, but by good luck I had found a person who was serious and funny at the same time, who just loved to learn, and who was amused by the paradoxes of human endeavors, especially as exhibited in language.

As it happened, my future wife was in the introductory philosophy course, too, although I didn't know it, and she later became Alexander's typist. I mention these details in the interests of full disclosure, not because it is relevant as a fact of the case of career choice. We really met through the literary magazine that a friend had started and that I later edited. I still pictured myself as a poet.

My interest in debate (and politics) was more socially evident to fellow New Mexican students, but it was a result of an earlier academic accident. Eighth graders at Monroe Junior High School in Mason City, Iowa, were expected to take part in various extracurricular amusements, and I fell into the hands of an ardent social science teacher, Dave Tripp, who believed in debate, the kind where you flip a coin to discover what side you are on. He thought that you could not properly hold a belief until you discovered what was truly to be said for other sides of an issue. Thus you had to learn to fashion the best possible argument for any issue at hand. Some teachers who believe they possess absolute truth think this is cynical, but I liked it, for I had the background for dealing with this attitude.

My father's family of Welsh Americans was much given to argument and dissent for the fun of it. In Wales, each subsection of the family seemed to breed its own nonconformist clergyman; their little circle of chapels is known as the Black Spot of Wales in honor of their heresies. The family also attracted some of those who revived the Welsh versions of what is covered in the medieval "Matter of Britain" and were sentimentally interested in restoring the glory of the old culture. That is, they gave fiery speeches to each other, and some of them rather upset outsiders (English), but they also told lovely stories of a heroic age and often sang. Family reunions in Wisconsin were large and lively, and as a child I thought that was the way life was supposed to be. As a matter of family course, one should learn to debate and tell stories, but in this country the skeptical nonconformist preachers turned into rather intense teachers.

Dave Tripp got me started in school debate, decided that I had talent, and sent me to Mason City High School to become part of their team. Their coach, Guy Crosen, gave us watered-down Aristotle as a pattern of argument; he also arranged for us to we have unlimited access to the stacks of the public library, a very good library memorialized in *The Music Man* by Meredith Willson. That was where I read the complete Bernard Shaw, Rudyard Kipling, Robert Graves, and Stephen V. Benét, among others. I also researched questions of political sovereignty, economics, and community organization, and thus I came to understand that libraries not only were a source of fun but could also be used for examining particular questions. I rather doubt that research was a part of the official school curriculum, but my later college work had little to add to what I learned in high school.

Because I am somewhat dyslexic and have terrible handwriting, I rarely took notes, and I refused to deal with the little boxes of file cards common to most high school debaters. The coach simply made me the final speaker, who had to pull arguments together and tie up the case for the audience at hand. As a result, I acquired the habit of recasting what other people said into my own systems of organization so I could always speak extemporaneously, and I had to become especially conscious of organizing strategies. The ancient rhetorics, after all, were intended for speakers.

Fortunately, my high school required almost no written work in English classes or elsewhere, so I was not penalized for hopeless manuscripts, and I became quite adept at planning argumentative discourse. I managed to sneak in a course in typing during my senior year—the school did not record it because I already had too many courses—but my typing is only marginally better than my handwriting. Professor George Arms once refused to put a grade on one of my typewritten literary criticism papers because he said he couldn't bear to show an "A" on such an awful manuscript; he also advised me to hand in papers early so that instructors would have time to discover that I might be making sense. I did not love the red-pencil addicts, but that was a personal reaction, not a result of formal indoctrination by later antiformalists. Much later, I learned to distinguish among scribal errors, social class and stylistic errors, and discourse errors. These errors have much different causes and consequences and need to be addressed in much different ways.

When I reached New Mexico, I found that I was well prepared as a debater, and the debate coach at the university was also an assistant dean who found money to finance our trips. We traveled all over the western United States and did well, so the coach was inclined to let us make our own curricular decisions. Debate, incidentally, was awarded academic credit, so just a few other courses were required for a major in speech. Most of the other speech faculty members were attracted to general semantics, so I read Elwood Murray, Wendell Johnson, S. I. Hayakawa, and even Alfred Korzybski, although I found him rather heavy going. The general semanticists are fond of cute slogans and games—provokingly funny commentaries on the world around us. They (and I) enjoy ambiguity, irony, metaphor, and other forms of duplicitous language, for this fundamental squishiness of statement is crucial to negotiation. Their techniques have been a constant source for my own teaching, and I still read *ETC* regularly.

The speech correction work required us pay attention to phonology; about the fourth time I tried to master the phonetic alphabet, it dawned on me that being somewhat deaf was a bother. Somehow, when adults had talked about birds singing or about the chatter of rushing water, I hadn't noticed that I didn't know what they were talking about. They seemed to know what they described, so I took the experience at their value. Children take adult knowledge for granted. Almost four decades later, when someone devised a hearing aid that matched my loss, I discovered what it meant to hear high-pitched sounds, especially consonants. Even now, I rarely decode the lyrics of a song. Still, in reaction, I had become aware that sensory systems give each of us a unique view of our external world, that any particular word may have quite different meanings for different people. It also explained to me why I preferred Latin to modern languages. The teachers didn't expect me to hear it spoken.

Latin in high school supplied to me much of what English classes did not. Virgil and Cicero opened the doors to serious poetry and devices of style. To be sure, I had a poem published in our fourth-grade newspaper, but in Latin I learned about meters—quantity and accent; even a deaf person can figure out rhythm. The drama of the periodic sentence delighted me. I also learned strategies of organization different from those in argument, even though Virgil in the *Aeneid* took a rhetorical stance in supporting an imperial case. I became aware of figures of speech, mostly through Cicero. I acquired a taste for history and myth, doubtless reinforcing my excursion into the novels and reworked myths of Robert Graves. Mostly, though, my Latin teacher, Florence Flynn, opened the vision of language change, how words and political power intersected in dialects. She may have thought of the exercises as leading to vocabulary building, but for me it was the basis of later study in linguistics, politics, and epistemology.

Rhetoric and poetics were thus inextricably linked. Those 19th-century departments of rhetoric and oratory staffed by clergy and writers would have been my ideal. I have never liked the quarrel that composition specialists have mounted with literary people, even though I admit that since the days of Francis Childs and George Lyman Kittredge, at least, departments of English have slighted the people who teach writing. I am saddened that English professors were inhospitable to people in speech and journalism. I liked the essay, even when New Critics ignored it. That it was convenient to major in speech, as well as philosophy, reinforced my taste, although at the time it didn't occur to me that there was a split.

I will not pretend that VA alone sent me to English. I liked literary studies, and the faculty of English at New Mexico supported activities in speech and lived in a world honoring the arts and various cultures. They may have preferred philosophy in the form of literary criticism, but no one thought it odd that I took more formal work. Professor Arms had led me into the New Criticism and close reading, but he also opened up a broad range of critics.

The community of students and faculty was also crucial. Veterans dominated; they were in a hurry, serious about learning, and not easily pushed aside. They mixed art and politics, journalism and literature, personal ambition and public service. Jene Lyon and Jetta Carleton were our special models of life as lived in language. Jene, a veteran, was a poet and printer, Jetta, a dancer and novelist. They constructed their home out in the dunes west of town; Jene was working on a degree in Inter-American Studies, founded the literary magazine, rebuilt the yearbook, and made his living in the print shop. The couple rather looked after the romance of my future wife and me, not so much as matchmakers but as mentors. Later, they went to New York and Washington, where Jetta worked on her fiction and made money in advertising, and Jene made and sold mobiles and then translated scientific works for the state department. Eventually they returned to Santa Fe, built a house and studio at 8,500 feet above the city, wrote, and printed handmade books. They were people who heard their own drummer, blended broad social and intellectual concerns, and enjoyed being in the company of others; to me they represented what education—especially education in the language—was supposed to confer on humans, and thus they provided a lesson in goals. Their example gave life to what might be understood as "composition."

Graduate school is another story, briefly told. It had almost nothing to do directly with teaching composition. A course in 17th-century literature at Chapel Hill enhanced my interest in style, additional work in linguistics at Iowa introduced me to Leonard Bloomfield's *Language* and various other technical works, and my own interest in prosody built on my background in high school Latin. Otherwise, doctoral work provided me with some history, some knowledge of literary works, and a basis for teaching Victorian literature and culture. It was the *Beowulf*-to-Virginia Woolf model of professional study, and I don't regret it, for it gave me a perspective on language and belief that shapes my sense of human motive. I acquired a timeline to which I could attach miscellaneous bits of knowledge as I lived on. Borrowing sensibilities from many times, places, and circumstances through literature is a crucial part of human existence.

If graduate study per se was irrelevant, employment as a graduate student teacher was not. Through a series of accidents that would appall any person now responsible for hiring or making graduate appointments, I found myself teaching two sections of business writing to juniors and seniors. My predecessor had just walked out halfway through the semester. The following fall, I became a full-time nontenured teacher in a required junior/senior technical writing program, with one course in sophomore literature thrown in as gravy. Fortunately, I had more experienced graduate students, William F. Carstens and Jim L. Fife, as mentors, and we used a single syllabus for all of the sections. Our "offices" were desks in the back of our classroom, which was "dedicated" to composition by virtue of an overhead projector and room scheduling. I learned by doing and by observing those a little ahead of me in line.

The course itself was very much formula-oriented, as was the other teaching in engineering, but we required a paper every time the class met, there was lots of participation in class sessions devoted to examining papers, and most of the tasks were directly oriented to professional audiences and assumptions. About one fourth of the papers required engineering drawings, which were "checked" by an engineering assistant. We also had lots of backup chatter from engineering faculty in their courses, so as a form of extra service we often read final reports written in other classes. We attended engineering faculty meetings and heard the speakers at their weekly luncheon club. I was chair of the luncheon club the year I finished my degree, and I recruited my speakers from the general education teachers in liberal arts as a way of helping the faculties meet each other. I have always felt that colleges have too many isolated subsections.

This course offered writing as a tool for doing the world's work, and the students were far enough along in engineering to imagine themselves in the roles we asked them to play. They did not want a "personal" voice; they sought the engineer's voice. They believed themselves to be highly rational, so they honored the claims of logic and structure. They were also socially conventional, so they were willing to conform to rules for mechanical correctness, even though they hated the rules that were set up for the program partly to reassure the engineering faculty that we people from English were not too arty. They instructed me in the idea that the crafts of writing may be ends in themselves for poets but are means to ends for most people, so I had to think in terms of the outcome of each piece of prose, no real problem for one trained in debate.

The year I might have entered the job market, the person who ran the technical writing program left the university. I had just had some exotic lung surgery and did not want to try out a new VA hospital, so I asked to take over the program. I suspect that Baldwin Maxwell, the chair of English, a Shakespearean and editor of *Philological Quarterly*, was relieved at not having to find someone else, and the College of Engineering figured it was better to stay with a known person. Suddenly I was hiring and training new teachers in a system that did not permit us to make appointments until after registration had confirmed enrollments, the day before classes began. I had a deal with Paul Engle that he would note which applicants to the writers workshop might relate well to engineering students so that they would be in waiting when I confirmed the need. They were often superior writers, so they also taught me a bit about verbal crafting even as I taught them things about classroom management. Collegiate rules drafted to accommodate creative writers, painters, and musicians also served to give us practical writers considerable room to move on our own, but I learned about writing administration in on-the-job training.

In a couple of years, Alma Hovey, who had been hired in 1923 by Hardin Craig and was also a speaker at the initial meeting of the Conference on College Composition and Communication (CCCC), and who was in charge of the upper-class writing courses in liberal arts, retired, so Maxwell added her courses to my program. She had had four courses, although she had taught them all much as the same tutorial course. Two of the course numbers allowed graduate students to register, and having double numbers allowed students to register for more than one course. I chose to turn the graduate numbers into separate courses—one with a strong base in rhetorical theory, the other in style. Because we did not require undergraduates to take linguistics, I added a subtext to the undergraduate courses to deal with a soft survey of sociolinguistics. No administrator ever inquired about what I was doing, so on my own I was creating a base for a program in nonfiction writing. That in turn meant that I had to be an autodidact, reading like mad to offer decent courses. My students were very helpful in opening new ideas to me, but so were Herbert Read, C. S. Lewis, I. A. Richards, Robert Graves, Don Murray, and (in a negative way) Rudolf Flesch.

Later, the two graduate courses developed into the base of the graduate options in rhetoric and composition, but the nearer term effect was to identify me on rather shallow grounds as the one who dealt in rhetorical theory for writers, and that led in two directions that eventually confirmed my academic specialties. Dick Braddock needed an associate for the study of research in written composition, and John Gerber needed a composition teacher for the Iowa version of the College Entrance Examination Board (CEEB) institutes. Both assignments turned into multiyear self-educational programs. I've recorded details about the institutes in an essay in *Composition in Context*, a collection of essays in honor of Don Stewart, so I will not expand on that part of my education here except to note that teaching experienced school teachers forced me to grapple with how humans acquire language. Piaget, Britton, Vygotsky, and Dewey entered my world through this door, as did Whitehall, Gleason, and Chomsky, as well as Christensen, Moffett, Kinneavy, and Jakobsen. Two books created in the shadow of the institutes, Walker Gibson's *The Limits of Language* and Martin Joos' *The Five Clocks*, also grabbed my imagination. There was other reading, but these pieces, read in the effort to design decent courses, shaped my attitudes.

Braddock had cochaired a National Council of Teachers of English (NCTE) committee on the state of knowledge about teaching composition; the committee had compiled a list of about 500 studies mostly drawn from schools of education and based on "scientific" methods. Someone was needed to actually read the studies and discover what had been learned. Braddock volunteered and brought in Lowell Schoer to evaluate research design and me to comment on theoretical assumptions, for as a practical matter he needed fellow Iowans. Project English, a new and venturesome federal program, put up money. For about 9 months, we met twice weekly to compare notes on our reading and to draft subreports. The studies we examined were relatively innocent of theory, but I learned a lot about design of quantitative studies—comparisons and enumerations. I realized that most teachers of writing merely did what had been done to them.

The resulting book, published by NCTE, was well received. Braddock hosted me at all sorts of NCTE and CCCC activities (he was an officer of CCCC while we were working on the reports), and I soon found myself on the first NCTE Commission on Composition and on the executive committee of CCCC, effectively two postdoctoral seminars.

The commission, chaired by Sister Mary Phillipa Coogan, met not only at the fall convention but also for 2 or 3 days in the spring. Walker Gibson, Wally Douglas, Alvina Treut Burrows, Bob Gorrell, Herman Estrin, Dolores Minor, and Priscilla Tyler, among others, provided constant instruction by means of discussion. One major effort was to produce a document, "The Students' Right to Write," with an accompanying opinionnaire to guide workshops and short courses. It was not earthshaking, and most of what we wrote would now be viewed as commonplace, but we learned a lot producing it. We foreshadowed some of what would a few months later turn up in "The Students' Right to Their Own Language."

Ed Corbett had asked me to chair a committee to draft a resolution on the subject, and the long process of preparing the document taught me a lot about language idolatry. The record of drafting the resolution and requiring some sort of general explanation of its reason for being is very complex, but in the end individual members of a committee supplied me, Liz McPherson, and Nancy Prichard a batch of moderately related and somewhat consistent substatements to draw together into a "supporting statement" for the resolution. Our quick study in sociolinguistics and political realism was better than a dozen courses, as we tried to negotiate a statement that might earn acceptance from the committee and approval from the membership of CCCC.

The immediate reality of civil rights politics dominated popular discussion and framed the committee's work. It was a racially and ethnically diverse group. Although the CCCC statement might not have existed without the racial politics and the examples were drawn mostly from Black English Vernacular, the underlying linguistic notions challenge much of the orthodox view of language held by traditionally educated Americans, including many in departments of English. Often, discussion of the document was confusing, because people who supported the civil rights movement did not necessarily accept the implications of sociolinguistic studies. We could not always tell whether the opposition came from covert bigots or linguistic imperialists, but the process of explaining took us into 2-year colleges that met in store-fronts, as well as into major universities, and challenged our broader theories of what education is supposed to offer to whom.

Another concern of the commission was also a crucial part of my education, building on the quantitative studies I had examined with Braddock and Schoer. As educational systems have tried to meet the needs of mass populations, politics has required more and more "objective" reporting of success. One effort to provide documentation was the National Assessment of Educational Progress (NAEP). In their first round of testing, they had produced a report unacceptable to members of the Commission on Composition. Sister Mary Philippa and Braddock had written hostile reviews for *Research in the Teaching of English*, and NAEP was eager to gain NCTE cooperation for the next round. I was drawn into meetings of NCTE people and NAEP psychometricians. In the discussions, we had hypothesized Primary Trait Scoring, a name offered somewhat inaccurately in the heat of discussion to indicate the constraints of rhetorical purpose. We held that the primary purpose of any piece of writing creates specific standards for excellence; one set of standards does not fit all forms of rating. Similarly, mere ranking (as in the first assessment report) does not provide enough information to make testing worthwhile for assessment. Although the psychometricians agreed that "one score point" (ranking) was not adequate, and although they had been involved in forms of holistic scoring used for granting credit, they really preferred the multiple score points of multiple choice testing and went along with our position somewhat under protest, probably assuming that we would not be able to make the procedure work. Indeed, we thoroughly messed up the meeting to design exercises, and so a larger effort was planned.

Eventually, Carl Klaus and I were designated to lead a team to develop new exercises and scoring guides that might provide useful descriptive material for samples of writing. Devising exercises for mass testing is a remarkably good discipline, for one must be unequivocal, or nearly so, in suggesting what one expects. Having already accepted the value of blurriness, doubting the truth implied by "clarity," I was not comfortable with the implications, but I was forced to articulate more clearly to myself the relationship between language and the reality it represents, the map and the territory. My earlier reading in general semantics was given an upgrade. I do not believe that we ever made sense to the psychometricians, but I learned a lot from them and from explaining our reasoning to teachers of composition.

I think I have more than made my point. My education as a teacher of writing was a matter of serendipity. I just did what seemed to be fun; I read books that answered questions I had at the time. When my professional colleagues wanted to enter practical negotiations about some issue, I was delighted to do the homework necessary to join the discussion. Like other autodidacts, I frequently find that I have not read some obvious material or have read exotic bits. For example, I had read substantially in the history of rhetoric and yet profited immensely from reading *The Rhetorical Tradition* by Patricia Bizzell and Bruce Herzberg; they filled gaps. I felt no great pressure to publish articles except as a form of direct teaching and persuasion, so I also felt free to draw materials from any experience and follow whatever tempted me. I offer this in sadness to new generations, for I cannot imagine that the academy as it now formed would allow mere curiosity and social do-goodism to define education. One must take courses and gain certification; one must submit works to referees before a dean or even a Department of English chair will consider that it exists. For all that, one composes the universe in language, so one never knows enough. Programs as such merely provide a point of departure, and it is the continual renewing and extending of one's base that makes a teacher of composition important. Alas, it probably also makes the "generalist," who is often praised but rarely sought as an authority on anything. As a token of goodwill, I submit not "Works Cited" nor even "Minimum Readings for Composition Teachers," but rather "Some Readings That Interested Me and More or Less Are on the Subject at Hand."

Iowa City, Iowa
January 22, 1997

WORKS ALLUDED TO

Abrams, Meyer H. *The Mirror and the Lamp: Romance Theory and the Classical Tradition.* New York: Oxford UP, 1958.

Aristotle. *Rhetoric. Poetics.* New York: Modern Library, 1954.

Bailey, Dudley, ed. *Essays on Rhetoric.* New York: Oxford UP, 1965.

Berthoff, Ann E., ed. *Reclaiming the Imagination.* Portsmouth, NH: Boynton/Cook, 1984.

Bizzell, Patricia, and Bruce Herzberg, eds. *The Rhetorical Tradition.* Boston: Bedford Books, 1990.

Bloomfield, Leonard. *Language.* New York: Holt, 1933.

Bosmajian, Haig. *The Language of Oppression.* Washington, DC: Public Affairs Press, 1974.

Booth, Wayne C. *The Rhetoric of Fiction.* Chicago: U of Chicago P, 1961.

Britton, James. *Language and Learning.* London: Allen Lane, 1970.

Burke, Kenneth. *Counterstatement.* Berkeley: U of California P, 1968. (Original work published 1931)

Chatman, Seymour, and Samuel Levin, eds. *Essays on the Language of Literature.* New York: Houghton, 1967.

Christensen, Francis. *Notes Toward a New Rhetoric.* New York: Harper, 1967.

Dewey, John. *Education and Experience.* New York: Macmillan, 1963. (Original work published 1938)

Diederich, Paul B. *Measuring Growth in English.* Urbana, IL: NCTE, 1974.

Gibson, Walker, ed. *The Limits of Language.* New York: Hill & Wang, 1962.

Gleason, H. A., Jr. *Linguistics and English Grammar.* New York: Holt, 1965.

Fisher, John. "Chancery and the Emergence of Standard Written English in the Fifteenth Century," *Speculum* LII (October 1977): 870–899.

Fries, Charles Carpenter. *The Structure of English.* New York: Harcourt, 1952.

Graves, Robert. *The White Goddess.* New York: Creative Age Press, 1948.

Howell, Wilbur Samuel. *Poetics, Rhetoric, and Logic.* Ithaca, NY: Cornell UP, 1975.

Johnson, Wendell. *People in Quandaries.* New York: Harper, 1946.

Joos, Martin. *The Five Clocks.* New York: Harcourt, 1961.

Kinneavy, James L. *A Theory of Discourse.* New York: Prentice-Hall, 1971.

Korzybski, Alfred. *Science and Sanity.* Lakeville, CT: International Non-Aristotelian Library Publishing, 1933.

Labov, William. *The Study of Nonstandard English.* Urbana, IL: NCTE, 1970.

Lakoff, George, and Mark Johnson. *Metaphors We Live By.* Chicago: U of Chicago P, 1980.

Lewis, C. S. *Rehabilitations and Other Essays.* New York: Oxford UP, 1939.

Miller, James E., Jr. *Word, Self, Reality: The Rhetoric of Imagination.* New York: Dodd, Mead, 1972

Morris, Charles. *Signs, Language, and Behavior.* New York: Prentice-Hall, 1946.

Ogden, C. K., and I. A. Richards. *The Meaning of Meaning.* 8th ed. New York: Harcourt, 1953.

Plato. *Gorgias. Euthyphro. Phaedrus.* New York: Oxford UP, 1938.

Polanyi, Michael. *Personal Knowledge,* 2nd ed., New York: Harper, 1964.

Read, Herbert. *English Prose Style.* Boston: Beacon, 1955. (Original work published 1928)

Russell, Bertrand. *A History of Western Philosophy.* New York: Simon & Schuster, 1945.

Sacks, Sheldon, ed. *On Metaphor.* Chicago: U of Chicago P, 1979.

Whitehall, Harold. *Structural Essentials of English.* New York: Harcourt, 1951.

Winterowd, W. Ross. *Rhetoric: A Synthesis.* New York: Holt, 1968.

Wittgenstein, Ludwig. *Philosophical Investigations.* Trans. G. E. M. Anscombe. New York: Macmillan, 1958.

CHAPTER THIRTEEN

The Education of a Wisconsin Farm Boy

Duane H. Roen
Arizona State University

I begin with a reflection on my vita, for it is marked by a pattern that promotion and tenure committees have noted and, when I stood for tenure, debated. That is, 39 of the 71 publications and 28 of the 67 conference papers listed on my cirriculum vita have multiple names on the byline. My love for such collaboration is a product of my early years on a Wisconsin dairy farm, where working together was a necessity. Many jobs on the farm required more than one person to complete, and other jobs, especially in the summer, had to be done in a hurry—before a rainstorm or before another job needed to be done. I worked with others on tasks almost daily, and I came to accept that mode of operation as normal—far removed from 19th-century Romantic notions of individual genius that pervade departments in the humanities. Work was, for me, something that needed to be completed; it did not matter who did it or who got credit for doing it. I feel much the same way today. Incidentally, I would probably still be farming today if a fire had not destroyed our barn and livestock in January 1962.

During the 1962–1963 school year, in Joyce King's eighth-grade language arts class at Baldwin-Woodville Junior High School, I knew that I wanted to become an English teacher. I had spent the previous seven grades in Willow Hill School, the same one-room Wisconsin country school that my father had attended in the late 1920s. As early as second grade, I had fallen in love with the act of writing, thanks mostly to *Let's Write*, a weekly show on a public radio station in Wisconsin. I still possess some of the pages on which those childish poems and stories appear. In eighth grade, though, Joyce King introduced me to the more formal study of literature and, especially, language. More appealing than the content of the class, however, was Ms. King's concern for me as a learner. By December of that year, I had decided that I wanted to be like the person in the front of that room—caring and nurturing. I am reminded of Joyce King each time I read bell hooks' descriptions of some of her early teachers, who were, in hooks' words, "on a mission" (2).

Even though my aptitudes lay in math and science during my public school years, my English teachers in grades 8 through 12 were the people that I respected and wanted to emulate most. If those people—Joyce King, Patricia Wiff, Ms. Grut, Cherry Grey, and Claire Stein—had taught math or science, I'd probably be a mathematician or scientist today. Through them, I came to value not only language, literature, and composing but also myself.

Because my father exerted gentle pressure for me to join the family business (a Ford dealership acquired several years after the fire), I began my undergraduate work at the University of Wisconsin-River Falls as a business and psychology major. By the end of my sophomore year, though, I escaped from business to return to English studies—as an English education major. During those years and through my first graduate degree, Nicholas Karolides, after whom my son is named, was the greatest influence in my professional development. He engaged his students in literature and in teaching in ways that I had never previously experienced. During my senior year (1970–1971), he introduced me to Louise Rosenblatt's *Literature as Exploration*. Years later, when he introduced me to Louise Rosenblatt at a National Council of Teachers of English (NCTE) meeting, it was obvious how much she had influenced him when he was her doctoral student at New York University in the early 1960s.

Teaching high school English in Wisconsin in the mid-1970s was a mixed bag. Although I enjoyed my students and colleagues, the rigors of teaching seven sections a semester (six of them writing sections); extracurricular coaching/advising in debate, baseball, forensics, and the student newspaper; and chairing both the high school English department and the district's kindergarten-through-grade-12 language arts team wore me out. I should have left New Richmond after my fourth year, but I hung on 1 more year— barely—until May 1977.

During my doctoral-degree years (1977–1981) at the University of Minnesota, my mentor, Gene Pichè, encouraged me to learn more about scholarship in English education and linguistics. In that degree work, I learned empirical methods, which I found appealing at the time because they allowed me to meld my interest in teaching English with my dormant interest in math and science. My experience at Minnesota also included introductions to the work of Janet Emig, Donald Murray, Mina Shaughnessy, James Moffett, Ken Macrorie, and Thomas Kuhn, which raised my awareness of process pedagogy, expressivist views of composing, cognition, writing curriculum, basic writing, and the nature of disciplinary shifts.

Although I spent only 1 year as an assistant professor at the University of Nebraska-Lincoln in a position vacated by Lillian Bridwell-Bowles when she went to the University of Minnesota, my association with Les Whipp, then director of the Nebraska Writing Project, was a fruitful one. It was then that I began seeing myself more in the world of composition than of English education. In the fall of 1981, I audited his version of the National Writing Project. In the spring of 1982, I offered a Nebraska Writing Project workshop for teachers in the Lincoln public schools. Whereas my studies and teaching at the University of Minnesota had helped me see the extent to which I had been a current–traditional high school writing teacher, my NWP work constituted firsthand experience in alternatives to current–traditional pedagogy.

I spent the next 11 years (1982–1993) at the University of Arizona. During my first year there, with funding from the Andrew W. Mellon Foundation, more than half my time was spent conducting in-service composition workshops for teachers at all levels and in all parts of the state. Because writing process pedagogy and writing across the curriculum were the two most requested workshop topics that year, I further developed my interest in and understanding of the former topic and experienced a steep learning curve with the latter. One of the more insightful and influential readings of the year for me was Maxine Hairston's *College Composition and Communication* (*CCC*) article applying Thomas Kuhn's theories of shifts in scientific fields to recent disciplinary changes in composition. Among my reading that year, Donovan and McClelland's *Eight Approaches to Teaching Composition,* Freedman and Pringle's *Reinventing the Rhetorical Tradition,* and Erika Lindemann's *A Rhetoric for Writing Teachers* helped me put diverse process pedagogies in dialogue with one another. My education in Writing Across the Curriculum (WAC) that year included Fulwiler and Young's *Language Connections: Writing and Reading Across the Curriculum.* That interest has continued, leading to two textbooks that I have coauthored with Stuart Brown and Robert Mittan.

During my years at the University of Arizona, I taught composition methods more often than any other course. The course was required for several undergraduate and graduate majors in English studies and education, including English as a second language (ESL). Although my doctoral work included all the courses for a minor in English as a second language, I was woefully ignorant of ESL pedagogy, especially in composition. I read as much as I could by the scholars who were doing work in ESL composing, especially Ann Raimes and Vivian Zamel. Some of those essays became part of my packet of course readings, but I wanted something more to offer my students. Subsequently, I coedited with my colleague Donna Johnson, a careful ESL scholar, a collection of essays on teaching writing to non-native speakers of English.

Throughout my life, I have been drawn to administrative positions of various kinds, so it's not surprising that I have done some administrative work in rhetoric and composition. During my early years at the University of Arizona, I guided first-year teaching assistants (TAs) individually and in groups ranging in size from 4 to 30. Working with TAs helped me develop a larger repertoire of strategies for explaining and discussing theory, pedagogy, and curriculum in the field, and it helped me understand how to work with colleagues in other fields in English studies—literature, creative writing, linguistics, English as a second language. At Arizona, I also helped build the doctoral program in rhetoric and composition, which I directed for 4 years—probably the most fun I have had in my career.

I left Tucson in 1993 to direct the writing program at Syracuse University. Although the job in Syracuse was exciting in many ways, I learned that I was not meant to live in a city that ranks behind only eight others for the number of cloudy days per year and that gets more snow per year than any other major city in the United States. (Syracuse got 178 inches of the white stuff my first winter there.)

In 1995, I left the northeast to become director of composition at Arizona State University. At this writing, it's 18 months later—January 1997. For the younger scholars reading this essay, I will note that moving across the country twice in the span of 2 years has many costs—professional, economic, and personal. First, the professional cost for me—and maybe some people can avoid this—is that I was a less productive scholar in 1993, 1994, and 1995 than during any other period in my career. Moving requires immense investments of time and emotional energy. Second, the economic loss involved in selling and buying two houses and moving household items across country in the span of 24 months is large—nearly $55,000 for my family. Third, I am not embarrassed—although perhaps I should be—to note that changing cities and jobs takes its toll on relationships between life partners and between children and parents. Although our family has been fortunate in that both parents now have jobs that are in some ways better than any they have had in the past, the moves have strained my relationships with my spouse and with my children for several years. It is clear to me that staying put in Tucson would have resulted in less emotional stress than we have experienced. Perhaps wiser people learn this lesson more quickly than I did.

Tempe, AZ
May 6, 1997

WORKS CITED

Brown, Stuart, Robert Mittan, and Duane H. Roen. *Becoming Expert: Writing and Learning in the Disciplines.* Dubuque, IA: Kendall/Hunt, 1990.
Brown, Stuart, Robert Mittan, and Duane H. Roen. *The Writer's Toolbox.* Boston: Allyn & Bacon, 1997.

Donovan, Timothy R., and Ben W. McClelland, eds. *Eight Approaches to Teaching Composition.* Urbana, IL: National Council of Teachers of English, 1980.

Emig, Janet. *The Composing Processes of Twelfth Graders.* Urbana, IL: National Council of Teachers of English, 1971.

Freedman, Aviva, and Ian Pringle, eds. *Reinventing the Rhetorical Tradition.* Conway AR: L & S Books for the Canadian Council of Teachers of English, 1980; rpt. Urbana, IL: National Council of Teachers of English, 1980.

Fulwiler, Toby, and Art Young, eds. *Language Connections: Writing and Reading Across the Curriculum.* Urbana, IL: National Council of Teachers of English, 1982.

Hairston, Maxine. "The Winds of Change: Thomas Kuhn and the Revolution in the Teaching of Writing." *College Composition and Communication* 33 (1982): 76-88.

hooks, bell. *Teaching to Transgress: Education as the Practice of Freedom.* New York: Routledge, 1994.

Johnson, Donna M., and Duane H. Roen, eds. *Richness in Writing: Empowering ESL Students.* New York: Longman, 1989.

Kuhn, Thomas. *The Structure of Scientific Revolutions.* 2nd ed. Chicago: U of Chicago P, 1970.

Lindemann, Erika. *A Rhetoric for Writing Teachers.* New York: Oxford UP, 1982.

Macrorie, Ken. *Uptaught.* New York: Hayden, 1970.

Murray, Donald M. *A Writer Teaches Writing: A Practical Method of Teaching Composition.* Boston: Houghton, 1968.

Moffett, James. *Teaching the Universe of Discourse.* Boston: Houghton, 1968.

Raimes, Ann. "Tradition and Revolution in ESL Teaching." *TESOL Quarterly* 17 (1983): 535-52.

Rosenblatt, Louise. *Literature as Exploration.* Rev. ed. New York: Noble & Noble, 1968.

Shaughnessy, Mina. *Errors and Expectations: A Guide for the Teacher of Basic Writing.* New York: Oxford UP, 1977.

Zamel, Vivian. "Writing: The Process of Discovering Meaning." *TESOL Quarterly* 16 (1982): 195-209.

CHAPTER FOURTEEN

Close Reading: Accounting for My Life Teaching Writing

John Trimbur
Worcester Polytechnic Institute

I left graduate school in 1972 to do political work. My time was up: I had spent 4 years in the American studies program at the State University of New York at Buffalo, I was ABD, and my graduate funding was gone.

The late 1960s were heady times in Buffalo. Lawrence Chisholm came up from Yale in 1968 to start an American studies program with an internationalist perspective that countered the Cold War-inspired American exceptionalism then prevalent in the field. Within a few years, American studies at Buffalo became what we would now call multicultural, with programs in women's studies, Puerto Rican studies, and American Indian studies headed by Iroquois traditionalists. In a celebrated case, Leslie Fiedler got busted on trumped-up drug charges—retribution by the local vice squad for the blossoming psyche-delic scene. Charles Olson had just left Buffalo, but Robert Creeley, John Logan, and Robert Hass were still at the university, and the poets I had been reading—Robert Bly (in his pre-*Iron John* phase), Allen Ginsberg, Ed Dorn, Gary Snyder, Denise Levertov, W. S. Merwin, Robert Duncan—all came to town for poetry readings that gathered the countercultural, antiwar, and utopian energies of the time and seemed to prophesy the formation of a new society within the shell of the old. Every imaginable leftist tendency had cadre on campus, from the old-line Stalinists of the Communist Party to the Yippies of the New Left. Following the Cambodian invasion and the killings at Kent State and Jackson in 1970, massive antiwar demonstrations closed down the university, firebombed the ROTC building, and moved into the streets of Buffalo to set up barricades and skirmish with the police.

So it was not that I wanted to leave Buffalo. I would have been happy to stay on—to continue teaching courses on participatory democracy, the Black Mountain poets, and cultural geography, to work on the New Left journal *Red Buffalo* that a group of us edited, and to be part of the scene. I did not exactly imagine I would have an academic career. I just thought the university was a good place to hang out. But my graduate student days were over, and I left Buffalo without a doctorate or any plans to get one and moved to California to work with a small Trotskyist group I had recently joined.

Now I mention all this in part to recall a moment in my life and in the political life of my generation. But there is also an irony here: Namely, if I had not left graduate school to do political work in the Spartacist League, I doubt if I ever would have become a writing teacher. Here is the story.

By the time I left Buffalo in 1972, campus activism had peaked. Nixon appeared to be winding down the war, pulling out troops while ordering the most ferocious bombings in history of North Vietnam. The New Left splintered, and Students for a Democratic Society broke up into Progressive Labor and Weatherpeople factions. The FBI annihilated the leadership of the Black Panther Party. Those of us in graduate school were left to contemplate what our educations and our relation to the academy could possibly mean in the absence of a mass student movement.

The people I knew responded in different ways. There was a kind of informal pipeline between Stanford, where I had been an undergraduate, and Buffalo, where a number of us ended up in graduate school. My best friend at Stanford and Buffalo went to Chile to study agrarian reform under Allende's popular front government, wrote a book about it, and eventually got a second doctorate in epidemiology. Another friend from Stanford left Buffalo with a master's in English and, after returning to school for social work, is now heading statewide mental health services in Oregon. A third took the idea of returning to the land seriously, left Buffalo to farm in Kentucky, and is now doing full-time organizing for the Community Farm Alliance he founded. An old friend from my freshman dorm days came to Buffalo after two years on a Rhodes scholarship and is now teaching high school English in the Bay Area. As for me, I got regrouped.

The regroupment of a small fraction of the New Left into old-line Stalinist and Trotskyist tendencies is a historical moment that is not well understood. Most accounts of the New Left give the impression that the student left simply broke up with the end of the draft and the removal of American ground troops from Vietnam. But that isn't really the end of the tale. By the early 1970s, a minority within the antiwar movement had become not just pro-peace but anti-imperialist and anticapitalist—actively pro-Communist in their sympathies for the National Liberation Front and North Vietnam. These were the people at antiwar demonstrations chanting "Ho, Ho, Ho Chi Minh/NLF is going to win" and "All Indochina must go Communist." This was the era of the Maoists, the cult of the Guevarist guerrilla, and Third World politics.

I had always been skeptical, however, about whether taking up guns in the countryside was actually going to work in an advanced industrial country. My political imagination was shaped by the French general strike of 1968 and an Old World revolutionary tradition of dual power and workers' democracy—the Paris Commune of 1870, the soviets of 1905 and 1917, the workers' councils in Barcelona in 1936, and the Hungarian uprising against the Stalinist state in 1956. Like many others of my generation, I had been deeply influenced by E. P. Thompson's *The Making of the English Working Class*, and it led me to traditions of working-class self-organization in the Wobblies (the Industrial Workers of the World), the immigrant labor press, and the citywide strikes in San Francisco, Toledo, and Minneapolis in 1934. Political affiliation, I discovered, was not so much a matter of theory as of tradition—of linking lives in the present to those in the past, of being responsible to the accumulated experience of past struggles, of keeping them in living memory. So, while other New Leftists joined various Maoist grouplets, the Communist Party, or the Socialist Workers Party, I got regrouped, into a small Trotskyist group called the Spartacist League (after Rosa Luxemburg and Karl Liebknecht's ill-fated revolutionary group that broke with the Second International during World War I). Like our predecessors in the 1930s, we had joined the party.

In 1972 I went back to California as a full-fledged member of the Spartacist League. I worked in the post office for 2 years delivering mail, sold the party paper *Worker's Vanguard* at political meetings and factory gates, did solidarity work for the Chilean left before and after the coup against Allende, and participated in various defense committees. I was supposed to be "leadership material" but turned out not to be particularly good at democratic centralism and party discipline. And I found life in a political sect claustrophobic and troubling. The Spartacist League-style of political intervention is highly polemical and abrasive in a way that did not really fit my personality. (There is some truth to the traditional charge that Trots are "splitters and wreckers": One goes into united fronts with other leftist groups ostensibly to participate in joint action but with the real intention of finding a point of principled difference in order to denounce one's opponents and try to recruit a person or two to one's own program.) By 1974, my career as a professional revolutionary was in the doldrums, to say the least, and party leadership thought that my wife (who was also in the party but disillusioned, too) and I needed a fresh start setting up a new party local in Philadelphia. So we agreed and moved back east.

One of the first things we did in Philadelphia was to sell the party paper at a screening of the Cuban film *Lucia*. As often happened at political events in those days, rival political groups also showed up to sell their paper. On this occasion, two members of another Trotskyist group appeared—people with ties to a current in the Trotskyist movement that we called Pabloist revisionism. (Michel Pablo was a romantic revolutionary figure who ran guns to the Partisans during World War II and took on a prominent role in the international Trotskyist movement following the war.) We baited each other in a humorous way and then watched the film together. Afterward, we went out for drinks and got to talking. It turned out that one of the Pabloists was at the time director of freshman English at a nearby college. He told me he was looking for someone to teach a section of basic writing, and I told him I was not qualified—that I was an ABD in American studies and had never taught writing before. He said it didn't matter, that he would give me some books to look at, that I would do fine.

And so I did it: I taught basic writing in the fall of 1974 at Rutgers as an adjunct, although I am not sure I actually did fine. But I loved it, and, as I say, the irony is that none of this would have happened at all if I had not left graduate school to do political work, for it was the revolutionary mystique of the Bolsheviks and Trotsky's Left Opposition—the Old World Marxist romance of a workers' commonwealth and the abolition of class society— that led me, indirectly to be sure, to that chance encounter and back to teaching.

* * *

As a general rule, if you want to teach writing, as I certainly did, you have to learn how to live in English departments. I was utterly unprepared: not that I had not read literature, but I knew little about the profession of literature as it is practiced in the American academy.

My work as an undergraduate was in history—at first European intellectual and cultural history, and then a shift in my senior year to American history with an emphasis on California and the West. I loved novels, and, during my undergraduate years, had read most of the American classics—although not as course work. It was just something I thought I should do, and I went systematically through Cooper, Melville, Hawthorne, Twain, Fitzgerald, Hemingway, and Faulkner. The same with European writers—Balzac, Stendhal, Flaubert, Tolstoy, Dostoyevsky, Gide, Kafka, Sartre, and Camus. Except for D. H. Lawrence, I pretty much skipped the British.

In graduate school, I took mostly history and American studies courses and directed reading in social and cultural theory. I started to read poetry seriously and hung out at the fringes of the poetry scene in Buffalo (which means I spent a lot of time in bars with John Logan and the students in his poetry workshop). Except for a course in which I was a teaching assistant for Leslie Fiedler, where we read Cooper, *Tarzan*, and Zane Grey's *Riders of the Purple Sage*, I stayed away from English classes. Frankly, I didn't see the point, because I could read all of that stuff on my own. To be honest,

I was intimidated and not at all sure about the point of literary studies. I knew, for example, that *Moby Dick* was a parable about 19th-century capitalism and that the whiteness of the whale was an ontological problem. Beyond that, however, I had little to say. I read literary criticism—the little that I did read, such as Matthieson's *American Renaissance*, Olson's *Call Me Ishmael*, Lawrence's *Studies in Classic American Literature*, Fiedler's *Love and Death in the American Novel*, Henry Nash Smith's *Virgin Land*, and the other studies of myth and symbol—in the only way I knew how, as social theory, which I believe literary criticism to be but which did not prove very helpful to me in my endeavor to live in English departments.

So even though I have a doctorate in English, which is largely due to the goodwill of Leslie Fiedler, who took on my dissertation when the American studies program at Buffalo ran into political problems getting its doctoral degree accredited, I have always felt I am just a visitor to the English departments I have worked in, observing habits, speech codes, and values that I know are coherent and rule-governed but that still seem alien and require effort on my part to remember. I keep forgetting the simplest things: for example, that you can't talk about the relation of English courses to students' professional aspirations without falling into the crassest kind of vocationalism that endangers the integrity of literature as a liberal art; or that talking about literature as a means to life lived intensely in its time will sound corny or middlebrow when it's linked to students organizing poetry readings or leading book discussion groups for senior citizens. And there are times, I must admit, when I forget the category altogether and imagine literature to be simply a form of writing that stands in an interesting and complex but not necessarily special relation to other forms of writing. Try telling your colleagues that you are not sure you see that much difference between teaching English and teaching chemical engineering. That's when I get the blankest stares of all—and when I feel like an extraterrestrial sent to Earth to ask naive questions about the nature of English studies.

As you might expect, I could accept this mission as an alien only after I had tenure and was promoted to full professor. Before that, it was too risky, and I did spend years trying to fit in. In fact, at one time, I went through a regime of self-improvement that I hoped would naturalize me as a citizen of English departments. I decided to read all of Henry James. I am not sure why I thought James would do the trick. Maybe it is the effect he achieves when one of his characters holds a glass or walks across the room in a certain way. Or maybe it is how his characters have their own particular privacy in his novels, when they leave for awhile and we are not allowed to follow them or to inquire into what they are doing. I love James' reticence and sense of propriety. At any rate, my James phase took place when I was commuting from Baltimore to Rutgers and had plenty of time to read on the train. So I did manage to get through most of the major novels.

Even better, I got what must be my only true literary education by talking endlessly about James with Donald Mull, who teaches at Rutgers and learned, as a student of John Crowe Ransom, to be the strictest kind of New Critic. I am not sure Mull knew it, but he taught me how to read literature, or, at least, how he read literature. It wasn't programmatic. It just came out of his own love of James—then, later, Joseph Conrad when I had grown tired of James.

What I learned from Mull sounds simple, but I believe it enabled me to survive in English departments. That is, before Mull's tutelage, I had been reading novels from a thoroughly realist perspective, as though they provided slices of life about people and history. And because I knew a good deal of history and social theory, I could often make statements about novels that were semi-intelligible to people in English departments. But with Mull, history and theory were inadmissible. Novels weren't made of the pictures from life I was seeing when I read but of words on the page, and they needed to be treated that way. So for the first time in my life, under Mull's direction, I began to understand what "close reading" might mean and how practical criticism might yield a kind of discriminating information about written language—how it was not just a set of formalist techniques but a way of being accountable for one's reading. Unknowingly, I had taken a tentative step toward rhetoric by way of the New Critics.

I must say that since those days with Mull, now over 20 years ago, my life in English departments has been a constant disappointment. I thought it was going to be fun. In my imagination, English departments would be filled with people like Mull who loved to read and talk about books, and I would keep learning how to read and eventually fit in. But cocktails with Mull has pretty much been the high point for me. English departments, I found, were filled with people you would describe as scholars, not readers. Faculty did not necessarily read widely, though they certainly read deeply in their fields. In my naiveté, I had missed altogether the fact that literary studies in the postwar period had been thoroughly professionalized.

Now, I realize that my thwarted expectations derive in large part from the unrealistic view that English departments are special places where people can get away with doing what they love to do, reading and talking about books. I know that this comes from an idealized vision of a leisured professoriate removed from the mundane world and that it flies in the face of everything I believe about academic departments being workplaces where faculty produce professional goods and services that are exchanged for the symbolic capital of recognition, prestige, and reputation. But I do not want to leave it at that.

My disappointment, I must say, has nothing to do specifically with my colleagues or the places I have taught but points instead to something quite different and more general—namely, that my own unschooled reading is part of a larger extracurriculum in which students and people of all ages make use of reading in their own ways. And this desire of ordinary readers to use literature, in Kenneth Burke's phrase, as "equipment for living" is frustrated in many respects by the exchange value of literary criticism in the academic market, where the point of reading is to produce careers.

* * *

I had been teaching basic writing for 5 years before I went to my first Conference on College Composition and Communication (CCCC) in 1979. I come from a generation of writing teachers who, by and large, were not trained in rhetoric and composition. There were not that many graduate programs at the time, and teaching writing and directing writing programs were still seen in English departments as rites of passage for junior faculty— the dues you have to pay before getting on with the real work of literary studies.

But I knew about all this only vaguely, because I had been teaching basic writing as a part-timer, both at Rutgers and at the Community College of Philadelphia (and later at the Community College of Baltimore), while I continued to do political work. I finally quit the party and decided to complete my doctorate so that I could try to make a life for myself in the teaching of writing. I say "try" because the job prospects in English departments were not good in the mid- to late 1970s, especially for an ABD with children and in need of full-time income. I bounced around, as people trying to make it in academia did at the time and do now, moving from part-time, per-course jobs to semester or year-long contracts, hoping for more. I remember the times my wife and I would talk about how long this insecurity could go on before I would have to leave teaching for something more permanent.

By the time I went to my first CCCC in 1979, I had a good deal of experience teaching basic writing, but I had no knowledge of rhetoric or composition. I thought of teaching writing as a matter of applied American studies. I gave writing assignments so I could find out what the students were thinking. I wanted to know. The students I taught were largely inner-city African Americans, many of them returning to school, more women than men. There is no way I can generalize about what I learned. (Because I had no idea composing research even existed, I certainly was not framing research questions.) I can say that the reading, writing, and talking we did brought me glimpses of a way of life in urban America—the role of Black Christianity, patterns of kinship and multigenerational childrearing, networks of sociability and mutual aid, problems with the law, the endless welfare bureaucracies, the alternating sense of hope and futility, the repeated refrain that better days must be coming because things cannot get any worse.

The students I taught in graduate school at Buffalo were traditional college-age Jewish kids from New York City and Catholics from western New

York, not too different from the kind of students you find in state universities everywhere—largely middle class or working class, not rich but not poor either. However, aside from the occasional writing class reserved for young White women coming in from the suburbs to train as dental assistants, the courses I was now teaching were in open-admission or equal-opportunity programs won through the struggles of the late 1960s and early 1970s to make postsecondary education a democratic right.

As Ken Bruffee says about the beginnings of open admissions at the City University of New York campuses, no one in writing programs was prepared for this kind of work. But I was convinced it was real work—a long-overdue attack from below on the colleges and universities as bastions of privilege. I saw the so-called literacy crisis *Newsweek* and other opinion makers had created in the popular mind during the mid- to late 1970s not as a matter of declining standards but of the wrong standards. To my mind, teaching in open admissions programs located my work in a tradition of popular education, linking it to the mechanics' institutes, the lyceums and chataquas, the workers' colleges, the founding of the land-grant universities, and the GI Bill. I began to imagine nationalizing all the private colleges and universities, instituting open admissions at Harvard and Yale, and guaranteeing students free tuition and a living stipend,

So when I got to my first CCCC meeting, I was puzzled by what people were talking about. I was unfamiliar with the terms people used so confidently—*recursive, tagmemics, invention, expressive and transactional* writing. I could catch on quickly enough to their meanings (except maybe tagmemics, which is one of those ideas I learn over and over but which keeps falling out of my head). Nonetheless, it became clear to me that I needed to begin studying again. Fortunately, I was just coming out of my Henry James phase, and I read back and current issues of *College Composition and Communication* (*CCC*) and *College English*, as well as Mina Shaughnessy, James Britton, Janet Emig, Peter Elbow, William Coles, and the collections available at the time, such as Charles Cooper and Lee Odell's *Research on Composing* and Gary Tate's *Teaching Composition*. Needless to say, I quickly joined the process movement, stopped talking about writing, and started talking about composing. More important, I began to see how people like Mina Shaughnessy and David Bartholomae applied the skills in close reading they had acquired in their literary educations to the matter of student writing—to hold themselves accountable to the ordinary texts they were reading. My lessons with Don Mull in the New Criticism were paying off in a way I had not imagined.

Looking back on this period of time I spent studying composition (rhetoric came later), there is something remarkable about it that I want to note, and that is the fact that in the late 1970s one could actually stay current with the field. I do not believe this is the case anymore. The proliferation of journals and book series, not to mention the conferences and discussion groups on the Internet, has made it very difficult, if not impossible, to keep up with current work in composition studies. And this doesn't even take into account what people feel they need to read in other fields. When "theory" hit in the 1980s, it only multiplied the amount of reading one had to do, and although we are now supposedly entering the era of posttheory, there is still all the work in cultural studies, feminist studies, postcolonial studies, literacy studies, African-American studies, gay and lesbian studies, and so on that it seems irresponsible not to follow.

I mention this not to be nostalgic or to idealize the pioneer days of composition studies, when people were making up the field. The point I want to make is simply that a kind of information overload has set in, along with an accompanying information guilt. A friend of mine who works in marketing research did a study for a vendor of scientific journals that found, among other things, that practicing scientists believe that, even though they are reading the same amount as or more than they always have, they are reading less and less of what they should know. I am starting to think that a similar situation is true in rhetoric and composition.

Now this situation is both a cause and an effect of specialization in the field. People complain that CCCC meetings no longer have the sense of a central burning issue, as was the case when Pat Bizzell and Bruce Herzberg debated Lil Brannon and Cy Knoblauch about writing across the curriculum, or when the cancellation of E306 (the first-year course Linda Brodkey designed) at the University of Texas prompted great controversy, or when Peter Elbow and David Bartholomae argued about writing with or without teachers. The last few CCCC meetings, in my experience, have been characterized by pockets of interest, where the like-minded gather around their own topics and preoccupations. The level of research and scholarship is high, but my sense is that everyone has just become more and more whoever they are, covering their corner of things, pursuing their projects, doing good work.

By no means do I want to suggest that specialization per se is the problem here. After all, from a certain perspective, basic works in composition studies, such as Janet Emig's *The Composing Processes of Twelfth-Graders* or Mina Shaughnessy's *Errors and Expectations* or Charles Bazerman's *Shaping Written Knowledge*, can be seen as specialized. The issue for me concerns how the specialized work of writing theorists, historians, and researchers is articulated to democratic aspirations and traditions of popular education.

When I started teaching basic writing, I believed I had found a new and important context for the kind of intellectual and political work I had always wanted to do. I felt that my work teaching was part of a larger struggle for a literate and participatory democracy. Today, for better and for worse, I feel I am part of a profession that has arrived.

* * *

In the preface to *The Errand into the Wilderness*, Perry Miller talks about the "sudden epiphany" he experienced as a young man seeking adventure in the Congo: "It was given to me . . . disconsolate on the edge of a jungle of central Africa, to have thrust upon me the mission of expounding the innermost propulsion of the United States, while supervising, in that barbaric tropic, the unloading of drums of case oil flowing out of the inexhaustible wilderness of America." I first read these enigmatic lines as an undergraduate in an American intellectual history course, and it has taken me years to understand how the experience Miller describes could shape his life's calling to account for the "innermost propulsion" of Puritan doctrine and its bearing on what used to be known as the American character. As a young history student drawn to the emerging New Left historiography, I had thought of Perry Miller, with his belief in the power of ideas, as the most diffident and apolitical of historians. Now I see that Miller's work began not so much with his method of expounding doctrine, as he kept saying, "on its own terms," but with a sense of accountability, a felt need to bear witness to a history that made the oil drums, in Miller's words, "tangible symbols of the republic's appalling power."

I have not read Perry Miller for years, but writing today has returned me to him and his epiphany. There is something that goes beyond that moment in American studies when Miller reigned as the leading scholar of American intellectual history. Nor is it just a matter of how the oil drums got to the Congo. This can be given in accounts of trade and political economies. There is something I intuit in Miller's epiphany about how the circulation of American power—that "innermost propulsion"—links lives to lives. Perhaps the crux is that, of the leading American-studies scholars of his day, Miller was "appalled"—and thereby held himself accountable.

I spent the summer of 1967 in Vietnam as an intern for International Voluntary Services, teaching English and working with Vietnamese youth groups. I was stationed 40 miles southeast of Saigon in Vung Tau, a resort town on the tip of a peninsula that extended into the South China Sea. It is an old fishing village where the former emperor kept his summer mansion and the French vacationed. The coastline is spectacular.

At night you could hear American artillery firing on a "random grid," lobbing shells into Viet Cong territory, and flares and tracer bullets from fire fights lighted the sky. Vung Tau was the only in-country rest and recreation center for allied forces, and at any given time 45,000 Americans, South Vietnamese, Australians, and South Koreans were in town for the beaches, bars, and brothels. Vung Tau, everyone agreed, was the safest place in South Vietnam because the VC made so much money taxing the houses of pleasure that military actions or urban terrorism made no sense. Young Vietnamese men—"Honda cowboys"—toured the four-square-block area of bars on their motor scooters, carrying young prostitutes in Western clothes and whiteface pancake makeup. In the other part of town, Vietnamese bartered in the traditional market—traditional people bitter and resigned to invasion and the corruptions of war.

I was appalled. I had been opposed to the war from the start, but I had never imagined how utterly destructive American power could be—what could issue forth from the "inexhaustible wilderness" Miller describes. When I returned from Vietnam for my senior year in college, I felt I needed to give an account. I looked for one in part in the study of history, and I abandoned the senior thesis I had started on French anarcho-syndicalism in order to shift my concentration to American history. More directly, I sent back my draft card in protest. I got drafted and was planning to refuse induction. By the fall of 1968, however, when I received my notice to appear and took the long bus ride from Palo Alto, there were so many draft resisters at the Oakland Induction Center that the officials in charge were giving us medical deferments to keep down the numbers of refused inductions and to avoid jamming up the court system. I was relieved, of course, but at the same time realized that I had simply been reclassified. Though I had tried, I was still not accountable.

For the past 5 years, I have been teaching at night in an adult literacy program sponsored by the South Providence Neighborhood Ministries (SPNM). SPNM functions as a kind of settlement house for recent immigrants from Southeast Asia, Latin America, West Africa, and the Caribbean. It provides basic social services, a food pantry, sewing classes, an after-school program, and adult literacy classes. I teach an advanced class of students with fairly high levels of proficiency in English. But the teaching is very different from the English as a second language courses I have taught in the past. The reason students come to SPNM seems to involve something more—or different—from the needs of undergraduates to work on their English in college. Perfecting the nuances of vocabulary concerning the weather—of learning to distinguish, say, between "sleet" and "hail" and "snow"—takes on a new meaning when the learners are struggling to provide winter coats for themselves and their children.

I bring readings to class, such as chapters from Sandra Cisneros's *House on Mango Street*, and the students write poems and put on plays. But just as often the curriculum comes from their lived experience—from the need to write notes to teachers, to offer condolences to a coworker whose wife has just had a miscarriage, to fend off the foreman, or to negotiate for plots of land in a nearby community garden.

These are adult learners, and although one of their goals certainly is to improve their mastery of English, I think they are also looking for a place to go, in a new world that is hardly hospitable to them, where they will be taken seriously—where they can do some work involving language that engages them as social and intellectual beings, where learning is sociable and provides a forum to associate with others. They are curious and want to know about each others' lives—about their food, their music, how they raise their children. An evangelical Christian woman from Guatemala asks one of the Cambodians in the class: "Do you believe in the one, true God?" "Of course," the Cambodian replies, "Buddha says to believe in all the gods."

Most of all, they want to articulate their experience, so others can understand life histories that are ignored in the everyday struggle to survive in a new country and discounted in the official discourse about immigration. Even the sensationalized media culture of tabloids and talk TV cannot assimilate their narratives. The Cambodian Buddhist tells about his year of slave labor under Pol Pot's regime. Another explains how he and his family hid for 14 months without papers in a refugee camp in Thailand, scavenging food and bribing guards. The Guatemalan woman's father was killed by the death squads because he stood up for Indian rights. He was buried in a closed casket because his face had been so disfigured by torture.

How to describe the movement of people that has brought my students to Providence? The terms seem inadequate: immigration, diaspora, displacement, global disruption. Many of my students have come to Providence to work in the jewelry industry for low wages in nonunion shops, sometimes on a piecework basis. These are people who were teachers, speech pathologists, small business owners, insurance salesmen, or farmers at home. Now they are polishing and carding jewelry for Penney's and Wal-Mart. The composition of the class keeps shifting—Haitians, Hmong highlanders, Lao lowlanders, Cambodians, Liberians, Salvadorans, Hondurans, Guatemalans, Mexicans—as the effects of poverty and political turmoil at home, the wars in southeast Asia, and the global economy are changing the face of South Providence.

I live a settled life now in an Italian working-class and lower middle-class neighborhood that borders on South Providence. We are plugged in to the local underground economy, where somebody's cousin can always get you a good deal if you need a new TV or you want your basement remodeled off the books. I have steady work at Worcester Polytechnic Institute (WPI) and a cabin in the Adirondacks. I have been lucky. Plenty of good teachers I knew when I was a part-timer never got that elusive full-time position. I am grateful for the chance encounter that started me teaching writing, and I owe a lot to people like Harry Brent, Ken Bruffee, Peter Elbow, Maxine Hairston, and Ben McClelland, who helped me along the way.

Given how clueless I was coming in to the work of studying and teaching writing, I think it is fair to say that without the "social turn" in rhetoric and composition, I would still be writing unpublishable material. (I was not getting anywhere in the 1970s trying to read Charles Olson's essay on projective verse and Jack Kerouac's "Essentials of Spontaneous Prose" as contributions to composing theory.) For the past 10 years or so, I have been trying to imagine how to extend in a useful way a theoretical and pedagogical practice that begins with Richard Ohmann's *English in America* and continues in the work of Patricia Bizzell, Lester Faigley, and my missing friend and comrade, Jim Berlin. In South Providence, in college classrooms, in books and journals, I want to know how to make my work accountable—to bear witness to the "appalling power" of late capitalism at a moment when the bosses are winning the class struggle on a global scale and working people everywhere need the intellectual and moral resources of literacy to find hope.

Cranston, Rhode Island
February 7, 1997

CHAPTER FIFTEEN

Love, Lust, Rhetorics
(From Double Binds to Intensities)

Victor J. Vitanza
University of Texas, Arlington

The last Sophist I call myself, for I am the last human being. No one converses with me beside myself and my voice reaches me as the voice of one dying. With thee, beloved voice, with thee, the last remembered breath of all human happiness, let me discourse, even if it is only for another hour. Because of thee I delude myself as to my solitude and lie my way back to multiplicity and love, for my heart shies away from believing that love is dead. It cannot bear the icy shivers of loneliest solitude. It compels me to speak as though I were Two.

—Friedrich Nietzsche

To know that one does not write for the other, to know that these things I am going to write will never cause me to be loved by the one I love (the other), to know that writing compensates for nothing, sublimates nothing, that it is precisely there where you are not—this is the beginning of writing.

—Roland Barthes

A cool heavenly breeze took possession of him.

—Nikos Kazantzakis

The opening quotation to this article is from X, 147, of the Naumann edition (*Gross* or *Kleinoktavausgabe*) of Nietzsche's works and has been translated by Marianne Cowan. I have taken it from Cowan's "Introduction" to *Philosophy*, p. 18.

Much that I have written about religion's treatment of Jesus Christ and God, I could have written about our discipline's, as well as other disciplines', treatment of Karl Marx and the God that Failed. All that I would have had to do is to switch from Kazantzakis' rendering of Christ to Lyotard's rendering of Marx in *Libidinal Economy* (see "The Desire Named Marx" 95-154). For such a switching, see my *Negation, Subjectivity, and the History of Rhetoric* 112-21.

LOGOS

Being asked to give an account of when and where and how I fell in love with—or was initially called (chosen) by—rhetoric, I un/just laugh.

I am called now to give an account of having been called! It's not that I mock such a question and opportunity and call. I am grateful to be asked. To be called again. To be given the opportunity to dis/engage in telling my stories. To come full circle.

Understand, however, that my stories are not sentimental, or centermental, ones. With tenderness, there is roughness and harshness and tearings of the body and wrenchings of the soul. Often, when rhetors rush in on an interpretive war (*polemos*), they act like Freudian children seeing their Freudian (family-romance) parents hot and thrashing, rubbing their bodies against each other, coupling, and so on. Often, when rhetors hear or read a cacophonous text, they want to purge it of noise and thereby fix it. Purge it of noise! Little do these rhetors understand the erotic passion and lust, tenderness and violence, in a word, the rapture (and other unmentionables) that is . . . the *Logos*—which calls us and gathers us together.

Martin Heidegger writes:

> λόγος means λέγειν as a saying aloud. . . . Who would want to deny that in the language of the Greeks from early on λέγειν means to talk, say, or tell? However, just as early and even more originally . . . it means what our similarly sounding *legen* means: to lay down and lay before. In *legen* a "bringing together" prevails, the Latin *legere* understood as *lesen*, in the sense of collecting and bringing together. Λέγειν properly means the laying-down and laying-before which gathers itself and others. . . . λόχος is a place of ambush [or a place for lying in wait] where something is laid away and deposited. (The old word ἀλέγω (*d copulativum*), archaic after Aeschylus and Pindar, should be recalled here: something "lies upon me," it oppresses and troubles me.) (*Early Greek* 60)

Heidegger sounds as if he's talking about, by way of etymological inventions, language copulating, giving off heat and occasional sparks, light that enlightens yet blinds us.

Heidegger continues: "To lay means to bring to lie. Thus, to lay is at the same time to place one thing beside another, to lay them together. To lay is to gather [*lesen*]" (61).

So that we (the two of us) might whisper sweet and bitter nothings to the other?

But let us spare ourselves from taking this calling in Freudian–Lacanian–Heideggerian terms and turns. Or at least make an attempt not to be tempted into these terms and turns.

RHETORIC-WHORE

Rhetoric has often been depicted as a whore. Body covered with diseases. But flesh covered with jewelry, vivid colors, perfumes. Body made up into a strolling fetish.

Well, again, let us also spare ourselves from taking this calling by way of insidious and invidious "Platonisms" tinged with Freudian-Lacanian terms and turns.

It is difficult, if not impossible, however, to avoid a theological notion of calling (vocation). As much as we rhetors try or say quite adamantly that "I will not!" engage in such thinking, we are called back. Such thinking in the calling lies in wait. And yet we rediscover ourselves individually saying, "I will not consume of that tree of faith and knowledge. Begone, both onto-logical and theological priggishness and boorishness!"

However, we rhetors cannot quite manage such a refusal, any more than Adam could refuse Eve or Christ refuse Mary Magdalene.

THEORY/PRACTICE

A few years ago, I was participating in one of those so-called think-tank groups. There were about 25 of us, by invitation only. (Many are called; few are chosen!) Participating in this group, talking with the others, was especially interesting because we were evenly divided between theory and practice. Inevitably, in this case, the practice people became very indignant with the theory people. This difference never got resolved because we were called (forcefully pulled and twisted) in very different ways. I must admit, the haggling between the two groups was at first interesting but very soon rather boring and tiring. There was not anyone getting hot and thrashing, rubbing his or her body against the others. No two were coupling! No Apollonian jumped a Dionysian, or vice versa. No Maenads arose in a frenzy. They un/just sat:

> Breasts swollen with milk,
> New mothers who had left their babies behind at home
> Nestled gazelles and young wolves in their arms,
> Suckling them. (Euripides *Bacchae* 699-702)

But what eventually became interesting is that someone in the group sug-gested that the theory people were probably Catholics or nonpracticing yet nostalgic Catholics and that the practice (*praxis*) people were Protestants. As we went around the lengthy table—seating 25 people—confessing our

identities, indeed, there was something to that distinction, although it did
not lead to our becoming ecumenical.

Yes, I am a rhetor-theorist-nonpracticing Catholic. And that . . . my dear
friends in rhetorics . . . is how I came to rhetoric, or rhetoric came to me.
I was called by the *Logos*. And it re/started—leaving the biological–psychological family romance aside—with the good nuns and the *Baltimore Catechism*. The questions (Who made me/you?) and the answers (God/Foun-
dationalism made me/you) were my once-upon-a-time propaedeutic.

I had this catechistic rhetoric to rebel-cum-revel against, but not as any
so-called Protestant might just rebel in some anemic, practical way! Not
through purification. Or purges. And counterpurges. Or through reactionary
methods. What is fundamentally unacceptable to me about Protestant rhetoric and politics is that they are the products of transalpine thinking. They
are cold, icy. What could the people of the north, of the Protestants, know
about passion? Their God was a vanilla, no-frills God. A no-music God! An
anti-Baroque God. Any prior connections with the Dionysians was totally
erased and denied by these so-called Protestants. If not, then the connections
were only faked, but not very well. About Protestants, there really is nothing
else to say.

What the world needs is love, love, excessive Dionysian love. We have
wasted enough time on this epiphenomenal theocracy called Protestantism.

Understand that concerning the question of God/Foundationalism and all
things X-cessively Baroque, the issue for me is not that I am against someone's
interpretation of God or his or her god terms. Or that I am an atheist (which
is too similar to theism for me to tell the difference) or that I am an agnostic
(which is too skeptical for me). The issue for me is not even to gather these
differences into ratios—that is, into their various permutations and combina-
tions. Instead, I am more concerned with the question of gods, innumerable
gods. You see, I am a nonpracticing Catholic-cum-a-pagan rhetor.

So when I say that I am a theorist, I do not mean theory as some solid
organizing principle that would give us knowledge. The Truth/truth. Or
even Consensus. Nor do I necessarily find any value in believing in negative
ontotheological principles or "negative knowledge" (DeMan 75).

By a pagan rhetor, I am best understood as following the call (vocation
and avocation) recorded through and by the nonlineage of Heraclitus,
Nietzsche, Kazantzakis, Deleuze and Guattari, Lyotard. (My affinities are
more with the 17th century, the early modern period, than with the 19th
and 20th centuries, the modern. Though Nietzsche is of the 19th century,
he is not; for after all is unsaid and undone, he is, as he says, posthumous
man. Though Nietzsche is from northern Poland, or Germany, he is not, for
he lived in and wrote so much of his work in Italy. Nietzsche is cosmopolitan,
as is Deleuze. My affinities are with Deleuze's readings of early modern
thinkers, for example, Deleuze's readings of Leibniz, but as reinterpreted by

those who are of the Mediterranean area, such as Mario Perniola's rereadings of the Baroque in 20th fin-de-siècle thinkers.) But I have only given the Continental nonlineage! There is always some more to tell. In the meantime, however, un/just call me a pagan rhetor.

This has been my way of saying, gathering all together, that I was called by the pagan gods (the *Logoi*). To rhetorics. *Rh*erotics = Rhetoric + Erotics.

PAGANISMS

Let us begin by saying—knowing that we will have to revise our saying—a pagan rhetor is not concerned with One or even with Many, but with a radical multiplicity. The uncountable. Excess. Xcess. XXcess. XXXcess. Gilles Deleuze gets close to explaining:

> The Gods are dead but they have died from laughing, or hearing one God claim to be the only one, "Is not precisely this godliness, that there are gods but no God?" [*Zarathustra* 294]. And the death of this God, who claimed to be the only one, is itself plural; the death of God is an event with a multiple sense. This is why Nietzsche does not believe in resounding "great events," but in the silent plurality of senses of each event [*Z* 241-45]. There is no event, no phenomenon, word or thought which does not have a multiple sense. A thing is sometimes this, sometimes that, sometimes something more complicated—depending on the forces (the gods) which take possession of it. (*Nietzsche* 4)

The "forces" that Deleuze refers to here are the various Wills to Power, which are the affirmations of differences.

Jean-François Lyotard also gets close to explaining:

> When I speak of paganism, I am not using a concept. It is a name, neither better nor worse than others, for the denomination of a situation in which one judges without criteria. And one judges not only in matters of truth, but also in matters of beauty (of aesthetic efficacy) and in matters of justice, that is, of politics and ethics, and all without criteria. (*Just Gaming* 16)

Historically situating what he means by paganism, Lyotard points to "a society of gods that is constantly forced to redraw its code. This is a theme that one finds among several Sophists and rhetoricians. Here are people for whom prescriptions are subject to discussion, not in the sense that the discussion will lead to the more just, but rather to the extent that a prescription cannot be founded" (17).

In Lyotard's reading—as well as Deleuze's—the gods do not speak from any "metalinguistic position from which the whole could be dominated"; he explains, the gods

> are not all-knowing. They just have their stories, that humans do not know. And humans have their own stories. And these two sets of stories are . . . not two blocks but two centers that send out their elements to negotiate, if one can call it that, on the boundaries. This is paganism. One does not know whom one is speaking to; one must be very prudent; one must negotiate; one must ruse; and one must be on the lookout when one has won. (43)

Let us listen to and keep our eyes ever on the chorus:

> The gods are crafty:
> They lie in ambush
> A long step of time
> To hunt the unholy. (Euripides *Bacchae* 888-90)

WHERE ARE WE NOW?

Have I left too far behind the theme of falling in love with—being called to—rhetoric? The ontotheological vocation of rhetoric? Or the paganic vocation of rhetorics? What's the difference? As we continue, my or rhetorics's discussions will become even more Byzantine. Serpentine. Baroque. Seduction is never put forth in a straight or in parallel lines. Seduction never stays within its frame, but ramifies out, spilling over beyond the frames. Seduction is not propositional, but is aphoristic and hypertextual, that is, bittersweet *eros.*

Thus far, in this mini-rebeginning, I have discussed the concept of paganism in terms of "force" and "having no criteria for judgment and consequently perpetually searching for and inventing provisions for just gaming." After all, paganism is about forceful seductions (*apate*, lying in the extramoral sense) and forceful encounters (whether with an object or a subject or any heretofore excluded middle possibility).

WHAT IS . . . ?

If I were to ask, What is this thing called "love" in the phrase "falling in love with rhetoric"? I would be asking, What is X? Which is the question, of dialectics and not paganism. Paganism is concerned with the question, What is this X *for me*? Deleuze explains:

When we ask the question "what is it?" . . . we not only fall into the worst metaphysics but in fact we merely ask the question "which one?" in a blind, unconscious and confused way. The question "what is it?" is a way of establishing a sense seen from another point of view. Essence, being, is a perspectival reality and presupposes a plurality. . . . Essence is always sense and value. (*Nietzsche* 77)

And therefore—now to the pointless, the intractable thing called love— Roland Barthes (a Nietzschean) picks up on this theme of force, perspectives, "for me," and writes in his *A Lover's Discourse*:

Instead of trying to define the other ("What is [X]?"), I turn to myself: "What do I want, wanting to know you?" What would happen if I decided to define you as a force and not as a person? And if I were to situate myself as another force confronting yours? This would happen: my other would be defined solely by the suffering or the pleasure [s/he, it] affords me." (135)

A lover of wisdom can never know or capture his or her object, though a lover can be seduced into the pursuit. No matter What the frenzy! No matter how(l) much one might plea! Accepting this conclusion allows one or many to become pagans. In matters of our loves for this or that or whatever we might be in transference with. *For me!* Although we have questions, we are wise when we come to understand that "the other is impenetrable, intractable, not to be found" (134). And let us thank the gods, for the other could only prove, in the most pedestrian terms, to be a disappointment and, in a word, boring. Tiresome! That is why, for me, the thing (*das Ding*) cannot be known. The *Logos* (cum *Logoi*) does not teach us what the thing (i.e., X) is. My teachers, RhEROTICs, have taught me Xcesses reveal themselves as truths.

And yet, as Nietzsche asks:

What if truth is a woman, what then? Are there not grounds for the suspicion that all philosophers, insofar as they were dogmatists, have been very inexpert about women? That the gruesome seriousness, the clumsy obtrusiveness with which they have usually approached truth so far have been awkward and very improper methods for winning a woman's heart? What is certain is that she has not allowed herself to be won—and today every kind of dogmatism is left standing dispirited and discouraged. *If it* is left standing at all! For there are scoffers who claim that it has fallen, that all dogmatism lies on the ground— even more, that all dogmatism is dying. ("preface" *Beyond* 2)

BELIEVING IN A WOMAN CALLED RHETORIC

Dear reader, do you hear echoes of Freud's "Mourning and Melancholia"? Or of Lacan's statement:

There is so little sexual relation that I recommend you read a very fine novel, *Ondine.* In it you will see that in the life of a man, a woman is something he believes in. He believes there is one, or at times two or three, but the interesting thing is that unable to believe only in one, he believes in a species, rather like sylphs or water-sprites.

What does it mean to believe in sylphs or water-sprites? Note that one says *believe in.* . . . To *believe in?* What does it mean? . . . Anyone who comes to us with a symptom, believes in it.

If he asks for our assistance or help, it is because he believes that the symptom is capable of saying something, and that it only needs deciphering. The same goes for a woman, except that it can happen that one believes her effectively to be saying something. That's when things get stopped up—to believe *in,* one believes *her.* It's what's called [courtly] love. . . .

Believing in a woman is, thank God, a widespread state—which makes for company, one is no longer all alone, about which love is extremely fussy. Love rarely comes true, as each of us knows, and it only lasts for a time. For what is love [of rhetoric] other than banging one's head against a wall, since there is no sexual relation? . . .

We believe her because there has never been any proof that she is not absolutely authentic. But we blind ourselves. This *believing her* serves as a stop-gap to *believing in*—something very seriously open to question. God knows where it leads you to believe there is *One*—it can even lead you so far as to believe that there is *The,* a belief which is fallacious. No one says *the sylph* or the *water-sprite.* There is a water-sprite, a sylph, a spirit, for some people there are spirits, but it all only ever adds up to a plural. . . .

A woman is a symptom. (*Feminine Sexuality* 169-70; Lacan's emphasis)

This statement by Lacan, of course, has been taken by women as an insult, but not by all women. For woman is a species. Rhetoric is not one woman. not the one, true, universal woman. No dogmatic stand is possible or, if so, can be successful. Within a species, there are many contending forces, goddesses, attracting and repelling an object. Radically many *rh*erotics, many contending forces. Fighting off dogmatisms.

Ah, and I said that I would not invent from Lacan!

RHETORIC, THE WHORE OF BABYLON

Let us return to our earlier discussion of rhetoric, love, and the depiction of rhetoric as a whore. And let us re/begin intertwining, weaving, our sayings together. But eventually, leaving Freud's and Lacan's modernism behind. Leaving mourning and melancholia, as the *Logoi* have been hinting at all along. Leaving the double bind, with which we have been in a whirlwind, spinning, and having ourselves cast out of it into X-uberance, the *atopos* to which the *Logoi* call me.

Richard Lanham reminds us:

> Rhetoric has usually been depicted as a woman, especially an overdressed
> one—the harlot rhetoric. We might begin liverishly by developing the com-
> parison. Students of rhetoric cannot have had much direct experience with
> harlots[!] Harlots do not paint to improve nature. They paint to invite a certain
> attitude. The cosmetics, since they are not referential, cannot be excessive.
> Their excess is their meaning—until, at least, all woman kind follows suit.
> Likewise their dress. It is not calculated to improve their figures—it usually
> distorts them—but to invite a particular sort of attention. Cosmetics and dress,
> then, in this puritanical [Protestant] comparison of the philosophers, are alle-
> gorical, not referential. (29)

Lanham continues in his discussion with an analysis of Ovid's *Ars Amatoria*,
which reads like Aristotle's *Rhetoric*, that is, like a book of seduction (50-64).
The object, Lanham says, in representing Ovid's words, is to "corrupt the
maid first" (50). The implicit contrast between Ovid's *Art of Love* and Plato's
Phaedrus (with the so-called non-lover, evil-lover, and noble-lover) is un-
mistakable. The sham of shams is Socrates as noble-lover! Socrates-Plato is
Shem the Penman to our being Shaun the Post. The ham of shams is Ovid's
lie-ing in wait so as to bring together (*legen, lesen*).

The question is not, What is it that "women" or wo/men want? but, What
is it that language (*Logos*) wants?

Have I been too obscure? Well, forgive me, dear reader, as I have attempted daily to forgive languages (*Logoi*) themselves. What wants to be
said by languages is never single. Languages do not want to be single, but
want to gather. In un/sitely mis/mannerisms. The *Logoi* seduce, grab us, at
times, gently, by the throat, and speak us. By the arm, and write us. Shake
us until we stutter and stammer our speaking and writing, our various pathic
intensities. It's the gods' spells.

DIONYSUS, CHRIST, AND THE *LOGOI*

A few years ago, I remember that the news, though never new, was that
particular, very fundamentalist Protestants were marching, with placards in
hand, denouncing the showing of Martin Scorsese's film *The Last Temptation
of Christ*. Of the *Dionysian* Christ. I saw them marching on TV. What a
hoot! These anemic ones, trying to deny, to suppress, the Mediterranean. I
had heard previously that Nikos Kazantzakis' novel was being filmed. I
turned off the TV. The news was tiresome. (The puritans in the United States
were denouncing the heresy that when Christ was confronted with constant
temptations, he could be actually attracted to and not just repulsed by them.
Could actually feel passion. It's sad to say, but Kazantzakis' own church,

the Orthodox church, also read the book as heretical. Most Christians probably do.) Eventually, I attempted to rent the cassette of the film several times but to no avail, because each time someone had poured acid into the cassette. Finally, I was successful in locating an undamaged copy, and I viewed it. Then I read the novel, which has been more important to me than having read Aristotle's *Rhetoric*, even George Kennedy's translation. Here, in this novel, was a portrayal of *Logos* as a double bind, as a seduction; was a portrayal of the *Logoi* as few Greeks since Heraclitus and a handful of Greek tragedians had attempted.

Is it not interesting that W. K. C. Guthrie, in a footnote, tells us: "Though the lapse of centuries makes it of doubtful relevance to the present discussion, it is interesting that Lucian could refer to Christ as 'that crucified sophist' (*Peregrinus* 13)" (34, n. 2). Doubtful relevance? Hell, Christ is more a Sophist than any of Guthrie's Sophists. For Kazantzakis' Christ, *Logoi* are more than just *dissoi logoi*, they are *dissoi paralogoi, polylogoi*. When *Logos* speaks, it giveth and taketh away. When the *Logoi* appear in Christ, they torment his body and mind. When struck, he grovels on the ground, in the dust. He dis/engages in a revelry. He is called, but it is a mixed call. He is called like Abraham to sacrifice Isaac; he obeys the call, but no intervening angel of the Lord-*Logos* appears with a ram to substitute for Isaac. Many die. (The question becomes, "You speak to me, Lord-*Logoi*, but what in either heaven or hell do you want?") For a Lacanian, Christ is an Hysteric (see Zizek); for a Nietzschean, Christ is Dionysus. Christ is not the second Adam. Christ is the third Dionysus (see Kofman).

It is in our interest to remember that Nietzsche tells us: "Dionysus has the dual nature of a cruel, barbarized demon and of a mild, gentle ruler" (*Birth* 73).

Che Vuoi?

"What is it that you want?" is the feverish driving force of the narrative.

While hanging on the cross, Christ, in his last temptation according to Kazantzakis, dreams that he is wedded to Mary Magdalene. Wedded. To his kin, yet a whore. (This came as no surprise to me, for Christ always hung out with the lumpen/proletariat.) Much, however, transpires before this last (?) temptation to establish a context that will reveal itself to be a turmoil.

The Gossip According to Kazantzakis

Earlier in the novelistic treatment, when Christ is with John the Baptist during the night, deliberating over what to do in terms of the "Revolution," John is depicted as the angry one and Christ the compassionate one. Each is called by *Logos* differently. Christ speaks:

"Isn't love enough?" he asked.

"No," answered the Baptist angrily. "The tree is rotten. God called to me and gave me the ax, which I then placed at the roots of the tree. I did my duty. Now you do yours: take the ax and strike!"

"If I were fire, I would burn; if I were a woodcutter, I would strike. But I am a heart, and I love." (*Last Temptation* 241)

Christ is troubled, however, not knowing what to do. He decides "to go speak with God in the desert" (242). Once in the desert and after undergoing much turmoil, finally, "a pleasant breeze blew" and he saw "in front of him a snake with the eyes and breasts of a woman [,] licking its lips and regarding him" (255). After much talk between the two, the snake asks:

"Do you hear what I'm telling you? Lift your eyes, give me some sign. Just nod your head, my darling, and this very hour I shall bring you, on a fresh bed—your wife."

"My Wife?"

"Your wife. Look how God married the whore Jerusalem. The nations passed over her, but he married her to save her. Look how the prophet Hosea married the whore Gomer, daughter of Debelaim. In the same way, God commands you to sleep with Mary Magdalene, your wife, to have children, and save her." (257)

In the last temptation, when Christ is hanging on the cross, unconscious, he apparently awakes, counting: "one, two, three . . ." (444). At last, an angel intervenes, telling him that he had not been crucified but only dreamed (445). And tells Christ that he is to be married (446). To whom? Mary Magdalene. When Christ sees Mary, the angel vanishes. Mary explains to Christ that the Angel of the Lord had appeared at the very moment he was to be sacrificed. (Here we have the return of the Abraham–Isaac story.) Now, they are safe. They embrace, kiss, "roll on the ground" (450). Christ sleeps (451). Mary, concerned about the still-possible threat to Christ, leaves him but is eventually caught by Saul, who would kill Christ himself, and his gang, who do stone Mary to death (453-54). Christ awakens and sees that the angel has returned and is told that Mary has been killed (455-56).

And yet, the story dreamline continues. To tell us that Mary is alive, that Christ lives with Mary and Martha and has children with them (458-66). The dream-temptation, apparently wanting to resolve itself, has Mary ask Christ, What is dreaming? "What are they made of? Who sends them?" Christ puts forth a theory of dreams:

They are neither angels nor devils. . . . When Lucifer started his revolt against God, dreams could not make up their minds which side to take. They remained between devils and angels, and God hurled them down into the inferno of sleep. (468)

Having listened to Christ's explanation, Mary, then, tells Christ—contrary to his thinking that he had escaped crucifixion—he is only in a dream while actually crucified! Christ is incredulous. Mary says, "the children . . . All, all—all lies! Lies created by the Tempter to deceive us" (468).

"Have I Been Understood?—Dionysus Versus the Crucified"

Christ has not only apparently been crucified but also has been wrenched in numerous directions, not knowing what is what: from John to the Snake to the Angel to Mary. All *Logoi. Dissoi paralogoi.* And they continue, for Christ meets Saul . . . I mean . . . Paul, who has been enlightened and is now ready to proclaim the Gospel (474). In their lengthy exchange, Christ screams out to Paul that he never knew or saw Christ crucified, because he himself is Christ, not the son of God, but of Mary and Joseph (476). Paul, in turn, screams out to Christ, telling him to be quiet and proclaiming about the nature of his own claim about spreading the Gospel, "True or false—what do I care! It's enough if the world is saved!" (477). Without any transition or adjustment whatsoever Christ now turns and says:

> "I said only one word, brought only one message: Love, Love nothing else."
>
> "By saying 'Love' you let loose all the angels and demons that were asleep within the bowels of mankind. 'Love' is not, as you think, simple, tranquil word. Within it lie armies being massacred, burning cities, and much blood. Rivers of blood, rivers of tears: the face of the earth has changed. You can cry now as much as you like; you can make yourself hoarse yelling, 'I didn't want to say that—that is not love. Do not kill each other! We're all brothers! Stop!' . . . But how, poor wretch, can they stop? What's done is done!"
>
> "You laugh like a devil."
>
> "No, like an apostle. I shall become your apostle whether you like it or not. I shall construct you and your life and your teachings and your crucifixion and resurrection just as I wish. Joseph the Carpenter of Nazareth did not beget you; I begot you—I, Paul the scribe from Tarsus in Cilicia."
>
> "No! No!"
>
> "Who asked you? I have no need of your permission. Why do you stick your nose in my affairs?" (478)

As I finish reading this section, once again, I am laughing (dancing) with tears in my eyes but will not laugh and dance the tarantella (Nietzsche *Zarathustra* 220, cf. 214; Burke "Dancing").

Ecce Homo

Now, why did I quote these various, long passages from *The Last Temptation*, which, as I said, I gladly substitute for Aristotle's *Rhetoric*?

The passages best describe in their enigmatic way . . . being called to rhetorics, falling in love (in lust) repeatedly with the *Logoi*. Falling in love with rhetoric!? Falling in (with) Christ's notion of love? Or in Paul's notion of love? Falling in love with rhetoric (*Logos*) or rhetorics (*Logoi*) or *rh*erotics (*dissoi paralogoi* or *polylogoi*)?

For me, it is no longer of any interest whether or not I can possess the *Logoi* (divide them [as in *diaeresis*], count them out at 28, or 16, or "to *ratio*" them—which would be but a rationing of them—and conquer and control them, own and dominate them), but for me it is important to understand and accept that I am possessed by *Logoi*. More so by *dissoi paralogoi*. The catechism(s) could never control the questions or answers. (What is X?, Who is X?, etc.) The catechism(s) only established the conditions for exploding the pathic possibilities. *Logos* became exploding *Logoi*. Became *dissoi paralogoi*. Although the various churches (and their propagations of the faith, propaganda, or reformations and counterreformations) attempted to fix the *Logoi*, they cannot. Although particular philosophers and rhetors have attempted the same, they cannot. Forget ratios! Communication theorists want *homeostasis* (a so-called comfortable steady-state). Some now want *autopoiesis* (reflexivity, self-organizing, and self-making). They are in *resentement* with *Logoi*.

There are in some of my allusions, quotations, performances (here, as elsewhere) a sense of both *homeostasis* and *autopoiesis* at work and play. Both are present dialectically in *The* (forever) *Last Temptation*. Both are the workings-out and playings-out of the *Logoi*.

The *Logoi*, however, want to flow across smooth spaces and not striated space. Un/just flow. Gods, I love all things that flow. I would rather read any day Henry Miller's *Tropic of Cancer* than Aristotle's *Rhetoric*. Rhetoric is a whore. *RhErotics*. And we are called to love and to lust (with) her. Accept it. Mary Magdalene is a whore. And we are called to love and lust and accept her. To accept all things that flow. To say Yes. But so many of us would have Rhetoric without an attitude. But that cannot be.

Do I have to explain all this?

In a novel (the new, novelty) that I found, after so many years, in *The Last* (First?) *Temptation*, I read: " 'I am Saint Blasphemer, and don't forget it,' Jesus replied with a laugh" (366). This schizo god (gods), with all of his/her attendants, is a riot. Christ, as depicted, is not the God of gods. But one of the gods of *Logoi*. This Christ, as one-cum-radical multiplicities, torn and wrenched in countless directions, as one being called by the various gods, each wanting him/her to love them, cannot know, would not know, which one to love over the other, but would give, instead, an affirming laugh. And refuse to be the "last man" (who would ask, What is the One? Or the Many?) and but dance. Laughingly. As Zarathustra says, "I would believe only in a god who could dance" (Nietzsche 153). Only in a god, while dancing, who believed in not only the eternal return of life but also of perpetual refoldings and unfoldings.

So my dear friends in rhetoric and writing, let's dance! not the Tarantella, but the Dionysian dance. Not the Tarantella, because it is the return and the revision based on being-reactionary. Forget Euripidean/Burkean drama. Forget this deca-dance. But the Dionysian because it is a self-overcoming (of *homeostasis*, as death, and *autopoiesis*, as narcissism). Because it is post-human (*virtual*), refusing the conditions of ideal or actual, denegating the negative dualisms, and but dancing the wild, savage differences. Christ, the third Dionysus, is not of this dualism, for he is the third Dionysus. One, two, and . . . stop expecting an ac*count* of XXXcess.

Ecce Ecriture

Do I have to explain all this? Okay, I will, with another writing lesson. When I last left them, Paul was haranguing Christ. Remember Paul was saying he would represent Christ as he himself (*autopoiesis*) willed. This issue of representation, how one is called to represent, is more complicated than the previous passage suggests.

Much earlier in the novel, Matthew the evangelist decides he is going to write down, record, everything that Christ says and does, "where he was born and who his parents and grandparents were, the fourteen generations." What happens, however,

> as he began to inscribe the first words on the paper in a beautiful hand, his fingers stiffened. The angel had seized him. He heard wings beat angrily in the air and a voice trumpeted in his ear, "Not the son of Joseph! What says the prophet Isaiah: 'Behold, a virgin shall conceive and bear a son.' . . . Write: [Then] Mary was a virgin. The archangel Gabriel descended to her house before any man had touched her, and said, 'Hail Mary, full of grace, the Lord is with you!' Straight away her bosom bore fruit. . . . Do you hear? That's what you're to write. And not in Nazareth; no, he wasn't born in Nazareth. Do not forget the prophet Micah." (349)

But Matthew stops writing in order to protest: "It's not true. I don't want to write, and I won't!" Then we are told:

> Mocking laughter was heard in the air, and a voice: "How can you understand what truth is, you handful of dust? Truth has seven levels. On the highest is enthroned the truth of God, which bears not the slightest resemblance to the truth of men. It is this truth, Matthew Evangelist, that I intone in your ear. . . . Write: 'And three Magi, following a large star, came to adore the infant. . . .' " (349-50)

Matthew responds: "I won't write! I won't write! he cried, . . . but his hand was running over the page writing" (350).

Later, Christ wants to see just what Matthew has been scribbling down about him. He reads. He screams out: "Lies! Lies! Lies! . . . I was born in Nazareth, not in Bethlehem." But then Matthew tells Christ about the angel who visits and dictates to him. Matthew says: "His lips touch my right ear." Christ, befuddled, says, "An angel? [and muses to himself] If what we call truth, [the gods] called lies. . . ." Then he finally says: "Write whatever the angel dictates" (391-92).

Therefore, today, as yesterday and tomorrow, I write what the *Logoi* dictate. It is no longer possible to be in *homeostasis* or even *autopoiesis*, but in *virtuality*. I fear, but accept, with much laughter, that I am on my way to becoming . . . a Techno-Erotic Pagan. (Let us raise our heads and laugh.) The second great Whitman of our age, Henry Miller, records: "there is no hope for us, *any of us*, but if that is so then let us set up a last agonizing, bloodcurdling howl. . . . Away with lamentations! Away with elegies and museums! Let the dead eat the dead. Let us living ones dance about the rim of the crater, a last expiring dance. But a dance!" (257). (Let us raise our heads and laugh the laugh of unbearable lightness.)

Arlington, Texas
January 11, 1997

WORKS CITED

Barthes, Roland. *A Lover's Discourse*. Trans. Richard Howard. New York: Hill & Wang, 1977.

Burke, Kenneth. "Dancing With Tears in My Eyes." *Critical Inquiry* 1 (1974): 1-31.

Cowan, Marianne. "Introduction." Nietzsche. *Philosophy*. 1-21.

Deleuze, Gilles. *Nietzsche and Philosophy*. Trans. Hugh Tomlinson. New York: Columbia UP, 1983.

DeMan, Paul. *Blindness and Insight*. 2nd ed., Revised. Minneapolis: U of Minnesota P, 1983.

Euripides. *Bacchae*. *Greek Tragedies*. Ed. David Grene and Richard Latimore. Trans. William Arrowsmith. Vol. III. Chicago: U of Chicago P, 1960.

Guthrie, W. K. C. *The Sophists*. Cambridge: Cambridge UP, 1971.

Heidegger, Martin. *Early Greek Thinking*. Trans. David Farrell Krell and Frank A. Capuzzi. San Francisco: Harper, 1984.

Kazantzakis, Nikos. *The Last Temptation of Christ*. Trans. P. A. Bien. New York: Simon & Schuster, 1960.

Kofman, Sarah. "Baubo: Theological Perversion and Fetishism." *Nietzsche's New Seas*. Ed. Michael Allen Gillespie and Tracy B. Strong. Chicago: U of Chicago P (1991): 175-202.

Lacan, Jacques. *Feminine Sexuality*. Ed. Juliet Mitchell and Jacaqueline Rose. Trans. Jacqueline Rose. New York: Norton, 1985.

Lanham, Richard. *The Motives of Eloquence*. New Haven: Yale UP, 1976.

Lyotard, Jean-François. *Libidinal Economy*. Trans. Iain Hamilton Grant. Bloomington: Indiana UP, 1993.

Lyotard, Jean-François, and Jean-Loup Thébaud. *Just Gaming*. Trans. Wlad Godzich. Minnesota: U of Minnesota P, 1985.

Nietzsche, Friedrich. *Beyond Good and Evil*. Trans. Walter Kaufmann. New York: Vintage, 1966.

Nietzsche, Friedrich. *The Birth of Tragedy and the Case of Wagner*. Trans. Walter Kaufmann. New York: Vintage, 1967.

Nietzsche, Friedrich. *Philosophy in the Tragic Age of the Greeks*. Trans. Mariann Cowan. Washington, DC: Regnery Gateway, 1962.

Nietzsche, Friedrich. *Zarathustra. The Portable Nietzsche*. Trans. Walter Kaufmann. New York: Vintage, 1968.

Perniola, Mario. *Enigmas: The Egyptian Moment in Society and Art*. Trans. Christopher Woodall. New York: Verson, 1995.

Vitanza, Victor J. *Negation, Subjectivity, and The History of Rhetoric*. Albany: SUNY P, 1997.

Zizek, Slavoj. *The Sublime Object of Ideology*. New York: Verso, 1989.

CHAPTER SIXTEEN

Technology/Writing/Identity in Composition and Rhetoric Studies: Working in the Indicative Mood

Kathleen E. Welch

University of Oklahoma

THE NEW PARADIGM

Composition and rhetoric studies have been constructing and enacting the New Paradigm, the merger of research and pedagogy, since the 1960s, when the the civil rights movement, the anti-Vietnam War movement, and the second wave of United States feminism coalesced around the writing milestones of Edward P. J. Corbett's *Classical Rhetoric for the Modern Student,* Richard Braddock, Richard Lloyd-Jones, and Lowell Schoer's *Research in Written Composition,* the Dartmouth Anglo-American Conference on the Teaching of Writing, and Janet Emig's research for the epochal *The Composing Processes of Twelfth Graders.* In this heated, revolutionary cultural context, amid democratic/liberatory movements of many kinds (movements that continue to benefit the entire nation in uncounted ways), writing pedagogy as a deep activity, as an activity of intellectual moment, came to occupy a center of attention in English studies and far beyond. Some of the best minds, including those mentioned above, as well as James L. Kinneavy, Winifred Bryan Horner, Maxine Hairston, and many others, devoted their formidable talents to this work. This effort was predicated on what we can call the New Paradigm, in which research and teaching interact so thoroughly that they are merged. The fruits of these scholars' labor, including the work of many of their students who now occupy faculty positions, have resulted in the proliferation of dynamic and visionary graduate composition/rhetoric programs and undergraduate writing majors and tracks across the landscape of United States universities. In fact, the New Paradigm places composition and rhetoric studies in the avant-garde of higher education reform. As Theresa Enos writes in *Gender Roles and Faculty Lives in Rhetoric and Composition,* the work that our field has performed with extraordinary success for the last 30 years is the vision described by Ernest Boyer in which scholarship broadens its calling and communicates with the general public (44-45).

Composition/rhetoric has not only this 30-year history but also has, of course, histories of 2.5 millennia during which the teaching of writing and rhetoric (not, of course, always together) has taken place actively across multiple technologies in the historical construction known as the West. At various points in the longer story (as opposed to the more accessible 30-year history), the power relations between research and pedagogy have shifted in important ways. At the gateway of the third millennium of the common era, the relationship between pedagogy and research in all fields undergoes inescapable change. Higher education is in a period of radical change because of the development of communication technologies; the smoldering power differentials of gender, race, and ethnicity; a changing form of patronage; and, for the traditional humanities, a pervasive sense of the uselessness of what has been offered as an automatic good.

Our current and phenomenally successful system of higher education, fueled by federal dollars and the independence of researchers to pursue their intuitive knowledge, undergoes changes in funding that inevitably change the nature of research. The increasing importance of corporate dollars in place of federal dollars leads to less academic freedom as we have known it, in that researchers in the sciences and social sciences are now prodded to be more "practical" and, ominously, in that some researchers in the biological and medical sciences now seek monetary gain from their discoveries (for example, with the demands for patents and remuneration for genetic discoveries). The relationship between the research university and the corporations that sponsor so much research (and whose overhead funding supports the humanities as well) grows stronger by the day; the ethics of these arrangements have scarcely been attended to.

The humanities have been a secondary presence in this loop since about 1970, when the so-called National Defense Student Loans were cut off to humanities students, so many of whom had publicly and impolitely challenged the government's secret war-making and other activities. We were downsized 25 years before most of the rest of the United States, when the job market in English crashed in the mid-1970s. Our second major downsizing began in about 1991, after the Ronald Reagan–David Stockman fiscal plan had a decade and a half to work into the fabric of education. As David Stockman recounted in his cynical autobiography, the Republican plan of the early 1980s was centered on halting the redistribution of wealth by allowing the rich to keep more of their money. This substantial reduction in the redistribution of wealth let loose a period of laissez-faire capitalism that continues to damage higher education in as yet incompletely analyzed ways. The faculty lines that were to have opened up in the 1990s (after the retirement of those professors hired to teach the baby boomers who swamped colleges and universities in the 1960s and 1970s) have disappeared, largely because the states have been so thoroughly starved by the Reagan budget plan. In this post-1983 situation, the humanities simply had no leverage to maintain lines. Lines that did become available found their ways to the sciences, the business schools, and other, more obviously useful, locations.

One of the reasons the leverage declined is that the general United States citizenry regards Literature, Art, and so forth as cordoned-off activities reserved for particular elites. In other words, the triumph of Modernism across symbol systems in the universities is almost complete. The result of the hegemony of Modernism brought unintended consequences: They made traditional arts and humanities appear to be useless. The masses of United States citizens are well aware of the condescension of this aspect of the Modernist project, of its antidemocratic basis, of its need for exclusion of citizens like the ones required to take humanities classes. The Modernist university has taught this lesson well; as a result, we have a citizenry (rightly) attuned to the uselessness of what many humanists do. When the post-Arnoldian successors of modernism sneer from their ivory towers that the United States is filled with couch potato anti-intellectuals, they need to stare into their mirrors. Who trained this purportedly pathetic group? They did.

When traditional humanists complain of alleged "illiteracy" (with a prefix that reinforces their own sense of health and entitlement) and cultural ignorance, they should reexamine their own syllabi, curricula, and ideologies. These traditional humanists taught our citizenry to fear or even to hate their own language and to believe that a special realm of "art" excluded them. I have discussed elsewhere the twinned, wizened formalisms of the current traditional paradigm and New Criticism.[1] Both attenuated, antihuman constructs led to the profound diminishment in which the humanities now reside. I argued, in fact, that these twins collaborated both in persuading the citizenry that their own language production was destined to be inferior to anything the "geniuses" of post-Romanticism could produce and, in current traditional rhetoric, in teaching students to be bored by, fearful of, or, in some cases, even to loathe their own language. These lessons have been learned so well that the humanities have nothing more than tepid lip-service support from university structures, funding agencies, and other sources of power. So far, the humanities remain merely tolerated.

Composition and rhetoric studies, however, have been exempt from this onslaught, as Martha Woodmansee and others have pointed out.[2] Wood-

---

[1] *Electric Rhetoric: Classical Rhetoric, Oralism, and a New Literacy.*

mansee has described the situation as one in which all areas of the humanities except one have undergone drastic reductions. That one field is composition/rhetoric studies, which, as Woodmansee points out, continues to flourish among the second series of downsizings, the 1990s version. Why is composition/rhetoric studies exempt? One of the various answers is that we have enacted the New Paradigm for our 30 years of growth as a discipline. In short, the public, which as a whole understands but cannot articulate that language study is vitally important, supports massive support of the teaching of writing and the research that accompanies and drives it.

Composition/rhetoric studies have vigorously declined to join the hierarchy that Enos and Boyer identify as so damaging to the general culture. Although we are immersed in university cultures that regard research as the peak, teaching as the valley, and service as the underground (so that it is invisible), composition/rhetoric scholar-teachers embrace pedagogy, work hard at it, share current research with students, and generally possess an identity (or what Diotima or Aspasia might call an *ethos*) in which pedagogy is definitive. Composition/rhetoric graduate training, for example, includes a large amount of material that is pedagogical and a merger of research and pedagogy. We tend not to hierarchize research and teaching (although some do because the climate invites it through the reward and prestige structure that Enos describes).

The New Paradigm of the merged pedagogy/scholarship now interacts with the new communication technologies.[3] Composition/rhetoric studies is awash in emerging technologies, including the proliferation of webbed environments and the stupendous possibilities they offer our students and ourselves. The histories of rhetoric and of writing practices are inherently tied to communication technologies, from ostraca (shards of pots that were relatively inexpensive) to papyrus and stylus, to rag paper and vegetable inks, to the Gutenberg press, to xerography, to cheap wood-pulp paper and chemical inks, to computers with words only to computers with words and pictures conjoined in a new vocabulary and grammar. Look at the curricula announced in course bulletins across English departments in the United States. Composition/rhetoric dominates the new technologies. It does so for at least two reasons: We realize its possibilities, good and bad, and its inevitability, and the rest of English studies has, for the most part, "appointed"

---

[2] Woodmansee, paper presented at Society for Critical Exchange/Sites of Writing, Cleveland, Ohio, February 28, 1997.

[3] Compare, for a moment, the technology programs and displays of the Conference on College Composition and Communication (CCCC) to those of the Modern Language Association (MLA). Whereas the former offers a dazzling array of technological pedagogy and research in demonstrations, in numerous panels, in site visits (for example, the demonstration of state-of-the-art technology by Arizona State University at the 1997 CCCC), the MLA offers next to nothing.

us to do this work that they regard as too onerous. Just as first-year writing is regarded by Modernist humanists as an unpleasant, ungenteel task (largely because of the perception that it is tainted by the secondary status of "mere" pedagogy) to be dumped onto the composition/rhetoric staff, so the new communication technologies are regarded for the most part as an unpleasant, unrewarding task that can best be thrown into the already-there-and-already-exploited writing programs.

But those humanists who see the teaching of writing and the teaching of and with new technologies as secondary, as beneath them, tend not to understand, to really understand, that scholar-teachers in composition and rhetoric remain fascinated by and committed to both.

The new communication technologies and the commitment to labor-intensive writing pedagogy are not the only aspects of the New Paradigm. No new paradigm can succeed unless profound inequities in gender, race, and ethnicity are met head on. It is imperative that composition/rhetoric scholar-teachers weave gender, ethnic, and race issues into all our classes, all our histories, and all our research. Most importantly, we must recruit persons from underrepresented groups into our ranks. Although the massive project of retheorizing rhetoric and composition is now being done by both women and men in numerous fields, it remains severely marginalized, as institutional sexism continues to operate strongly in the academy as it does in other areas.

Our progress in making scholar-teachers of color and issues of race and ethnicity more central in composition and rhetoric studies is our biggest challenge at this time. It is worse even than the limited progress of many women scholar-teachers. The New Paradigm characterized by the last 30 years of composition/rhetoric studies must focus on African American rhetors, orators, and writers, as well as the many cultures and linguistic traditions of the hundreds of Native American nations, bands, and tribes. In addition, enormous work remains for us (perhaps in collaboration with Spanish studies) in the area of Latina and Latino rhetorics, writing practices, oralisms, and so on.

OBSTACLES TO THE NEW PARADIGM

Composition/rhetoric studies have, then, looked to the future and to the ethical necessity of treating pedagogy as a central and defining activity in higher education and not as a secondary one that interrupts research. Nevertheless, the obstacles to the enactment of our agendas have been enormous. Two of the primary obstacles that I would like to explore here are continuing race, ethnic, and gender inequities, and a deep, almost unconscious and reflexive hostility by many traditional humanists (and some cultural studies scholars) toward the success of rhetoric/composition studies and our intellectual energy and connection to cultures.

We have proceeded past the second-wave American feminism (beginning about 1970) that often assumed (in that era of fabulous exuberance) that all women are feminists and that all men are misogynists. The women-and-language debates have discounted this convenient but inaccurate binary. The number of feminist men in composition/rhetoric studies has always astounded me since I began working in the field as a graduate student at the University of Iowa more than 20 years ago. Obviously, composition/rhetoric studies has had its own gender skirmishes. However, from my vantage point, I have seen numerous men join many women in wielding their power to make academic processes work so that women (almost all of them White) have been placed in tenure lines, tenured, and promoted. Even though these numbers remain alarmingly small, as Enos has demonstrated with her data, progress for White women has been made.

But women in composition/rhetoric are what I have described as *Double Others*.[4] I write now from a position of profound privilege, as the second woman in my university's English department to become a full professor. My situation resonates with the position articulated by Louise Wetherbee Phelps and Janet Emig in *Feminine Principles and Women's Experience in American Composition and Rhetoric*:

> The circumstances in which even privileged women still work, though, lengthened the project [the book] beyond our expectation. At one point we faced the classic dilemma of women struggling to reconcile the claims of multiple commitments—the moment when a direct conflict requires them to choose.
> . . . in the last two years of this project, each of us encountered extraordinary crises threatening the health and very survival of our programs, requiring us to respond with every reserve of resourcefulness and care we possessed, at the cost of delaying completion of the volume. This dilemma is one imposed often on women in our field, as it is on so many other women in our society. (xii)

Almost every woman I know in composition/rhetoric studies has faced this problem. We have to stop our work in the New Paradigm, the merger of research and pedagogy, to face one or both of the following issues: programmatic challenges (almost always from colleagues in English) and gender-, race-, and ethnic-based challenges by those who maintain with religious fervor a commitment to a White, Modernist canon of uselessness, a dogma of a purportedly objective Truth and Beauty (expressed so strongly by

---

[4] Paper presented to the Coalition of Women Scholars in the History of Rhetoric and Composition, Conference on College Composition and Communication, Nashville, Tennessee, March 1994.

traditionalist humanists such as William Bennett and Lynne Cheney, both of whom have worked shrilly and diligently to dismantle the agency they each headed in Reaganland, the National Endowment for the Humanities (NEH).[5]

One of the more alarming issues that faces the New Paradigm as it has been constructed by composition/rhetoric studies is the number of people, especially women, who do not get tenure. As has been the case for many years, many junior faculty members, men as well as women, are given so much service (frequently service that is grounded in rigorous intellectual training) that does not "count" that they are denied tenure.[6] An enormous number of highly talented, committed, hardworking scholar-teachers have been let go by departments that did not value their work, even as they used up the intellectual resources of those people. A related problem occurs for the many, many women who achieve tenure and one promotion and then remain at the associate professor level well beyond the years that they should occupy it. In both cases, the culprit is partly the crushing amount of work in pedagogy, research, and service that is assigned to composition/rhetoric studies, efforts that are gobbled up by institutions but, as many have noted, frequently not rewarded.

White women and men and women of color frequently are "behind" where they want to be or could be in their own intellectual journeys of vision and collaboration. Ethics require that projects—whether research projects or pedagogical experiments that merge teaching and research—be dropped when a writing program or graduate composition/rhetoric program is threatened with deletion or profound diminishment or when women and minorities are being blatantly harassed or discriminated or retaliated against.[7] Mountains of paper and virtual narratives exist on these persistent problems. They all add up to the delay that Phelps and Emig described.

These twin obstacles are the indicative mood to which my subtitle refers. We cannot work toward our subjunctive mood, our could-be world of democratic critical literacy through the deep pedagogy of writing. Instead, over and over, we are stalled. This stalling of progress through the obstacles of maintaining academic due process in promotion and tenure cases, of main-

---

[5] Bennett, Cheney et, al., have succeeded. The budget of the NEH, which they worked to dismantle completely, has been reduced to almost nothing. The pundit careers of these two Truth and Beauty objectivists, the former holding a doctorate in philosophy and the latter a doctorate in English, have flourished.

[6] Tenure workshops are held yearly by the Coalition of Women Scholars in the History of Rhetoric and Composition. The workshops I have led have been characterized by women who were denied tenure and who wanted to tell their stories. Another category consists of women who are about to compile their dossiers and know almost nothing of how their institutions' tenure policies work (either the published criteria or the power relations that determine their careers according to their double-otherness).

[7] In one summer, I was consulted about three allegations of stalking of White women faculty in three states. Stalking, of course, is a felony in most states.

taining composition/rhetoric programs that are regularly undermined, and of helping women and minorities to be treated equally characterizes our discipline at this time. With more work to be done now, especially with the addition of technology (again, a wonderful addition, but one that requires tremendously greater person power), we do not need these challenges. The long discussion in our field about secession from English remains compelling because of these obstacles.

As Enos, Kinneavy, Horner, Sharon Crowley, and many others have pointed out, the general public regards the teaching of writing as a central mission of the discipline of English. Our colleagues in English for the most part do not. Amazingly, even those who support our work have no idea what we do, although composition/rhetoric specialists can describe and discuss the work of our colleagues in cultural studies, traditional literary studies, and so on. And so we live in the indicative mood ("what is there" is a stipulative definition of rhetoric that I have addressed elsewhere). If we could only be released from these battles, think of the improvement in cultures we could make. Enormous energy, vitality, and intelligence are now uselessly expended by composition/rhetoric scholars on skirmishes with those who maintain a belief that reading is superior to writing, that whiteness is superior to any other color, and that research is superior to and utterly different from pedagogy. That is the indicative mood we face every day.

DEMOCRATIC IDENTITY

The New Paradigm of the merger of scholarship and research rests on the idea that leading-edge research should be shared with our students, that we should guide them and prod them with the most recent research. This desire to share with students, to interact with them dialectically, derives from a profoundly democratic spirit that pervades composition/rhetoric people. Basic writing, first-year writing, and the new pedagogies of webbed environments are three examples of areas shunned by a large portion of the professoriate across many fields. We in composition/rhetoric embrace these and other areas. In my own program at the University of Oklahoma, called Composition/Rhetoric/Literacy at the graduate level, we see students and faculty as committed to a freshman writing course as to a doctorate research seminar. A number of years ago, an applicant for an assistant professorship expressed great concern that she would not have enough access to basic writing students if she joined us. This nonhierarchical vision appears to me to be the norm.

This democratic vista, to echo Whitman, brings with it the challenge of daunting time constraints. When a program commits to outstanding freshman writing, to state-of-the-art undergraduate writing courses and graduate composition/rhetoric courses, it has undertaken an enormous burden. Add to this burden the dizzying load of administrative obligations (that includes keeping up with what other programs are offering, keeping up with research in "service," and so on) and you have one tired faculty group. The third addition, discussed in the previous section, the endless political battles over gender and race and attacks on writing/rhetoric programs, means that nearly all our programs throughout the country are extraordinarily overworked. Outstanding composition/rhetoric programs have disappeared because of the pressures I have described. National recognition for important advances in composition/rhetoric has not saved many of these programs, even as the general culture continues to expect this kind of work. The strong and intellectually vibrant composition/rhetoric section at the University of Iowa Department of English provides one example of a superbly successful program (Iowa doctoral recipients in composition/rhetoric now occupy many faculty lines) that was downsized nearly out of existence in the 1980s. Louise Wetherbee Phelps has recounted her story in *Feminine Principles and Women's Experience in American Composition and Rhetoric*. One could name a half dozen important, successful, intellectually important composition/rhetoric programs that had established themselves only to be deleted.

Tellingly, the democratic impulse that defines the identities of so many composition/rhetoric workers is the very force that leads us to take all these activities so seriously. With the rapid addition of technological pedagogy and research, our democratic desire to learn the new technologies and to teach them in the most effective ways (for the culture at large as well as for individual students and faculty members) has led to even more severe constraints on our time.

Our first-year writing programs and advanced writing classes are using technology in advanced ways. Graduate teaching assistants at the University of Oklahoma now vie to teach in webbed environments and regard it as a plum assignment that they must work toward. However, in many cases, for faculty there is little reward for these massive self-training efforts in working up new courses that both examine technology epistemologically and deploy those technologies. Interestingly, many highly traditional literary scholars have performed outstanding work in moving their fields' knowledge base onto CD-ROMs and the Internet, not only setting up chat rooms but also transferring databases of their fields. The "libraries without walls" on the Web expand daily, offering those with access, time, and functional computer literacy extraordinary opportunities to be autodidacts.

BLIZZARD COURSES

Although we have made wonderful, energizing, hopeful progress in so many ways (see, for example, the *Rhetoric Review* data on the proliferation of graduate courses; see also the gender and rhetoric and composition course material on the Web as well), we in composition/rhetoric face a problem that confronts all our colleagues: Curricula, students, and faculty remain so White that we appear to be in a blizzard. Whiteness is the only thing that can be seen in this situation. The three areas—curricula, students, faculty—are of course closely connected. Scan university and college bookstores to see the books that are ordered. This kind of reading quickly reveals the values of a given department. Composition and rhetoric studies needs to take concerted action against this persistent problem.

One pedagogical/research effort that addresses this problem is an experimental graduate course taught in fall 1997, Histories of Feminist Rhetorics and Writing Practices, offered simultaneously at the University of Oklahoma Department of English and the Ohio State University Department of English. In this course, conceived at meetings of the coalition of Women scholars in the History of Rhetoric and Composition, three professors—Andrea Lunsford at Ohio State University, Cheryl Glenn at Pennsylvania State University, and I at the University of Oklahoma—taught three "pods" intended to inject race and gender issues directly into the received rhetorical tradition and the historicizing of writing practices. The pods consist of classical rhetoric and writing practices (Sappho, Diotima, and Aspasia and constructions of race in the ancient world); late 19th-century and 20th-century selections (Ida B. Wells, Margaret Fuller, and others); and the situation right now. The plan was to provide a model syllabus and structure, including the use of new technologies.[8]

To stop the blizzard, we must recruit people of color much more actively in rhetoric and composition studies. This move includes, of course, a substantial commitment to the mentoring of junior faculty and students of color. As Angela Davis has taught us, racism damages not just its proponents' object of hatred and derision; it also damages the holders of this pernicious worldview. It is the duty of those of us in higher education to fight this cultural illness.

LIVING IN THE SUBJUNCTIVE MOOD

Even as we are bogged down by the setbacks imposed on composition/rhetoric scholars by those who believe that writing is a skill as transmissible as the learning of car repair, we must maintain and add to our new

---

[8] It is important to note that although the classes communicated electronically with the remote sites, a teacher was physically in each class. One challenge of the new technologies is the issue of distance learning that decreases the student-teacher ratio. Many people, especially legislators, have responded to distance learning with utopian zeal because they think that a great deal of money can be saved. This issue relates, of course, to the starving of state-funded higher education by Reaganomics and its aftermath. Legislators have no choice but to search for alternatives.

vision—what could be, what should be. The composition/rhetoric democratic vista must contain the vision of gender equality, race equality, and ethnic equality. The *kairic* moment is now.

Norman, Oklahoma
June 3, 1997

WORKS CITED

Braddock, Richard, Richard Lloyd-Jones, and Lowell Schoer. *Research in Written Composition.* Urbana, IL: National Council of Teachers of English, 1963.

Corbett, Edward P. J. *Classical Rhetoric for the Modern Student.* 3rd ed. New York: Oxford UP, 1990.

Davis, Angela Y. *Women, Race, and Class.* New York: Vintage, 1981.

Emig, Janet. *The Composing Processes of Twelfth Graders.* Research Report #13. Urbana, IL: National Council of Teachers of English, 1971.

Enos, Theresa. *Gender Roles and Faculty Lives in Rhetoric and Composition.* Carbondale: Southern Illinois UP, 1996.

Phelps, Louise Wetherbee, and Janet Emig, eds. *Feminine Principles and Women's Experience in American Composition and Rhetoric.* Pittsburgh: U of Pittsburgh P, 1995.

Welch, Kathleen E. *Electric Rhetoric: Classical Rhetoric, Oralism, and a New Literacy.* Cambridge, MA: MIT Press, in press.

Welch, Kathleen E. "African American Voices, Gender, and the Question of Rhetoric." Coalition of Women Scholars in the History of Rhetoric and Composition. Conference on College Composition and Communication. Nashville, March 1994.

Woodmansee, Martha. Paper presented at Society for Critical Exchange/Sites of Writing. Case Western Reserve Univ. Cleveland, Feb. 1997.

On Being a Writer, Being a Teacher of Writing

Edward M. White
California State University, San Bernardino

Writing, Paul Goodman said, is a way of being in the world. Somehow, I knew that very early. When the conversation turns to who we are deep, deep, inside, I reply that I am a writer first and everything else—teacher, grandfather, piano player, and so on—after that. That is why everything I have written on writing is influenced by the writer's sense of control: We shape events, control reality, define feelings by putting them on the page. Writers make reality and so are more in charge of what goes on than are other people. I am always happy to take the minutes at important meetings. That way I can shape what happened to become what I saw happening. If we don't like how things are going, we change them. The great thing about being a writer, John Barthes says in *The Friday Book*, is that we can turn our worst experiences into money. I take that yet further. The great thing about being a writer is that we can exchange mere reality for the sturdy truth of our prose. Real life, the saying goes, is for those unable to put up with the rigors of fiction.

I engage in some deception as I say this. A writer in American society is someone who makes a living at writing, and I, alas, although author or editor of nine books, have never made more than a pittance—though a steady pittance—from publishers. Again, a writer carries a Romantic image that goes with the word, a maker of poetry and fiction, working in solitary inspiration, enraptured by communication with the muse. Not me. I have flourished as a pedant. Not just a routine pedant, let me add, but for the last two decades as a teacher of composition, and, to expose my sores yet further, a writer on assessment, the measurement of writing skill, often of the inept. Nothing, the classics tell us, is alien to the writer's humanity or, we might add, to the writer's word processor, although composition studies still remains alien to most of the old guard in most English departments. But teaching writing, even writing research to serious and ambitious graduate students, is to occupy the lowest rung of the prestige ladder in English departments. The latest twist in my career as teacher and writer has taken me to the hack work of academe, according to some, and writing assessment, the hack work of the hack work. But I get ahead of myself.

First there was the broken piano, then the power of the press, then the wisdom of the teacher. An underlying motif is the way writing allows us to shape our world. I became a writer first, a teacher of writing next, and now, as retirement opens new opportunities, the writing takes over again. By accident, the story of my writing is in part the growth of the discipline of composition studies. But it is no accident that a writer's story constructs the story of writing.

THE PIANO ROLL BLUES

My brother and I could afford the moving charges for our replacement piano, offered free by a local church, and we looked with pride at the hulking upright now awkwardly centered in the living room of our cramped Brooklyn tenement. Two musical teenagers we were, pooling the money we made by delivering flowers and groceries in the neighborhood. Unfortunately, the movers refused to take away the beaten and broken old piano that would not stay in tune, still in place against the wall. Our parents, unlettered, broke, and worn down, were both at work. My brother, older by 4 years and a dignified 17, decided that we would simply take the old junk piano apart and put it in the trash.

I won't repeat here the week-long saga of two boys hacking and slashing at an old piano and trying to fit it into trash cans. Brooklyn in the 1940s was a borough of small neighborhoods, and we became local legends, heroes of a sort to boys for miles around, envious of the frenzy of destruction we went through. The important moment for me came afterwards, the living room back to its normal state of disrepair, the electricity and water restored, the downstairs tenant mollified, the building janitor paid off by our furious father, by a whole dollar as I recall. "I think," I remember saying, "I should write this down." I not only wrote it down, but a month later I stood in that same living room holding a check for $25 from the Youth Editor of the *Christian Science Monitor*, which published my account, even keeping the title I gave it, "The Piano Roll Blues." (I had no way of knowing that the scores of newspaper articles and reviews I would later write would all be given headlines by editors more concerned about making the lines fit than making the meaning resonate.)

Has there been a triumph to match that day? I think not. Shaping moments like that must occur early on. I asked my father half a century later, months before his death, his mind almost gone, what was the best moment of his life. He didn't hesitate. It was a month after he quit school at the age of 13 to work in the post office, when he brought home his first paycheck. The whole family, he said with pride that looked back 75 years, moved into an apartment with an indoor bathroom. He fell back into his sickly sleep, and I remembered my own moment of glory at 13 holding that check, pay for writing, and gloating at my name on the printed page. "I am a writer," I remember saying, "that's what I am."

The feeling was one of power. The event, just weeks away, had begun to fade in everyone's memory, even in mine. But on the page it was newly created and forever new. I had made reality different and I knew it. In my newfound identity, I joined the high school newspaper, where my monthly column gave me some status, never close to that of the football players, of course, but not where my nearsighted, unathletic frame would normally have placed me in the schoolboy rankings. And on my first day at New York University (NYU), I joined the college weekly newspaper, which I would later turn into and edit as a daily. Yes, I was a writer. Fame and fortune lay ahead.

"SEE ME AFTER CLASS"

But how was a boy from the slums of Brooklyn, commuting from home to college on a full-tuition scholarship, to wind up rich and famous? Writing was well and good, but the world was there to be dealt with. I remember one day, early in the year, brandishing my press card to cross a police line in front of a nearby tenement that had caught fire and was still burning fiercely as I happened upon it. Firemen were hauling hoses and brandishing axes. Smoke was billowing from the upper stories, and the electrical smell of burning wires made my nose pinch. The police officer gave my press card a cursory glance, shrugged, and waved me into the building; he had more important things to do. I wandered through some burned-out apartments, feeling exhilaration. See how the power of the press card let me through! I said out loud. Dirty water was dripping through the ceiling, the smoke made it hard to see, and the cries of the firemen seemed to come from all sides. My exhilaration passed quickly, replaced first by apprehension (Migod! I'm lost inside a burning building!) and then panic. Somehow, I found an exit and stood for a moment outside again, trying to feel once more the power of the press. I just felt like a fool. Being a writer was going to take more than I had bargained for.

The only role model of success that I had was an overbearing uncle, a lawyer whose ostentation and bad taste (he and my aunt agreed that pink ceramic elephants should be the unifying motif throughout their splendid house) struck me as the pinnacle of human achievement. NYU had a prelaw program for undergraduates that seemed to be my destiny, but the required freshman English course proved my salvation. By great good luck, I wound up in the class of Professor Hans Gottlieb, who wrote at the bottom of my first freshman theme, "See me after class."

I was shaken. Was the writing, my writing, my identity, so bad that he had nothing else to say? What would happen to me? After class, I timidly knocked at his office door. He looked at me though wire-rimmed glasses, not unkindly. "White," he said, "you don't belong in this class." So my fears were justified, I thought, I needed remedial writing, I had been fooling myself all along. . . . But Gottlieb had barely paused. "You already know everything I plan to teach here." I gradually realized what he was talking about: ". . . so come to my fiction writing class instead." We would have our little conspiracy, the professor and I, so the registrar would never find out I was not actually taking freshman composition. But I would in fact be writing fiction, *advanced* fiction, whatever that was, instead of freshman themes. And so I wound up creating stories, toying with reality, week after week, in a small writing workshop, while my prelaw courses seemed increasingly unreal. But I was still unprepared for the ominous "See me after class" that appeared at the bottom of a story handed back to me that spring, even though Gottlieb had become for me a friendly and supportive figure. "What now?" I wondered, anxious as always about whether I really belonged at all in the university. Gottlieb had come to know me better than I knew myself, as it turned out. He asked me to sit down and describe my plans for the future. I did, matter-of-factly; it was the familiar narrative that all my relatives heard with nods of approval. But Gottlieb scowled.

"*Why* do you want to be a lawyer?"

"Well," I answered, giving the only answer my culture had prepared me for, "lawyers make lots of money."

"That's not a good enough reason," he responded.

I was stunned. What other reasons were there?

It was Gottlieb who showed me that I could actually make a living at the activity I had made a part of my identity. I did not have to work at a job I hated, as my father did, so I could write in my spare time. I could actually become an English professor and be paid for what I loved to do. By the time I left his office, I had resolved to change my major to English, to minor in languages, including Latin, and to enter graduate school. I think sometimes that such crucial conversations do not happen very much any more. Certainly it would not have happened for me if I had had the usual harried teaching assistant, showing signs of frantic poverty, talking to me in the corridor because no office was available, hastening away to teach another class on another campus. The professor as role model was too distant, too unknown, too literally inconceivable for me to understand that kind of life as a possibility until that conversation showed me I could reach beyond the limits of my small world.

THE POWER OF THE PRESS

The student newspaper for Washington Square College of New York University was a better-than-average weekly, due largely to the talents of the editors who came before me. I remember Sandy Nemser, who later became an important figure at *Newsday*, and Irv Chavkin, who, under a more Americanized name, still appears on CNN reporting from Hong Kong or Bangladesh. Stan Asimov was there, too, a good writer with a better-known brother—although not to me. Years later, at a social event at Harvard, I was introduced to Isaac Asimov, who, even in the 1960s, had produced dozens of stories and works on science. Immersed in the Renaissance at the time, I pondered his name. "Asimov," I said. "Are you any relation to Stan?" The famous writer looked stunned, then broke into great peals of laughter. "He's the only one in the world," he said, pointing incredulously at me, "who knows my brother and not me!" Alas, I failed to be duly impressed. After all, I was a writer, too, and he had said he worked in science fiction, another low-status field.

We had a faculty advisor for the newspaper, I suppose, but even as editor I could never remember who it was; we certainly never thought about checking with anyone but our fellow student editors. Our staff was small but very good, and, as my generation became editors, we decided to band together with the two other student weeklies published by NYU schools downtown, pool our funds, and become a daily. To our amazement, we were able to bring it off. But once we attained the goal, we had to face the difficulties of putting out a daily with the usual unpaid staff; we never imagined the salaries that some undergraduate newspaper editors make these days. But what training in writing we went through! We found ourselves in a pressure cooker, where writing was always first-draft work, to be published tomorrow. There was always news in downtown New York, and I can remember evenings (long before word processing) sitting at a typewriter in an alcove at the printer's, with copy boys tearing out paragraphs as I wrote them to bring to the Linotype operators so we could start the printing run in time to be available in the morning. There was no going back, no time for revision, because the early parts of the story were already in type as I was writing the ending. We never articulated how we felt, but those of us working on the daily felt an enormous sense of professional power. We could not sell the paper, supported as it was by student funds, but every morning, everywhere we looked, people were reading what we wrote the night before.

Two events stand out from those heady undergraduate days. The first came with the New York newspaper strike. Such strikes have become routine these days, but in the mid-1950s they were unheard of. Every single daily in the city disappeared with one exception: our school newspaper. The first day of the strike, our business manager announced with glee that instead of 4 pages, we would have 16 the next day. There was sudden silence. "How can we fill 16 pages?" I asked, looking around the room at the half dozen stalwarts who essentially put the paper together. "No problem," he replied, "I'll fill it." And he did, with Macy's and Gimbel's and S. Klein and the other stores whose sales were now falling on deaf ears. The next day we were 64 pages, all but two of them ads. Enough, we declared; we were still a school newspaper. The business manager didn't mind, he just raised the rates.

And so, for several weeks, our little NYU paper was the only daily in town. Word spread quickly, and businessmen would stop at Washington Square to pick up a copy on their way to the office. That year the *New York Review of Books* began publishing, moving into the vacuum created by the absence of the *New York Times Book Review*, and that was the most significant effect of the strike. After the strike we went back to business and size as usual, but the *New York Review of Books* has since become part of our national cultural landscape. Nonetheless, the power we felt during the strike had gone to my head. Later that year, I was interviewed by a team of dignitaries for a Rhodes Fellowship, which I did not get. One interviewer, a quiet man with a piercing look, asked me several questions about what we did during the strike. I was ready to inform him about our role, suitably inflated, and had no trouble telling him a great deal about what it was like to put out a daily newspaper. He seemed vaguely amused by me. On my way out, I asked the secretary who he was, because I had not caught his name. "Oh," she said, "that's Mr. Ochs, editor and publisher of the *New York Times*."

More stressful but ultimately more satisfying was our conflict with the president of the university, Henry Heald, soon to become president of the Ford Foundation, and his assistant, Major General Howells, the hero of the Berlin airlift. We had asked for trouble when our April Fool's edition ran a picture of Heald, always rather lugubrious, sideways, proclaiming his death. But we knew we were in for it when we were summoned to Heald's office after running a series of stories about the university bookstore. The bookstore had fallen on hard times for several reasons: The clerks were rude, the prices were higher than those at competing bookstores around the university in Greenwich Village, and its operating hours were not convenient for all students. To protect the bookstore, the general had decreed that professors were not to be allowed to release their book orders to the local bookstores, as had been the practice for generations. Numbers of the faculty told or wrote us in confidence that this was outrageous, just part of a militarized administration that they detested. And the local bookstore owners told us that the general was trying to put them out of business so the university bookstore could have a monopoly. We ran some stories about the stalwart immigrant bookstore owners of Greenwich Village, culture heroes devoting their lives to helping students; their livelihoods were now in peril. One of our editorials pointed out that the general was using the same tactics that the Soviets and the Rockefellers had used: abolish competition and then control the market. Is that why, we asked in an editorial, he had preserved freedom in Berlin against a Soviet blockade?

My coeditor was an interesting and likable fellow named Bob; I wish I could recapture his last name. He had lost the use of his legs after a childhood bout with polio but managed perfectly well with a mechanized wheelchair and hand controls on his car. Nobody pushed Bob around, he liked to say, as he wheeled himself through the inhospitable university. But we were hushed by the visible power in the president's office: the sheer size of it, the carpets, the sherry set out on a sideboard, the quiet hum of endowments that vibrated in the room. Heald was as warm and friendly as he ever got, telling us how much he admired what we had made of the newspaper. "But you are really harming our university by attacking the bookstore day after day after day," he concluded, with something like a smile. Howells hovered in the background, like a fighter plane escorting a bomber.

Bob replied quietly, "We don't see it that way, sir." He went on to speak of the protests we had heard from the bookstore owners and the faculty. I chimed in, rather clumsily, "Forbidding competition just isn't the American way, now, is it?"

Heald was flushed now and turned to the general. I realized with a start that neither of them were used to being opposed in anything they said or did. This was as painful and difficult for them as it was for us. I can't remember what Howells said, but it did contain a veiled threat to our funding—which was through the student council and quite out of his reach. I remember Bob dramatically whipping his wheelchair around and heading for the door. Heald stepped back into the picture and tried to cool things down. He was actually pleading with us to stop attacking his policy. And we refused.

Two days later, Howells issued a bulletin to the faculty reversing his previous order; the local bookstores were able to order books and compete with the university bookstore, and everything returned to normal. We reported the story and congratulated the administration in an editorial, but we never reported our meeting, and surprisingly, as I look back, we did not gloat in print about our triumph. I suppose we didn't need to gloat. We knew that we writers actually ran the world, that we had more power than university presidents and big-shot generals.

THE LOGIC AND RHETORIC OF EXPOSITION

In graduate school at Harvard, the best students in English became teaching assistants (TAs) in the literature program of the department. Only the losers wound up teaching the freshman writing course, which we knew as Gen Ed A, now more neatly called Expos, short for expository writing. I was torn, because I knew what I was supposed to do. So I did both as I worked away on my dissertation on Jane Austen's fiction: I dutifully assisted Professor Al Friedman in the Ballad and Folklore course but put my main energy into teaching the freshmen who were beginning the adventure of a Harvard education. Again, I had great good luck. The director of the program was Harold Martin, later president of Union College, a genuine scholar of composition in those pre-composition studies days, and his assistant director was Richard Ohmann, later to write his socially progressive history of *English in America.* Our texts were two books they had jointly put together, the first book I had ever seen on rhetoric or writing, *The Logic and Rhetoric of Exposition,* and an anthology of writing, *Inquiry and Expression.* My fellow teachers were graduate students from various parts of the university, including the law and medical schools. We had weekly meetings to discuss what we were doing, filled with revelations for me. As I write, almost 40 years later, I have the two books in front of me and realize how profound their influence was on everything I have done since. Although I was completing an English doctorate, I knew nothing whatsoever about teaching writing, a condition of English graduate education in literature not much changed now, 40 years later.

I wish I could remember more from the class I taught in the fall of 1958, not least because the FBI recently told me that the serial killer known as the Unabomber was one of my students. I can recall nothing of him, and, happily, he apparently harbored no resentments toward me, but I do remember other students who suffered from my first efforts at teaching. I was trying to put together my identity as a writer with my job as a writing teacher. In the first place, I wrote far too much in the margins of my students' papers, exhorting them to write as I did. In the second place, I had no idea at all of how most students struggle with their writing, so I was mostly puzzled by what I saw on the page and by how I was supposed to respond to it. Remember, I had never taken a college first-year writing course, thanks to Professor Gottlieb, and, like many untrained writing teachers today, was drawing on my high school experience in English classes because all my college work had been in literature, not writing. Thank goodness I had both Martin and Ohmann, the text, as well as Martin and Ohmann, the people, to help me out. But there was no escaping the fact that Harvard then was a hard, structured, and forbidding place, in which we teaching assistants had a clear part to play. Our job was to judge the writing products of our students and to exhort them to write well by explicating model texts from our reader and by pointing out errors in the papers they gave us, hands trembling, every week or so. We were to grade all papers, of course, and to grade the first papers in September with the same rigor we would bring to the last ones in June.

I cringe now as I think of the heartache I brought to my 20 eager freshmen (there was but one woman in the class and she rarely showed up), all high school valedictorians who had never seen a grade below A in their lives. The first set of papers I handed back at the end of class during the second week were all marked D or F, with the exception of two Cs. I saw the stricken faces looking at my diligent and cruel markings, fled to my office, and shut the door. But there was no escape. I opened the door to a hesitant knock and there, neatly lined up, was the entire class, waiting to speak to me.

The first one in was a big blubbery boy who wobbled as he sat in the chair beside my desk. He tried to speak three times, but each time he broke into tears and no words came out. I told him to get on the end of the line outside and I would talk to him later. The second on line was, blessedly, one of the two Cs, a preppy whose jacket cost more than my entire wardrobe. He sat down confidently, pulled out the wing tab of my desk, perched his feet on it, took out his pipe and lit it calmly. "I thought you should know, Mr. White," he said, emphasizing the *Mister*, "that my thought has been formed principally by my intense study of the theology of Paul Tillich." He looked at me for a response.

"A very impressive writer, he is, indeed," I responded. "And a genial host. I had dinner with him last night."

A nice moment, that. As it turned out, my Danforth graduate fellowship included the appointment of a mentor, and mine had turned out to be Tillich. Most of the conversation at dinner had gone well over my head, to be sure, but that didn't matter now. The student's jaw had dropped. I had topped his carefully prepared opening ploy. We started to talk about his paper. He actually had no problems with his grade and just wanted to impress me. He never wavered throughout the entire year, drawing his gentleman's C while the other students wrote better and better and wound up with the top grades they deserved; after all, these were the best students the nation could produce. Neither they nor I imagined that there could be a more humane way to help them than the harsh grading and commentary I inflicted on them.

The following year, as I reflected on my harrowing experiences teaching the first year, I resolved to do things differently. By then I had become the editor of a little graduate student newsletter, and I used that as an excuse to beard in his den Frank Keppel the dean of the Harvard School of Education. He was an imposing man, soon to become Secretary of Health Education and Welfare in the Kennedy administration. He wondered why I had made an appointment to speak with him. My opening was well prepared and, I thought, unanswerable:

"I don't understand why we teaching assistants in Arts and Sciences, just starting out as teachers, don't have any contact with you here in the School of Education," I began. "Don't you have anything to teach us? And if you don't have anything to teach us, why are you here?"

He was not devastated. Actually, he seemed rather amused.

"Are you teaching now?" he asked.

"Yes," I replied.

"So how is it going?"

"Well, it's okay now, but last year was just terrible."

He nodded his head. "So it took you a year to get your feet fixed under you. Not too bad, now is it?"

I tried to recapture the bravado with which I entered the room. "But don't you have something here to teach me that would have made that first year easier?"

"Not really," he said, slowly. "Oh, we could give you a lecture or two on assessment or classroom management, that kind of thing. But the really important learning about teaching you have got to do for yourself."

He went on to tell me that his school of education was there for scholarship, for training of school administrators, for development of policy. Teacher training? He did not really believe in it and thought most of it was a waste of time. Colleagues in the same field serving as mentors—the way Martin and Ohmann were—were the best help for teachers anyone had come up with. He smiled, finally, indicating that we were done. "So find your own way," he said as I left.

"WRITING FOR NOBODY"

After completing my dissertation on Jane Austen at Harvard, I taught for 5 years at Wellesley College. I have written elsewhere about the social and intellectual issues that in retrospect seem important to me from those years, teaching literature and writing to the highly privileged ("Class and Comfort," 1998). I followed the normal pattern for a young English teacher in those days, publishing articles mined from my thesis, doing some bibliographical work on Thackeray with our most noted faculty member (Walter Houghton), and even publishing some fiction. I was a writer, yes, but I was becoming a conventional lit-crit man, one who would turn out slightly original articles and an occasional book giving new readings of the familiar canon. It was hard to be excited about such a future, although it was a comfortable enough prospect, and the fiction could perhaps be an outlet for less conventional leanings. I never for a moment considered composition as a field of study or as a subject for scholarship; hardly anyone did in those days. I needed to move to California for that to happen. As it happened, one day, from distant and unknown San Bernardino came an invitation to apply for a job in a new state college that would open in the fall of 1965. I was immediately struck with the possibility of a different sort of life. Now, when I tell young faculty about my asking permission to leave Wellesley in the middle of a 3-year contract that might have led to tenure, I receive uncomprehending looks. But those were days of plentiful academic jobs, and I never imagined that the situation would change as dramatically and catastrophically as it did soon after I packed up my family to head west. The sheer adventure of opening a new college was particularly attractive, because Wellesley in those days was dominated by a strong, vaguely military group of women who treated all of us younger faculty like irresponsible children. I felt incredibly lucky to have a frontier to conquer, despite its supposed disappearance 50 years earlier.

I have many powerful memories of those Wellesley years—spending afternoons with visiting writers such as Katherine Anne Porter and Eudora Welty, enjoying lunches with creative colleagues such as May Sarton (long before she left the closet) and the poet X. J. Kennedy ("call me Joe"), playing squash rackets with economist Marshall Goldman and Americanist Patrick Quinn, stupidly turning down an invitation from historian Ed Gulick to have dinner with Martin Luther King, Jr., in order to finish grading a set of freshman papers, delighting with my growing family in the serene and lovely campus, and so on. But somehow I knew that I had better move elsewhere. Wellesley was too much like the Bower of Bliss in Book II, Canto XII, of Spenser's *Faerie Queene,* a staple of our survey-of-literature course: too comfortable, too easy, too self-satisfied with its own place in the world.

So I joined 20 interesting faculty and some 200 students for the opening year of what has since become California State University-San Bernardino. I soon became chair of a fledgling English department, but the title was a joke in the first year because we were a department of four, including the dean of humanities and the dean of the college. The teaching of writing was now a major part of our work, and I slowly came to realize how easy and how different that task had been at Wellesley than it was at the state college. It is much easier to teach material and processes to people who already, in some sense, know them to begin with, as the Wellesley students did. The new students I encountered at the state college forced me to rethink what I thought I knew about composition.

For example, there was Hilary, an 18-year-old working-class young woman who saw our new college as the route to a better income. She sat in the back of the room silently as I gave my first assignment and then handed in a page and a half of writing I had never seen the like of before, the kind of error-filled prose that Mina Shaughnessy a decade later would teach us all to learn from. I had no idea what to do with Hilary at our first conference, so I tried suggesting that she take "remedial writing" at the local community college. Through her tears she told me that she had already done that three times and she would rather die than do it again. I was speechless, yet, unschooled in composition though I was, I saw I would need to try something different.

"Tell me," I said gently. "Just tell me what you were saying to me in the first paragraph."

"I checked the spelling twice," she replied, weeping.

"No, forget that. What were you trying to say?"

"Say? What do you mean? Every sentence has a verb."

And then it came to me with blinding clarity: For Hilary, writing was not a means of communication at all, not really connected with learning, and certainly not a way of achieving power. Communication took place face to face or over the telephone. Writing was a teacher's trap, a cruel exercise to expose her inadequacies. As she wrote in a later paper about the purpose of writing, "They make you write so they can *getcha.*" So her job as a writer, as she saw it, was to avoid making errors, and her repeated forays into remedial workbook instruction had solidified that view.

I worked hard with Hilary, who wound up with a C by the end of the term and with some sense that college reading and writing had to do with developing ideas and gaining power over her world. She reminded me in some ways of the Wellesley students I had left behind, although she would have been next to invisible to them: She was intelligent and articulate in person, polite and interested in doing well in school, eager to make a good impression and to get good grades. But the class differences between her and the Wellesley coeds were painfully obvious. Her family was not contributing any money to her college expenses, and she was working 40 hours a week as a checkout clerk to send herself through school. She had never traveled much, except to the nearby beaches and mountains, and books were not part of her life. She spoke in the dialect of the inner city. Her goals were modest: She hoped to get a degree in business and move up to a middle-management job in retailing. Her fiancé was a mechanic, and she knew that she would need to help support the family even after the children came. Martin and Ohmann had not prepared me for Hilary; indeed, nothing I had read or experienced since leaving Brooklyn was much help. Yet she was very important to me, not just because I wanted to help her but because she seemed to symbolize the entire reason the state college existed—to offer to ambitious working-class people some of the opportunities for education that had been reserved for the privileged.

As with the privileged private-college students, writing was a performance for Hilary, but not a performance for which she had been prepared. It was more of an irrational and useless *rite de passage* for her, one of many in a higher education system not really designed for people like her. She was ready to be called "remedial" and to experience repeated failure, but she had a dogged determination that went beyond anything I had seen at Wellesley. My job now was to make writing a meaningful activity for her, if I could, not just a series of conventional motions. Until that happened, and it did, Martin and Ohmann and all my prior experience were of no use at all. I was reading the critic R. P. Blackmur at the time, and I was well aware of his caution (later amplified by Richard Ohmann) that the teaching of "basic skills" can actually give just enough reading and writing ability for a population to be effectively controlled. If all that Hilary took from the composition class was a sense of neatness and linguistic propriety—the goals of "remedial writing" in those days and of too many of its descendants in these—the class would be neither liberal nor educating, merely confirming her class status and helplessness. For these reasons, I tried hard to find ways to convey the sense of power that writers feel. But this was incredibly difficult, for these first-generation students did not think of themselves as writers, nor did they feel any power over their lives. How, I kept asking myself, could we teach writing so that the students would feel the work meaningful and themselves powerful?

And so, all on my own, I came across the oldest idea in rhetoric, that awareness of audience is central to writing. I had, of course, heard of Cicero and Quintilian in my Latin courses, even read bits and pieces of their work. But my first awareness of classical rhetoric still lay years in the future. As was the case for so many of us who stumbled into composition studies, we had to discover for ourselves what we ought to have learned in the course of our studies or our early teaching. My first article on composition was published in *College English* in 1969, a little piece on the bored voice and inattention to tone that made reading freshman writing such a chore. I called the piece "Writing for Nobody" and urged the readers of student writing to give assignments that mattered and to respond in a personal and human way that established a real audience. "Nice article," one of my colleagues said. "It sounds like the introduction to a composition text." Well, I thought, why not? Neither fame nor fortune had yet come my way, but I found myself enjoying the teaching of writing, and I thought I might have something to say about it. A textbook would be a creative way to bring my teaching and writing together.

THE WRITER'S CONTROL OF TONE

The publisher D. C. Heath had put out a series of little paperback books in the 1960s on special subjects for writing courses that I found very attractive. I thought I might add to the series with what we would now call a set of rhetorical categories; at the time, I merely considered them topics for class teaching. In the light of my *College English* article, I thought I could put together a plan for a book to teach the concept of tone, that is, the relation between writer and reader, the necessity for considering audience. A Heath sales representative stopped by my office as I was pondering the idea and seemed very interested in it. He told me he'd be back in 2 days to pick up a prospectus for the book; actually, he suggested, it might even be a small series of books. Then he told me what a prospectus was and what one should look like. That afternoon, I wrote up a three-page plan and gave it to our secretary.

The next morning, a sales representative named Peter Phelps, working for the publisher W. W. Norton, came by to tell me about the forthcoming Norton books for writing courses. As we were talking, my secretary brought in the prospectus and put in it on my desk. Peter immediately perked up. "Looks like a prospectus," he said. "Can I see it?"

I told him I had prepared it for Heath and wasn't sure I should.

"Have you signed a contract with Heath?" he asked.

"No."

"Then why not give us a chance at it?"

I was surprised but pleased. Instead of the publisher doing me a favor by considering my work for publication, I was instead giving this publisher an *opportunity* to publish my work. I liked the change in attitude. Sure, I told Peter, I'll make you a copy. And 2 days later, I had a contract in hand from W. W. Norton to publish the volume on tone, with an option for two more just like it. I called Heath and told the editor I needed an answer within a week, only to find out that it would be months. I told the editor I was signing with Norton. He sighed, saying he wished Heath could make decisions that quickly. (Later on, under editor Paul Smith, they did.)

Peter was promoted to an editorship in New York, in part as a reward for signing me up as a Norton author, and he helped *The Writer's Control of Tone* (as the book became when it appeared in 1970) to be a consistent and handsome volume. The article from *College English* indeed became a major part of the introduction, and the book was a modest success; it sold about 40,000 copies, if I remember correctly, before it went out of print about a decade later. Those were the days of cheap paperbacks, though, and I made about 10 cents a book, so the royalty checks were slim indeed. Nonetheless, I had finally produced my first book. The shiver of pleasure that went through me when I walked into class in 1970 and saw an entire class with my book in hand was a clear echo of what I felt at age 13.

The tone book had a focused curriculum: It sought to help students gain control over the relationship of writer to reader using personal-experience materials. The second book in the series was trickier: It sought to teach students to analyze texts by reading popular-culture material critically. I wanted to call it *The Writer's Control of Analysis* because I saw it from a curricular angle. Peter, on the other hand, saw it as a collection of readings on popular culture and saw that as its central concept. He wanted to call the book *Popular Culture* and give it a garish cover of hot yellow and bright red lettering on a black background. Naturally enough, we could not agree on a title, even as the publication date drew near. Finally, he called me and, cordial as ever, pointed out that in cases of disagreement our contract specified that the publisher would decide on the title. "We're going to call the book *Pop Culture*," he said, "unless we come up with something better before closing time today."

"But don't you see," I argued, for the hundredth time, "It's not about pop culture. It's about the whole tradition of pop culture and how it conveys a set of values."

Peter paused, anxious to leave his New York office. "Well, then, how about *The Pop Culture Tradition*?"

It was the best idea yet. The book, garish cover and all, came out in 1972 and is still in print as of this writing. It sold one copy last year.

INSTANT SOPHOMORES

I had almost finished my third small textbook for Norton when events moved me from my obscurity in San Bernardino onto a much larger stage. The multicampus institution now called the California State University (CSU) had emerged as a result of the California Master Plan for Higher Education, a grand design that saw higher education as a three-tiered structure. At the top was the richly funded University of California (UC) with its nine campuses, Research I institutions all, focusing on graduate education and the doctorate. On the bottom tier were the community colleges, over 100 of them, offering the first 2 years of higher education at a cut-rate price, giving the opportunity (sometimes the illusion of opportunity) to many who could not afford or not qualify for 4-year institutions. The middle tier was CSU with (then) 19 campuses (now 23), appropriately nicknamed "the people's university." CSU campuses accepted the top one third of high school graduates (as opposed to the top one eighth at the UC), had roughly a third of a million students, and awarded more master's degrees and teaching credentials than any other institution in the country. Occupying the middle position has caused and still causes all kinds of organizational problems for CSU, most particularly with funding, which is considerably lower per student than it is at UC. Faculty have a particularly uncomfortable position, because the teaching load is very high, virtually full-time work in itself, yet professional activities such as research and publication are normally expected despite lack of support funds or time. Nonetheless, the faculty are often serious teachers and scholars, and the CSU administration is forever seeking to make its mark in a world that pays it scant attention. Unfortunately, the almost unblemished record of clumsiness on the part of the central administration—unblemished to this day—has diminished its attempts to be educational leaders.

In the summer of 1971, CSU system administrators, with typical wisdom and foresight, became confident that a great faculty shortage lay ahead and decided to press for credit by examination, that is, to allow students on a large scale to "test out" of required course work. For the tests, the administrators turned to the Educational Testing Service, which delivered a series of shoddy examinations that two campus presidents agreed to accept as valid for all general education work. It apparently never occurred to the system administrators or to the presidents of San Francisco State or California State University-Bakersfield, to mention this undercover move to the faculty, although it was well publicized to incoming freshmen. Some of us on the faculty did, however, get to see the short and simple multiple-choice exams that were creating hordes of what the newspapers came to call "instant sophomores" out of a bemused freshman class. We were outraged. We were used to foolishness from our chancellor's office, but this was an out-and-out betrayal of higher education itself.

The chairs of CSU English departments did, however, meet and know each other. This was a time for us, as teachers and writers, to exert some power. I had been writing book reviews for the *Los Angeles Times,* and others of us had been working for various San Francisco newspapers. It was easy for us to call our newspapers' attention to the degradation of standards the tests represented, particularly when we pointed out that students were receiving a full year's worth of credit for freshman composition by passing a test that called for neither reading nor writing. Under such circumstances, journalists—as writers—became our allies. We agreed unanimously to a resolution, duly reported in the press, expressing our shock (or was it outrage? I do recall a long debate over which word was best) over the situation.

That resolution was, however, diplomatic enough to give the chancellor an easy way to retreat, and he took it with pained sighs of relief. We accepted the premise that some entering students might already know what we teach in our first-year composition courses, but we argued that the faculty should be in control of assessment and the awarding of college credit. The administration agreed to drop the testing fiasco and, instead, to fund the development of a system-wide examination run by the faculty to award credit for qualified students. There was no time to savor our victory, although it did remind me of what occurred at NYU 15 years earlier. We now had to make good on our rash proposal that we were the ones to assess whether entering students knew what we had to teach. I remember well the sinking feeling I had as all eyes at an executive committee meeting of our English Council turned to me. None of us knew anything at all about assessment, but I had been guilty of publishing textbooks in composition—an activity as strange for the chair of an English department in those days (or, indeed, these) as showing a professional interest in janitorial services. I might be ignorant of assessment, as we all were, but I could learn because I had demonstrated interest in writing as a study. I grudgingly agreed to produce a report on assessment of writing, figuring that in 6 months I would be back to my usual writing and teaching. None of us even dimly suspected that composition studies was in the process of being born, that the report I finished in the summer of 1972 would launch me into the middle of these new developments in English studies, as well as into the middle of our chancellor's office, or that my teaching and writing would take a wholly new direction.

ASSESSMENT OF WRITING

The major issue in writing assessment, I soon discovered, was the place of multiple-choice tests, the fill-in-the-bubble tests that dominated all testing in those days and that even today remain the dominant force in all American assessment of students. As a writer, I had no question about where such tests belonged: in the trash. It was obvious that the activity of mind called for by a multiple-choice test has very little to do with what a writer does putting words on a page. But I needed to put my own views aside for a bit to find out what was known in the world of writing assessment. I found precious little, almost all of it dealing with young schoolchildren. But I did discover why so little writing was going on during writing tests: Work was just beginning on ways to score the writing consistently and fairly.

I have written at some length about the development of holistic scoring and my role in the rapid acceptance of essay testing once reliable and economical scoring became practical (see my *Teaching and Assessing Writing*, 1994, particularly chapter 13). The first edition of that book, based on my experience developing and administering several statewide writing testing programs, appeared in 1985, and it was widely and favorably reviewed as the first real guide to direct writing assessment. I was, for the first few years after my appointment as a test administrator, only an "expert" by appointment, but as time went on I learned enough about the practical and then the theoretical aspects of assessment to give workshops at scores of campuses all over the country. I found to my surprise that I was expected to be an expert not only on writing assessment but also on the other emerging issues in composition studies: writing across the curriculum, writing research, teacher training, and the relation between literary theories and composition studies. As I discovered more and more about this new field, I began writing about it, and the writing helped me find out yet more.

I discovered the Council of Writing Program Administrators (WPA) in the course of applying for and then writing about a research project that was funded in 1980 by the (then) National Institute of Education. I had become curious about the place of writing programs in higher education and about the relation of a collegiate writing program to the writing ability of students on campus. The 5-year research project used the CSU as its sample and sought correlations between student writing performance at the end of the first year with the kind of writing programs that each CSU campus had in place. As we developed findings, we published them in the WPA journal, and I began to attend meetings of this relatively specialized group—as it happens, the principal researchers and thinkers in composition studies. Thinking of this group as audience, I published a book on writing programs that appeared in 1989: *Developing Successful College Writing Programs.* I had noticed that most university administrators and faculty considered their campus writing program as consisting of only a first-year composition course. But my campus visits, including program evaluations, had convinced me that virtually every institution of higher education had a wide-ranging but unrecognized writing program that went well beyond that course: a system of assessment that could include preenrollment placement or equivalency and extend to graduation certification; support services, including tutoring in a writing center and in special enrollment student services; some variation of writing across the curriculum involving faculty development and upper-division writing courses in the disciplines; and so on. The president of the WPA at that time, Lynn Z. Bloom, a professor at the University of Connecticut, then asked me to administer one of the important WPA programs, a con-sultant-evaluator service for campuses, a most interesting coordinating job that I pursued for the next 6 years.

Meanwhile, my home campus, in an act showing real foresight, had established a master's degree program in English composition, a carefully designed program that immediately attracted a substantial enrollment. I be-gan devoting most of my teaching energy to this new program, developing courses in literary theory for writers, writing research, and writing assessment. The first time I taught a course in writing assessment, I called William Lutz at Rutgers University for help in picking the required reading.

"I'm embarrassed to be using so much of my own writing," I told him. "What do you use?" Lutz had administered the New Jersey assessment program at the same time I was responsible for the CSU program; we had come to know and like each other and had combined to give a number of workshops. A *College English* interview in the mid-1970s had identified us as leaders of the new field of composition studies. He laughed out loud at my question.

"Everyone else uses your books," he said. "They're the only ones *to* use. I don't know how you could teach the course without them."

LOOKING FORWARD

Writers control their reality by shaping the past, as I have said; they also have a hand in shaping the future, at the very least their own future. One taste of that future came from editing and contributing to a volume of essays by leaders in the field, *Composition in the Twenty-First Century: Crisis and Change*. The volume emerged from a WPA conference organized by my two coeditors, Don Daiker and Lynn Bloom, and its vision of the future of composition studies is, well, mixed. All of higher education faces an uncertain future, and composition studies may save English departments or may disappear along with English departments. Perhaps I had a clearer view of the future when I agreed to teach a graduate seminar in writing assessment for advanced graduate students at the University of Arizona in 1994. Because I would be commuting from California, close to half of my instructional time would be spent on the computer.

I found the experience exhilarating. The students were excellent, and as a group we worked out the place of computer conferencing in the course; it was a powerful supplement to instruction, but only a supplement. I wrote a cautionary article about the experience for the "distance learning" issue of the *American Association for Higher Education Bulletin* ("New Bytes"). We should welcome the support of technology, I argued there, but we should not imagine that technology can replace the human interaction of student with teacher. Clearly, writing will continue to grow as an essential subdiscipline within (or even outside of) English departments, and, just as clearly, writing instruction will be profoundly affected by technology, as well as by the shifting demographics of undergraduate students. But in another sense, the writer must never forget the real human reader who, whatever machinery may intervene, is the audience for the writing. The power of the writer is the ability to shape reality by affecting the perceptions of a reader, not merely to order machinery about.

I elected early retirement, imagining that I could at last become a full-time writer. But the pleasure of teaching was in my blood. The CSU has a special option called the Faculty Early Retirement Program, which allows retired folk to continue to teach part time for 5 years while receiving their pensions. How could I resist? In addition, I have begun teaching extraordinary students in the doctoral program in Rhetoric, Composition, and the Teaching of English at the University of Arizona, in company with a congenial and creative faculty. Meanwhile, writing projects extend a decade or more into the future: a second edition of the writing textbook *Inquiry,* which Lynn Bloom and I edited in 1993; another text in early draft patiently awaited by Prentice-Hall; another WPA conference to become a book (tentatively titled *Composition 2001*); and perhaps an extension of this self-indulgent memoir into a book of its own. I am charmed by Lynn Bloom's fancy that as long as a book is under contract, one cannot die; a writer's recipe for immortality indeed.

As I reflect on the professional life sketched here, I am struck at my repeated references to good luck and happy accidents. In a sense, those are the right terms for the unexpected confluence of my life as a writer and teacher and the growth of composition studies. But in another sense, everything was set up by my realization at the age of 13 that I was a writer. That realization, along with the sense of power it gave me, allowed me not only to go with the flow, as we say in California, but also to seize the moment and make it run. We sometimes speak of our goal as teachers of writing to "empower" our students. The metaphor works for me, since it is writing that lets us shape the flux of incident into a coherent and meaningful reality. I was empowered early on, and the joy that came with the sense of power has never faded; indeed, it continues to grow. If composition studies maintains that goal, it must thrive in a future that threatens to diminish our humanity and our control of our lives. The more we can help our students see themselves as writers, the more they will be able to stand fast and assert the power of language to resist foolish authorities and to give meaning to their own experience. I see this as the central thread of my own life, so naturally I declare it the worthiest of goals for our field of study.

San Bernardino, California
May 7, 1997

WORKS CITED

Bloom, Lynn Z., and Donald A. Daiker, and Edward M. White, eds. *Composition in the Twenty-First Century: Crisis and Change.* Carbondale: Southern Illinois UP, 1996.

Bloom, Lynn Z., and Edward M. White, eds. *Inquiry: A Cross-Curricular Reader.* Englewood Cliffs, NJ: Prentice-Hall, 1993.

Martin, Harold C., and Richard Ohmann, eds. *Inquiry and Expression.* New York: Holt, Rinehart & Winston, 1963.

Martin, Harold C., and Richard M. Ohmann. *The Logic and Rhetoric of Exposition.* New York: Holt, Rinehart & Winston, 1964.

White, Edward M. "Class and Comfort: The Slums and the Greens." In *Coming to Class: Pedagogy and the Social Class of Teachers.* John McMillan, Alan Shepard, and Gary Tate, eds. Portsmouth, NH: Boynton-Cook-Heinemann (1998): 283-95.

White, Edward M. *Developing Successful College Writing Programs.* San Francisco: Jossey-Bass, 1989.

White, Edward M. "New Bytes Need New Bottles: Fitting the Computer Into the Curriculum." *AAHE Bulletin* 48.4 (1995): 11-14.

White, Edward M. *Teaching and Assessing Writing: Understanding, Evaluating, and Improving Student Performance.* San Francisco: Jossey-Bass, 1985. Revised and expanded edition, 1994.

White, Edward M. *The Pop Culture Tradition.* New York: Norton, 1972.

White, Edward M. *The Writer's Control of Tone.* New York: Norton, 1970.

White, Edward M. "Writing for Nobody." *College English* 31 (1969): 166-68.

CHAPTER EIGHTEEN

The Long Look Back

Winifred Bryan Horner
Texas Christian University

I am not certain just where my fascination with language began. Perhaps it started with my climb into my brothers' treehouse at our family's summer place in the Missouri Ozarks to lose myself in a book. Perhaps it began with my mother's reading Dickens aloud to us—always with a dictionary at her side, which we consulted frequently. Perhaps it began with the quarter I won for the best essay on storms in the third grade. But I do know that language in all its mystery and power has been one of my enduring interests for as long as I can remember.

I grew up in St. Louis with three older brothers and spent the summers reading and writing bad poetry in the cabin on the Meramec River that my parents bought with the Horner family as a summer retreat from the city. There were four boys in the Horner family, one of whom I later married, so in effect I spent a good part of my life with seven older brothers. Our principal leisure activity was reading; our main aquatic sport was trying to drown each other in the river. They used to duck me under the water and then pull me up by the hair to see if I was still breathing. I did plenty of ducking in return, but I was at a disadvantage because I couldn't grasp their hair as they did mine. As a result, along with my love of language, I grew up with a fierce sense of competition, a deep-seated survival instinct, and a fervent desire to be in the swim.

My husband shared my interest in language and always encouraged me to continue my reading and writing. On the first day in our first apartment, I had spent the day washing our clothes and most of the afternoon carefully ironing his undershirts, T-shirts, undershorts, and socks. That night at dinner he asked me what I had been doing that day. "Well," I replied, "I ironed your underwear, and I had to dampen those cotton socks before I could get them to come out smooth." He looked at me thoughtfully and then said very seriously, "Tomorrow, why don't you read a book and write something and then let's talk about that at dinner." I have been reading books and writing ever since.

After World War II, I settled in to bake and cook and have babies, just as Betty Friedan described. After 12 years of married life and 4 children, I supplemented our income by doing the only thing that I knew how to do from my home. I did freelance writing. I had two ways of getting my reading and writing done. Whenever I sat down, the children thought I was a reading machine, and they would present me with five or six books, so I did much of my writing standing up at the buffet in the dining room. I finally invested in a playpen, so my 2-year-old was at least slightly contained. That worked all right until the 4-year-old cried because he wanted to get in the playpen as well. Finally, I put myself, my typewriter, and my books in the playpen and gave the children the run of the house. I did manage to achieve some very modest fame in our local community by selling a few articles, but after four children I decided that there had to be more in life than smelly diapers, crying babies, and dirty dishes.

One night, I met the professor who was head of the freshman English program at the University of Missouri. Over cocktails, he suddenly asked me if I liked students. Of course I liked students. "I would like to talk to you about doing some teaching for us." It took me some time to think that one over—about 2 years, as a matter of fact. I still had difficulty doing much thinking outside of the playpen, but in due time I went in to see him at the university.

He looked at me in complete bewilderment. It was obvious that he had no idea who I was. He had completely forgotten our conversation of 2 years ago that had sustained me through so many hours in the playpen.

"But we never hire anyone for teaching freshman comp unless they have a master's degree."

I remember my first trip to the library after I started my master's degree. I stood in amazement in this huge building watching all of the young students rushing around, knowing just where to go and just what to do. I was 40 years old, and I was terrified. Home and the playpen were so much safer. But I learned that day something that I have not forgotten. Most new and unexplored territory is frightening, but it is the only way I know to break the barriers of your mind, to expand your world. It was the beginning of my academic career—as a part-time temporary adjunct faculty, which was the appointment I received when I completed my master's degree.

I learned a lot in those early years of teaching freshman English. In my first semester, I taught a class in the chemistry building in a room that had seats in a stepped incline and a raised platform on which I stood. The room was always cold where I stood and warm toward the back, and usually the back two rows were sound asleep before the hour was over. One day, it was obvious from the discussion that none of the students had read the assignment. As a new teacher, I was determined to make an impression and to wake up the back rows. I announced with authority that I intended to walk out and that while I was gone they were to read the assignment. I slammed my book shut, gathered up my papers, strode across the platform, and stepped down—into the wastebasket. My foot was irrevocably stuck. I had two options: I could take my shoe off and limp out with one foot bare or drag the wastebasket with me. It was a sobering moment for a new teacher. I never taught from a raised platform again—either literally or metaphorically.

Several weeks later in the same class, I opened my textbook and realized that I had prepared the wrong material—I had not done the assigned reading. I tried to decide whether to bluff it through or to admit my mistake. I had learned something from wastebaskets about humility, so I told my students what had happened. "So you must tell me what the assignment was about." And they did, discussing and arguing about the main points and the structure of the argument and why they agreed or disagreed with the thesis. It was the best class that we had all semester. From that day, I learned to listen and learn from my students.

I continued teaching, working my way into a full-time position, continuing my writing, until I was awarded tenure some years later. At that time, it was assumed that because I knew how to write, I would automatically know how to teach it. That was a mistake. I was a good teacher, but most of what I knew about teaching writing I had learned from current textbooks (an idea that makes me shudder now) and from my own experience—not always bad, but not good enough. In a way, I had come to the end of my knowledge, and I was painfully aware of it.

I continued reading and writing. My early writing had been about my children. I remember one article that I wrote about how to work with a 2-year-old—I wrote it while my own 2-year-old was noisily destroying the house. But after the children started to read, I had to stop writing about them. They were embarrassed. So the subject of my writing shifted as my interests changed. But beyond my children and the daily routine, I had no real subject.

Twelve years later, our youngest son went to the university. With three children in college and one married, I thought my time had come. I wanted to go back to school. I didn't have to—my position was secure—but what really drove me was that I wanted to learn more about how to teach writing, how people interact through language, how language reflects our culture and empowers us as human beings.

At the time, I couldn't put a name to my interest. I tried linguistics, but that seemed too narrow; I tried literary criticism, but that seemed too vague.

Then a friend in the speech department remarked offhandedly, "Oh, you mean rhetoric!" And, of course, she was right. I had one colleague in the English department who had gone to graduate school with Richard Young and Pete Becker, and he suggested that I read *Rhetoric: Discovery and Change,* which they had coauthored with Kenneth Pike (New York: Harcourt, Brace & World, 1970). I telephoned Richard Young, and we talked for almost an hour and a half. It was the combination of linguistics and rhetoric in that book that gave me my first insight into the nature of language—but I wanted more. At that time, there were no graduate programs in rhetoric; but at the age of 50, I entered the University of Michigan program, where, with the help and advice of Richard Young, I embarked on an interdisciplinary program in linguistics and English-language. I enrolled in courses in the speech department, the linguistics department, and the English-language program. I took my first rhetoric course from Rich Enos and discovered that what I lacked in youthful agility of mind was made up for by the kind of discipline forged through the everyday tasks of raising a family and holding a job and just having lived a little longer.

For me, those studies opened a new and wonderful world. I learned the power of language, how relationships are defined by titles—the difference between introducing myself as Dr. Horner or Professor Horner or Win Horner or Win—how language has sexualized women with terms like *mistress, madame,* and *professional.* One of the worst put-downs among teenage boys is to call another boy "a woman." I learned how language can trivialize by calling a Black man "boy" or women "girls" or men "boys." "What are you boys planning to do this afternoon?" Can you imagine addressing that remark to a group of men going into an important business meeting? I learned that language can be a powerful weapon used to include or exclude and that in teaching students how to use language, I was empowering them. I read and studied the great treatises on rhetoric that Aristotle defined as the art of persuasion. I studied Aristotle, Cicero, Quintilian; I read lectures on rhetoric by Joseph Priestley and Adam Smith, and I learned how to mount a logical argument and how to shape a treatise for a particular audience, to first gain their goodwill, and above all to establish my credibility. And I thought finally that I was going to learn all about how language worked. Then I discovered that all my reading had only taught me just how much I did not know. I enrolled in graduate school to find answers; what I found instead were more questions—a discovery that may be the beginning of real knowledge.

But aside from Dick Young and Rich Enos, I did not know any other students of rhetoric in my discipline of English. As far as I knew, there were just the three of us. There was one graduate student, Jim Zappen, who was interested, and we used to eat our lunchtime sandwiches together and talk rhetoric. That made four of us. At about that time, I went to Modern Language Association (MLA) conference and was excited to read about a meeting of the Rhetoric Society. When I inquired about the location, I was told that I needed to ask Win Horner—that she would probably know. When I finally located the meeting, there was only a handful in attendance, but I sat next to Ed Corbett and we talked. Now there were five of us. It was a small but exciting group. Things were looking up.

I was more than 50 years old when I walked across the stage and received my doctorate. It was the end of examinations, but it was only the beginning of paper deadlines. It was only the beginning of my reading, the beginning of my language studies. Today I continue to read; I continue to question. My dissertation was on speech act theory, so I felt that there was still much for me to learn about rhetoric. My first publication was a bibliography on rhetoric, which gave me an opportunity to read all that I had not had time for in graduate school. I continue to learn by listening to my students, my colleagues, and my friends. I continue to read in order to write so that I can join in the conversation of scholarship around the world. I wanted to be a part of the growing community of scholars who, like me, wanted to know how we use language and how it uses us.

Today we are in a language revolution—we used to think that it was quaint that Aristotle thought delivery of an oration was the most important element of a speech and that Quintilian spent five pages on how best to drape the toga when arguing a case in front of the Roman senate. But in an electronic world, delivery has taken on new importance. In the presidential debates, points were won and lost on the color of the tie, the cut of the hair, the slope of the shoulders. Newscasters noticeably shuffle and stack their papers at the conclusion of a broadcast, even though every word they utter is written on the TelePrompTer in front of them, out of view of the TV audience. The stack of papers that they handle might just as well contain a grocery list or a letter to a friend. Cicero told us that the rhetorician needed to know everything, but he couldn't have envisioned a world where information on anything and everything is at our fingertips. What we need today is a defensive rhetoric, to understand the electronic tricks of TV advertising, to judge political reasoning, to evaluate information on the World Wide Web.

That is what I study today—that is what I try to teach—how to use language and how not to be used by the language of others. Today we know more about language, but the questions are still there. Today there is an army of scholars in departments of English studying rhetoric and composition, where at the beginning there were so pitiably few. Today I am engaged in that continuing quest to know more about language, to understand better. But today there are many voices out there, and it is no longer a lonely endeavor.

Columbia, Missouri
May 3, 1997

CHAPTER NINETEEN

Have Rhetoric, Will Travel

Stuart C. Brown
New Mexico State University

*I can do you blood and love without the rhetoric, and
I can do you blood and rhetoric without the love and I
can do you all three concurrent or consecutive but I
can't do you love and rhetoric without the blood.*
　　　—Tom Stoppard (*Rosencrantz and Guildenstern Are Dead*)

SUMMER

Eight mule deer crowd around the molasses block in the yard. From the front deck of our cabin, I watch a big doe rear up on her hind legs and kick the others away.

On a hike up Graveyard Canyon, I look at elk track, trying to distinguish them and their scat from deer and open range cattle grazing the Lincoln National Forest. A bear print is fresh enough to have the morning's rain still in it. Wildflower and bird books weight the day pack. Maps are stuffed in the side pocket. I wear a T-shirt that has an illustration of the Milky Way galaxy and an arrow pointing to a tiny dot labeled "You Are Here."

This is the summer of my sabbatical. I am reading the rhetoric of a different world. I do not think much about the academy I have left behind for the next year until a friend sends the Loeb Quintilian, the four volumes found in a used bookstore. Cicero's *Rhetorica ad Herennium* comes as a bonus. Deep in New Mexico's Sacramento Mountains, I am surrounded by

50 square miles of forest and canyonlands cut with logging roads and an occasional ranch. Other than in the dictionaries found among the 200 or so residents of my small community, *rhetoric* is a missing term.

Browsing the Loeb, I am drawn to the passage "From the discussion of our own person we shall secure goodwill by praising our services without arrogance and revealing also our past conduct . . ." (*ad Herennium*, I.v.8, 15). I think about my contribution to this collection and what goodwill, reader, you are expected to carry away with you. I write this chapter knowing the august company it joins. Many of the contributors to this collection formed my education in rhetoric. I read them in graduate school at the University of Arizona. Some visited campus, putting faces and voices to the words I read in courses, in the library, in the books gathered. I still learn from them. They and others are too many to name.

But I am reminded of debts. With Duane Roen's guidance, I began attending and presenting papers at the Arizona English Teachers Conference and, in 1986, the Conference on College Composition and Communication (CCCC). (Last year, Duane came up after a presentation and remarked, "You've gotten a lot better; I remember when you first started giving papers, and you were terrible.") Charles Davis, then director of composition, opened windows of experience into the role of the administrator, deeply embedding in my mind his philosophy of the centrality of a writing program in a university and of the high mission such a program could accomplish. A couple of years later, Theresa Enos introduced me to the difficult and too often thankless task of editing one of the best journals in the field. Both she and Duane have been and remain role models as teachers, scholars, and members of the profession. In 1990, Bill Bridges at New Mexico State University took on a freshly minted doctoral recipient, hiring me for their then-new doctoral program in rhetoric and professional communication. Reed Dasenbrock, 5 years later, would shepherd me through the tenure process. I could not have had better mentors or a better apprenticeship. Along the way, I fed on rhetoric, intellectual sustenance in sips here and gulps there.

AUTUMN

I had no plan for a career, much less in the academy, much less in rhetoric. With an undergraduate degree in English, I had flirted with going to law school, been a financial analyst in the health care and education division of the largest appraisal firm in the world, managed the business side of a heavy-duty truck parts company, and restored historic houses. Rhetoric happened as a happy accident while I was teaching freshman composition and pursuing a master's in fine arts degree in creative writing. One summer, the essayist Nancy Mairs took me on as a "student teacher" in a technical writing class and opened a whole new dimension to the teaching of writing. Now, after 8 years of graduate school, two terminal degrees, and 6 years of being a faculty member, I have a career, but I am still not sure I have a plan.

Fifteen miles away as the raven flies is the National Solar Observatory at Sunspot. I pass by it on the 1½-hour trip to town for groceries. A graduate of our master's program with emphasis in technical writing works there. She makes me think of the places rhetoric has taken me. For the past 5 years, I held a course release time to work with the Center for Economic Development and Research Assistance (CEDRA) at New Mexico State University; in this capacity, I traveled to the Navajo and the Jicarilla Apache reservations, to Teseque, Pojoaque, Santa Clara, and Laguna Pueblos doing workshops and writing proposals, feasibility studies, and market analyses. CEDRA also took me to Sandia National Laboratories, where I studied corporate culture, developed market research for waste management technology, and researched software feasibility. I worked with the city of Las Cruces, with local businesses, and with agencies in the state government. Applied rhetoric.

Here in the high country, however, I discover I am at a loss trying to explain what rhetoric is, what I do for a living, to a new friend who is the deputy sheriff here. I talk about the *lingua franca* of police work, the rhetorical nature of his job; he goes away puzzled. I work with a cabinet-maker and with a plumber, apprenticing in trades that roughen my language as much as they callus my hands. We do not talk much about my other life. I'm introduced as the English teacher, the Piled Higher and Deeper Professor, Mr. Peabody from the *Rocky and Bullwinkle* cartoons. I am told a joke: A new employee arrives to work in a hardware store. He is told to sweep the storeroom. He protests, "But I have a college degree." "Then," replies his boss. "Let's start with the basics; this is a broom." My life at the university, the study of rhetoric, is a mystery to these people, even as they welcome me into their own professions, their community.

I once began a course on modern rhetorical theory with the question, "What is rhetoric?"; my final exam was one question: "What is rhetoric?" I got back almost unanimously, "It's all rhetoric," and was pleased. In retrospect, I wonder if I failed, reading Quintilian's admonishment: "It will be, however, the duty of the rhetorician not merely to teach these things, but to ask frequent questions as well, and test the critical powers of his class" (Loeb, Book II, v. 13). Have I asked enough questions of myself as I profess rhetoric?

I see myself as a "second-generation rhetorician," one trained by rhetoricians imbued with both the history of rhetoric and the rich flowering of the profession in the 1970s and 1980s. A generalist in an age of specialists. I remind myself how lucky I have been. To find the right teachers, to hit the job market at its peak, to go where I wanted and do well there, teaching what I wanted, publishing, making a good living, the days begun early and finished late. I admit to a certain unease now. I study doctoral programs in rhetoric and composition, the job market, the perception of faculty in the world outside the university. Programs have proliferated. Journals and books arrive faster than one can keep up with. A recent CCCC program guide reveals that the field keeps growing both in size and the scope of its concerns.

Each month I come down from the mountains and return to the university to meet with students working on dissertations, preparing for exams, planning course work. I pick up mail, professional journals, a month's worth of the *Chronicle of Higher Education*; I catch up on department doings and the grinding machinations of the university, the gossip. Each time I am reminded of the profession and my concerns for it. Anne Berthoff, gracefully declining my pestering requests to contribute to this collection, reminds me, "Don't sugarcoat things." In my files I find the following list of "worries":

- The lack of undergraduate programs in rhetoric and composition.
- The failure of the profession to reach outside the academy (although there are some efforts with adult and workplace literacy programs).
- The continuing battles with literary studies over ideologies and resources.
- Despite the efforts of the Council of Writing Program Administrators (WPA), the lack of professionalization at many schools in their writing programs and by their administrators.
- Graduate students who are entering the profession because of the perception that jobs are plentiful (and some who enter the profession but would really rather be doing other things).
- The continuing (and increasing) uses and abuses of part-time instructors of writing.
- The seeming disjunction or even competitiveness among historians, theorists, and practitioners.
- The inclination toward narrow scholarly specialization and the danger of reductionism.

I read in the *Chronicle* about universities now being seen as "mature industries" after years of growth. Is rhetoric as a discipline following the same cycle? How will rhetoric be positioned in an academy now sorting out resource allocation and mounting pressures for accountability?

WINTER

In the journal I keep—my wife teases about the *New Yorker* cartoon she found with the balloon "Dear Diary, sorry to bother you"—rhetoric is notably absent, filled rather with the doings of the natural world and the people of this small community and the new skills I am acquiring. I learn to read the grain of various wood, to lay waterpipe so it won't freeze, and to study flame in a furnace. I join the volunteer fire department and write for the monthly newspaper. I encounter people scrabbling for next month's rent or scamming to fill the propane tank this month. I see some of the rhetorics here, but they seem remote from what I profess. I mull over these rhetorics and their relation to the ones I put before my students in Las Cruces.

Winter has set in. The wood stove spits and flares as it consumes alligator juniper, pinyon, and pine. Each morning I break ice off the water trough for the deer. I set out corn for them and keep the bird feeder full for Steller's and pinyon jays, nuthatches, finches, and grosbeaks. Each night, a gang of raccoons comes like thieves to raid the dog food bins on the back porch. I keep an eye (and ear) out for a large bobcat that has taken up residence nearby.

In the previous year, I was promoted and tenured. I still taste the blood. The scrutiny and evaluation and summation of what I have done and who I have been. Not to mislead you—I had no problems; my department was as humane and fair as anyone could ask. But I see the vita materials accumulated in two milk crates sitting like a Gorgon in my office at school. Years of courses taught, writings published, reports produced. My academic life fixed on page after page after page.

The files contain, in retrospect, a bewildering variety of inquiries. In two collections of essays coedited with Theresa Enos, we tried to come to terms with what rhetoric is, to present rhetoric in all of its plurality. In another collection of essays coedited with Carl Herndl, we provided inquiries into the many rhetorics of environmentalism. In two textbooks coauthored with Duane Roen and Robert Mittan, we presented material to engage students in writing across the curriculum. I would sit on panels at CCCC with James Berlin, Anne Berthoff, Wayne Booth, Jim Corder, Jimmie Killingsworth, Janice Lauer, James Murphy, and Richard Young, starstruck and in awe. I have studied the rhetoric of cartoons, the nature writings of Joseph Wood Krutch, the rhetorical techniques of direct mail solicitations, the rhetorical theories of George Campbell and I. A. Richards, and the interplay of ethos and ethics in technical writing. From where I write now, I see a copy paper box overflowing with projects underway and speculations that may never go anywhere.

My department head calls. It is January. He is asking for my fall teaching requests. Sabbatical is half gone. I mull over the last 6 years of courses taught. Composition and technical writing and business communication. Children's literature and southwestern literature and environmental rhetoric. The graduate seminars in rhetorical criticism, ethics and ethos, nature writing, history of rhetoric, computers and writing, document design, research methods in composition, and others. Another bewildering variety.

I remember past students and what I have done, and not done, to them. Some are more haunting than others. In the introductory course to graduate studies in English that I teach often, I assign entering graduate students to imagine a "day in the life of" one of their professors. One returned with a portrait of leisurely coffee and croissants, a late-morning bicycle ride to campus in a tweed jacket, intensely intellectual (but amiable) conversations with colleagues before going off to teach students who are lively and engaged and prepared. Reading this aloud to our class, she stopped mid-paragraph and began to laugh at her naiveté. But tears lay under that laugh, and she would leave the master's program the next semester, returning to the life of an investment counselor.

I study the clear, cold night and find stars one can only find at an altitude of 8,000 feet. Part way through this chapter, I falter, dry up in confusion about its progress, its aim. I give it to my wife, who returns it with the following comment.

> *S.,*
>
> The tone of the piece is good, and the occasional inclusions of natural descriptions are well done. I'm not sure what the focus is, however, and this is because I'm getting a lot of different "feints" that don't seem to deliver. You've isolated different worlds and experience—your own as a graduate student new to the discipline, the quotidian experiences of academic life, and the intended contrast to the natural world and to Timberon's human communities. I think you need to choose which of these "new" rhetorics you are most intrigued by (and which of them will most intrigue a reader), and to use that central metaphor as a way to reexamine what rhetoric does in the world.
>
> I'd suggest you look more often at the natural world as one made up of different communication systems—ones that are largely closed to you—that you can only interpret. In other words, we "read" the tracks of animals, but those markers are not left for us to read. And there is a great deal of that system we cannot even interpret—scent markers for example—because we haven't the "equipment."
>
> Your use of Quintilian seems to indicate that there are questions of contemporary rhetoric's usefulness in the larger world that you feel are as important now as they were to the very different world of the Roman citizen. Perhaps, if you want to explore what "citizenship" is in the larger republic of the natural world (and this would use your descriptive talents as well as tie in with the Green Culture book), that would be a better approach. I really don't think the academic stuff serves to engage the reader—it sounds like a prose *vita*. You could still use some of the work experience you're having here to illustrate the "natural citizen" approach, but instead of going into details of how work operates, use examples of how these kinds of work position the individual within the natural world—explore the many contradictions of those conflicting experiences. In other words, though we can see the beauty of creating a pine bookcase, and the skill, what about the beauty of the wood (trees) used to make it? How and why do trees become "lumber,"

just as individual species of animals become "pork" instead of pig, "venison" instead of deer? Explain the defensive postures the woodworker has about the spotted owls—how does this contrast with his interests in preserving nature, and how might a rhetorical approach to this conflict be of some value? What I'm suggesting is that, whether or not your rhetorical approach to "conflict resolution" between the human and natural worlds gives you the results you hope for in this specific environment, there may be some benefits in the long run. What, for instance, does it do to change your idea of rhetoric's possible mission (connect with Charles Davis' work with writing programs, or the CEDRA work with Native Americans, and so on) to see the natural communication complex as closed systems to which you can, nonetheless, bring some mission of interpretation and activity? Explain the plan for the Timberon nature preserve, for an example. Anyway, that's all I can think of so far.

My wife is a wise and perceptive reader, one whose advice I usually follow. Her comments here have given me much to consider. But in this case I am not sure I have a straight story to tell, that following a focus is apt here. I find only anecdotes and ellipses at this point in my career, pebbles and tufts of grasses and seedling trees that do not yet form a landscape.

SPRING

Spring is coming to the high country, and this chapter is late. The 1997 CCCC in Phoenix is next week, and I will miss it and the many people I have come to know who gather there. I am still trying to puzzle out rhetoric and my relationship to it.

I respond one afternoon to a fire call, my first wildlands fire loose in the duff of pine needles, winter-dried grasses, and oak scrub. It is a small one, less than half an acre and easily controlled because there is moisture in the soil from last week's snows and because there is no wind. Coincidentally, I am reading Norman Maclean's stunning *Young Men and Fire*, about 13 smoke jumpers killed in the 1949 Mann Gulch fire in Montana. Later, soot covered and still exhilarated, I return to Maclean and find, "For a long time, our story becomes the story of trying to find it, and like most stories of the woods this one must begin with the ground and with some guidelines to tell in which direction to look (since compasses only tell the directions, not which one to follow)" (164). I do not find closure, but I do find resonance.

Kenneth Burke writes of humans as *homo narrans*, or, as I interpret him, "storied creatures." Rhetoric, I am only just realizing, is the compass by which to follow those stories, our own as well as those of others. It is a gift I do not yet fully appreciate, still touched with the wonder of it. I have followed rhetoric to many places. I suspect it will take me to many more.

May 22, 1997
Timberon, New Mexico

WORKS CITED

[Cicero, Marcus Tullius]. *Rhetorica ad Herennium*. Cambridge: Harvard UP, 1954.
Maclean, Norman. *Young Men and Fire*. Chicago: U of Chicago P, 1992.
Stoppard, Tom. *Rosencrantz and Guildenstern Are Dead*. New York: Grove Press, 1967.

Afterword

Jacqueline Jones Royster
Ohio State University

If, as Stuart C. Brown says via Kenneth Burke in this volume, humans are "storied creatures," then *Living Rhetoric and Composition: Stories of the Discipline* is very human indeed. It is filled with stories, 19 of them in fact, of men and women who have entered the field of rhetoric and composition in various ways, across four decades, through several geographic sites, from several ideological viewpoints, with various and sundry interests. They have entered the field, perhaps not so coincidentally, during the very decades that, in addition to framing their own stories, also frame the coming of age of our discipline itself.

In "field years," rhetoric and composition (or, indeed, the multiple ways by which we name ourselves in this area these days) has reached a chronological milestone. It is old enough, that is, it has matured enough in theories and practices, in time on task to have professors who themselves have grown as teachers and scholars as the field has invented itself and perhaps even exceeded our imaginations. The grafters of this volume are marking this milestone by eliciting accounts that address basic questions: "How did you come to 'love' rhetoric and/or composition?" "How did you come to dedicate your life to the teaching of writing?" "What has it been like to make a life in this field?" "What does your vision of the future, or even the past, foretell?"

The answers embedded in this volume are as different as the storytellers themselves, and by this feature the book underscores the need to resist overgeneralizing about who we are, where we are coming from, or what our work is about. From these stories, we might say, for example, that in our formative years models of language use matter, that across our lives the contexts of language production matter, that there are variable circumstances that demonstrate how a richness of language engagement matters, that the availability of graduate programs specific to professional interests matters, that, as always, gender (and other identities, as well) matters.

From these stories, we might also say that college majors seem to have mattered less for some of the contributors here than seems indicated today by graduate school admissions policies, procedures, and/or processes; that once these contributors got into a college, class differences seem to have been "consumed," to have been capable of mediation through acts of literacy and seem thereby to have been less important than our contemporary research and scholarship suggests; that regardless of the personal histories and experiences chronicled here, we notice that all of the contributors identify watershed moments, pipers to pay, and accidents or coincidences for which they are grateful. The continuities and discontinuities posited here seem indeed to be palpable across their lives, as well as many of ours, and to enrich individual tales as we try to make them larger, more instructive beyond our own selves.

The cautionary tale, however, is that in continuities there are typically differences and in differences there are often continuities, a fact that should suggest that we not flatten the stories that we tell about ourselves but bring instead even more texture and vibrancy to them, especially as we envision or imagine placing those tales within the presence of others not yet told. The expectation of more to be rendered and more to be made meaningful suggests that we consider why we are "storied creatures," what we gain by engaging in such acts so consistently and with such investment. If a goal is to speak of our past, then we seem to gain when we use *past* with an -*s*. If a goal is to use what we have discovered about language and language learning in making a better future in the interest of better teaching, research, and scholarship, then we benefit from an open-ended sense of what discovery means. If a goal is to gain greater interpretive power for the past, the present, and/or the future, then we benefit from finding ways to see what is there, to figure out what is missing, and to fashion and articulate viewpoints that do not lend themselves to overgeneralizing.

We start, though, with some stories—as Duane Roen, Stuart Brown, and Theresa Enos are helping us to do—and we go forth with yet another professional challenge. What sense can we make of these chapters as the authentic tales of our colleagues, as threads in the richly endowed fabric of a profession, as part and parcel of stories that we can retell in sharing with those who want to be and do "like us"? What sense can we make, collectively and as individuals, about who we are, what we do now, have done in the past, and are likely to do in the future, and, of course, for some of us, about the differences that we can make for ourselves and for others?

We begin with our stories. We rise to the challenges of sense-making. We move on, not always forward, but surely on.

APPENDIX:

Annotated Bibliography:
A Guide to Professional Development

Entries composed by Steve Beatty, Rebecca Busker, Chitra Duttagupta, Theresa Enos, Judith Kish, Jim R. Koncz, Krista Long, Jeremy Meyer, Rong Su, and Viktorija Todorovska.

Banner, J. M., Jr., & Cannon, H. C. (1997). *The elements of teaching*. New Haven, CT: Yale University Press.

Lengthy reflective essay by two long-time professors in history and classics. Focuses on teaching as a philosophy at all levels, from elementary education to the university. Includes anecdotal examples of educators who are either successful or problematic teachers. Speculates on the nature of teaching by dividing teaching into various elements, such as authority, ethics, order, imagination, compassion, patience, character, and pleasure. *JM*

Boettcher, J., & Cartwright, C. P. (1997). Designing and supporting courses on the Web. *Change, 29*(5), 10+.

Identifies basic principles of designing and supporting courses on the World Wide Web. Notes the movement from synchronous instruction (everyone together in the classroom) to asynchronous instruction, increased student-to-student dialogue, and increased student-to-resource dialogue that occurs in Web-based courses. Fairly elementary treatment of the topic but does include a list of further resources in designing and supporting Web-based courses. *SB*

Boice, R. (1992). *The new faculty member: Supporting and fostering professional development.* San Francisco: Jossey-Bass.

Argues the need for professional development programs for junior faculty. Discusses the three largest obstacles facing new faculty members—collegiality, teaching, and writing—and provides solutions for overcoming these obstacles, such as ways to mentor with senior faculty, enhance weak teaching skills, and support writing. Provides a model by which new faculty can develop themselves by becoming actively involved, creating a regimen, learning self-management, and networking. Discusses what is necessary for building institutional development programs. *KL*

Boufis, C., & Olson, V. (1997). *On the market: Surviving the academic job search.* New York: Riverhead.

A collection of 40 essays by recent doctoral recipients on searching for tenure-track jobs in today's highly competitive job market. A realistic look at the frustrations of the job search. Also includes sections on the application process, job interviews, and alternative careers. The first-person accounts are sure to be enlightening for those who plan on entering the job market in the near future and include some practical advice for job candidates. *SB*

Boyer, E. L. (1990). *Scholarship reconsidered: Priorities of the professoriate.* Princeton, NJ: Carnegie Foundation for the Advancement of Teaching.

Calls for improvement in undergraduate instruction in U.S. academic institutions through renewed emphasis on good teaching. Urges combining research, cross-curricular learning, teaching, and application of learning in an inclusive model of scholarship. Raises critical questions on the role of higher education in American society and the goals of colleges and universities. Includes useful data about faculty responses to the Carnegie Foundation Survey. *CD*

Caplan, P. J. (1992). *Lifting a ton of feathers: A woman's guide to surviving in the academic world.* Toronto, Ontario, Canada: University of Toronto Press.

A guidebook for female graduate students and faculty with commentary on and practical methods of surviving and thriving in academia. Chapter topics range from the "Unwritten Rules and Impossible Proofs" in academia to "What You Can Do: Suggestions for Specific Situations" on dissertations, job hunting, hiring, promotions, and so forth. Appendices provide information on the gendered nature of academia and suggested guidelines for hiring, promotion, and tenure committees. *JK*

Coiner, C., & George, D. H. (Eds.). (1997). *Thes family track: Keeping your faculties while you mentor, nurture, teach, and serve.* Springfield: University of Illinois Press, 1997.

Explores how the necessary rigors, benefits, and limitations of the academy infringe upon, but can be balanced with, the homelife of academic caregivers, single parents, adjunct faculty, and graduate students. Includes anecdotal testimonies offering advice and strategies on dealing with biological clocks and tenure timetables, providing care for abled and disabled children, acting as surrogate parents for students, and caring for the elderly. Investigates independent scholarship and nontraditional career options. *JRK*

Enos, T. (1996). *Gender roles and faculty lives in rhetoric and composition.* Carbondale, IL: Southern Illinois University Press.

Combines personal stories of writing teachers with hard data. Offers documentation that lower-division writing courses in colleges and universities are staffed primarily by women who receive minimal pay, little prestige, and lessened job security in comparison to their male counterparts. Provides information about writing programs, teaching, administrative responsibility, ranks, ages, salary, tenure status, records of publications, and promotion and tenure guidelines. *TE*

Ferber, M. A., & Loeb, J. W. (Eds.). (1997). *Academic couples: Problems and promises.* Springfield, IL: University of Illinois Press.

An edited collection containing scholarly, anecdotal, and statistical exploration of academic couples of all varieties: married, unmarried, White, Black, homosexual, heterosexual, and so forth. Discusses the current conditions and history of academic couples, as well as their status within the academy and typical levels of productivity. Examines the positives and negatives of programs for, administrators' views of, legal and financial conditions of, and policies for academic couples. *JRK*

Glassick, C. E., Huber, M. T., & Maeroff, G. I (1997). *Scholarship assessed: Evaluation of the professoriate.* San Francisco: Jossey-Bass.

The follow-up report to Boyer's 1990 *Scholarship Reconsidered,* this book—expanded to include 14 countries—continues the exploration of the professoriate. The Carnegie Foundation is recommending four courses of action in assessing scholarship: establishing character expectations of all scholars; providing six criteria for measuring, evaluating, and documenting scholarship; suggesting that all scholarship be subject to peer review; and asking that faculty support these evaluation criteria and offer suggestions where appropriate. *JRK*

Gerlach, J. M., & Monseau V. R. (Eds.). (1991). *Missing chapters: Ten pioneering women in NCTE and English education.* Urbana, Illinois: National Council of Teachers of English.

Combines bibliographic information about 10 women who have influenced educational methods in English. Part 1—"Paving the Way"—recounts early difficulties faced by women in a male-dominated educational system; "Working Together" discusses cooperative methods employed by female academics during and after World War II; "Looking to the Future" examines how efforts by four women professionals affect contemporary and future educational methods. *JK*

Griffin, G. B. (1992). *Calling: Essays on teaching in the mother tongue.* Pasadena, CA: Trilogy Books.

Reflects on the author's self-portrait as a woman and a feminist in academia. Separated into three parts—"The Fortunate Fall," "Vocation," and "First Person . . . Singular." Punctuated by excepts from early 19th-century journals by women, the author's journals, poetry, and fiction, which serve as an impetus for commentary on the place of the author and other feminists in the academic world. *JK*

Jarvis, D. K. (1991). *Junior faculty development: A handbook.* New York: Modern Language Association.

Encourages and assists senior faculty members and administrators in creating development programs for junior faculty. Discusses both the professional and practical reasons for establishing such programs. Provides information on faculty incentives, evaluation techniques for tenure and promotion, creating dossiers, the early development of good research and writing habits, improving teaching, and the importance of institutional service. Gives examples of both adequate and inadequate development programs. *KL*

Kernan, A. (Ed.). (1997). *What's happened to the humanities?* Princeton, NJ: Princeton University Press.

Commissioned essays investigating the profound changes in the humanities that have taken and are taking place during the last half century. Explores how and why budget cuts, technological advances, the proliferation of non-traditional students, and the decreasing academic status of the humanities themselves have occurred and how they have resulted in the formation of new relativistic epistemologies and a fundamental change in how we view books, libraries, and reading itself. Includes a statistical overview. *JRK*

Lambert, L. M., Tice, S. L., & Featherstone, P. H. (Eds.). (1996). *University Teaching: A guide for graduate students.* Syracuse, NY: Syracuse University Press.

A collection of 15 essays by graduate students, professors, and academic professionals across many disciplines, ranging from areas of the humanities to education to the physical sciences. Addresses such practical areas as classroom practice and basic teaching pedagogies, from the large lecture to the art studio. Includes sections on building an inclusive classroom, developing personal portfolios, and balancing personal lives with teaching and learning responsibilities. *JM*

Lewis, L. S. (1996) *Marginal worth: Teaching and the academic labor market.* NJ: Transaction Publishers.

Discusses how the academic labor market works, why teaching is not seen to be as prestigious as research, what students' attitudes toward school and faculty are, what faculty's perspective toward teaching and students is, how merit is defined, and the failings of academic administrators. Looks at factors that affect rewards in academia. Argues that many faculty teach because of intrinsic rewards and that trying to motivate faculty with material rewards may, in fact, be dangerous. *KL*

Lodge, D. (1979). *Changing places: A tale of two campuses.* Harmondsworth, England: Penguin Books.

The first of Lodge's novels set in academia, *Changing Places* concerns the misadventures of two academics in English literature—one from England and the other from America—who switch places for a year as part of an exchange agreement between the University of Rummidge, an English university of middling size and reputation, and Euphoric State, a wealthy American university. Set in 1969, *Changing Places* skewers English and American higher education and educators. *SB*

Lodge, D. (1984). *Small world: An academic romance.* New York: Macmillan.

The second of Lodge's novels set in academia, *Small World* picks up the leading characters from *Changing Places* a decade later (1979) and follows them and a young Irish lecturer along the literary circuit from a small, poorly attended conference at the University of Rummidge to the huge, end-of-the-year MLA convention in New York. Along the way, Lodge takes satiric aim at conferences, academics, graduate students, endowed chairs, and literary theory, to name but some of his targets. Highly recommended. Less dated and much funnier than *Changing Places. SB*

Luey, B. (1995). *Handbook for academic authors* (3rd ed.). Cambridge, England: Cambridge University Press.

This practical handbook contains a wealth of very important information for anyone who ever hopes to publish, whether within academia or outside of it. It gives prospective authors advice on how to prepare successful proposals, approach publishers, and negotiate contracts, as well as advice on how to prepare a manuscript, obtain permissions for using outside material and artwork, revise a dissertation, and so forth. The tone of this book is very direct and personal, which makes the content easy to understand. The book reveals the workings of the publishing industry, especially that part of it that deals with the publication of scholarly books and journals, and as such is an excellent guide for anyone who does not have extensive experience with the scholarly publishing industry. *VT*

Lynton, E. A. (1995). *Making the case for professional service.* Washington, DC: American Association for Higher Education.

Argues that professional service should overlap with traditional notions of teaching and research and that "service" should encompass a broader philosophy of institutional commitment from faculty members. Argues further that definitions of service must be tailored to each individual university and recommends that each department establish guidelines for evaluating service activities. Includes several examples of service activities from several research universities, as well as several policy statements from universities. *JM*

Maguire, M. H. (Ed.). (1995). *Dialogue in a major key: Women scholars speak.* Urbana, IL: National Council of Teachers of English.

Provides transcribed interviews/conversations with nine female scholars—from Australia, Barbados, Canada, England, the United States, and New Zealand—on issues ranging from language and learning to political concerns within individual countries and in the international academic community. Each conversation is considered an individual entity within an overriding framework of international dialogue concerning women in academia. *JK*

Olsen, G. A., & Taylor, T. W. (1997). *Publishing in rhetoric and composition.* Albany: State University of New York Press.

A collection of essays that address "joining," "shaping" and "negotiating" the scholarly conversation through publishing articles, chapters, monographs, and textbooks. Discusses the relationship between scholarship, teaching, and writing, gender issues, dissertations, professional expectations, commodification, planning and producing a textbook, reader, or edited collection, theoretical issues, historical studies, work habits, electronic scholarship, graduate students, and mentoring. Addresses how scholarship in rhetoric and composition is considered in English Departments. *JRK*

Palmquist, M., Keifer, K., Hartvigsen, J., & Godlew, B. (in press) *Transitions: Teaching and writing in computer-supported and traditional classrooms.* Norwood, NJ: Ablex.

This book, which successfully brings together theory and practice in the field of computers and writing, is useful both for teachers who are grappling with the problems of teaching in networked environments and for researchers interested in the theoretical issues in the field. Based on studies of teachers making the transition between a traditional and a networked classroom and new teachers beginning to teach in a networked classroom, this books offers a very detailed and insightful discussion of the study findings, as well as extremely useful advice for teachers who are trying to make those transitions themselves. In addition to discussing such issues as classroom design and theoretical assumptions about teaching writing, which influence the teaching of writing in networked classrooms in very significant ways, the book is full of practical advice for teachers and sample lesson plans, as well as the results of a survey completed by students taking writing classes in computer classrooms. The book is an excellent resource for anyone teaching in a computer classroom. *VT*

Phelan, J. (1991). *Beyond the tenure track: Fifteen months in the life of an English professor.* Columbus, OH: Ohio State University Press.

Records 15 months, January 1987 to March 1988, in the life of English professor James Phelan from Ohio State University. Provides fragments from his personal life, as well as his professional life as a university professor. Intimately discusses the pressures of the academy, from academic bureaucracy to student confrontations to the struggle to publish. Attempts to show the reader academic life from a different point of view. Offers both criticism and applause for the institutional structure of academic life. *KL*

Richardson, L. (1997). *Fields of play: Constructing an academic life.* New Brunswick, NJ: Rutgers University Press.

A compilation of personal essays, poems, drama, and autobiographical stories addressing issues of writing, theory, praxis, and life outside the academy. Examines how the conditions under which we write shape what we write, which, in turn, formulates our own and others' perceptions of ourselves; situates writing and texts within—and outside of—departments, disciplines, social movements, communities, and families. *JRK*

Showalter, E., Figler, H., Kletzer, L. G., Schuster, J. H., & Katz, S. R. (1996). *The MLA guide to job search: A hand book for departments and for PhD candidates in English and foreign languages.* New York: Modern Language Association.

This book provides information on the job-seeking process for doctoral recipients and candidates in English and foreign languages in the academic and nonacademic job markets. It gives advice to departments on making the hiring process more effective, offers strategies for candidates, and attempts to show how doctoral recipients can apply their skills to nonacademic jobs. It also discusses the outlook of the academic and professional job market in English and foreign languages. *RS*

Sid W. Richardson Foundation Forum. (1997). *Restructuring the university reward system.* Fort Worth, TX: Author.

Surveyed 156 universities across the United States to determine how universities reward faculty in tenure, promotion, and merit decisions. Concludes that university faculty do not perceive teaching or service to be as important as research in these decisions. Discusses these perceptions, their origins, and their impact on the future. Suggests changes in determining faculty tenure, promotion, and merit based on public and political demands, as well as survey respondents' suggestions. Acknowledges the possible barriers to the recommended changes. Argues that these changes are necessary to restore public trust and confidence in higher education. *KL*

Toth, E. (1997). *Ms. Mentor's impeccable advice for women in academia.* Philadelphia: University of Pennsylvania Press.

Modeled after the acerbic, witty advice of Miss Manners, this book offers guidance to women as they travel the road of academia from graduate school to tenure and beyond. The questions and answers are compiled from Ms. Mentor's column in *Concerns* and cover such diverse issues as dealing with hecklers during presentations, establishing woman-to-woman mentorship, juggling the demands of family and career, confronting sexual harassment, finding the increasingly elusive job, navigating the waters of department politics, and even dressing for success. Ms. Mentor answers all questions with humor while still managing to give serious advice. Most critically, she mixes strong feminist ideology with pragmatism: although she never hesitates to expose the gender bias of academic practices, she warns academic women (particularly young, untenured academic women) to choose their battles carefully. *RB*

Tokarczyk, M. M., & Fay, E. A. (Eds.). (1993). *Working-class women in the academy: Laborers in the knowledge factory.* Amherst, MA: University of Massachusetts Press.

An anthology providing a discussion on the language employed when defining "working class" and on the role of women in academia. Divided into five sections—"Belonging," "Pockets of Experience," "Going to Class," "Ways In and Ways Out," and "Epilogue." Contains 19 articles on how issues like socialization and politics in academia are perceived and received by working-class women. *JK*

Young, J. R. (1997, October 3). Rethinking the role of professor in an age of high-tech tools. *Chronicle of Higher Education,* pp. A26–A28.

Young argues that the roles required of a professor in a high-tech model of higher education are different from those required in the traditional model. He suggests that the traditional roles of a professor—course designer, lecturer, discussion moderator, and evaluator—may be unbundled in the high-tech model. For example, the production of course material and evaluation may be done by third-party organizations. He notes that there may well be pressures to cut labor costs by reducing the number of faculty and creating virtual universities. *SB*

Author Index

Subject Index